C000062141

LIVERPOOL'S 5-STAR HEROES

OFFICIAL STORY OF THE KINGS OF EUROPE

Sport Media
A Trinity Mirror Business

Published in Great Britain in 2005 by:
Trinity Mirror Sport Media,
PO Box 48, Old Hall Street,
Liverpool L69 3EB

Executive Editor: KEN ROGERS
Editor: STEVE HANRAHAN
Art Editor: RICK COOKE
Production Editor: PAUL DOVE
Sales and Marketing Manager: ELIZABETH MORGAN
Writers: ALAN JEWELL, GAVIN KIRK,
DAVID RANDLES, CHRIS McLOUGHLIN, WILLIAM HUGHES, JAMES CLEARY
Designers: GLEN HIND, COLIN SUMPTER,
BARRY PARKER, LEE ASHUN

ISBN 1905266057

Printed and finished by Scotprint, Haddington, Scotland

This is the exact moment on May 25, 2005,
when the Liverpool players realised their dreams and
became Champions of Europe for the fifth time

For many, the way our heroes pulled off
the greatest comeback in European Cup
final history still hasn't sunk in

Like the trophy a new generation of
legends brought home from Istanbul,
this official historic book is
YOURS TO KEEP...

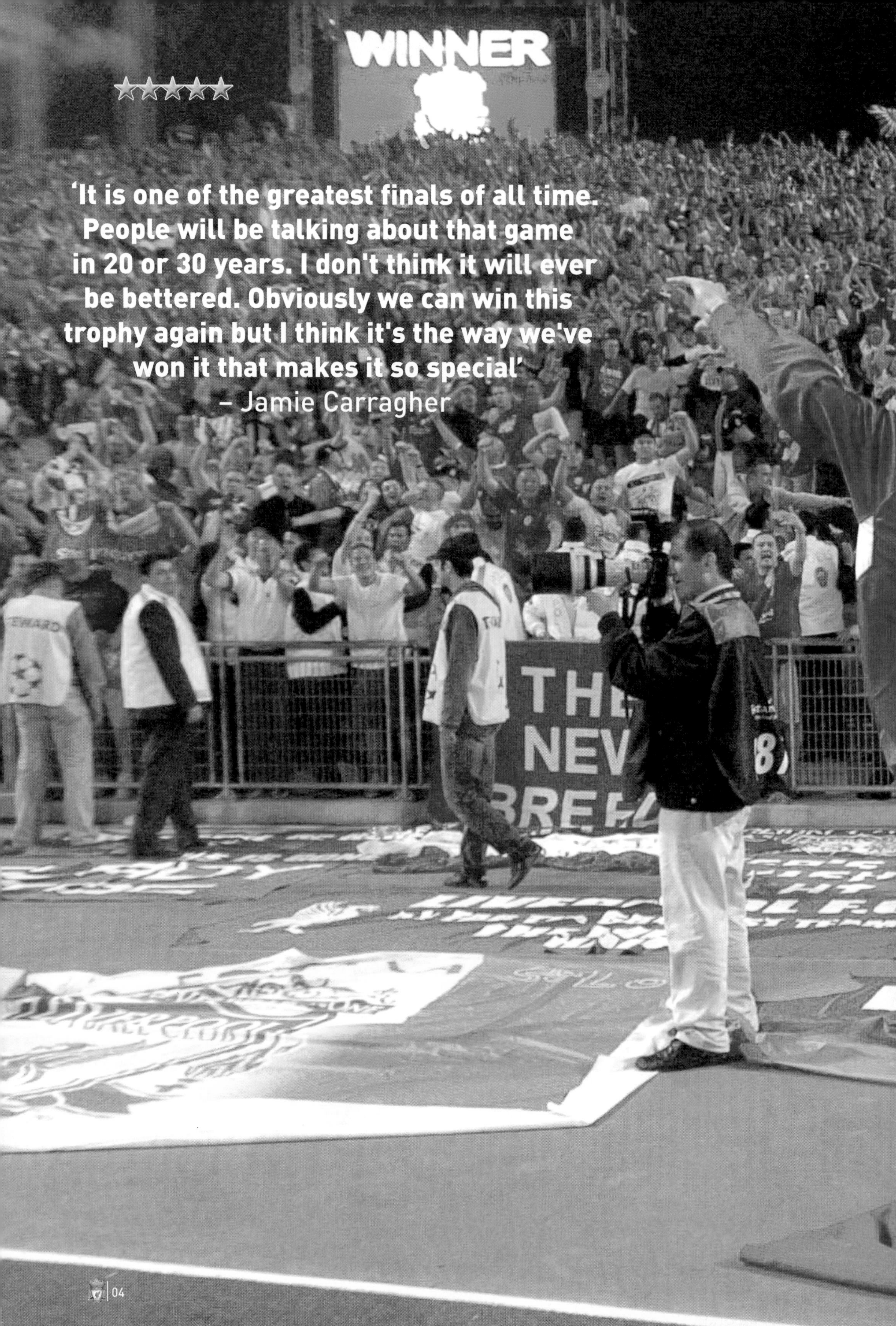

'It is one of the greatest finals of all time. People will be talking about that game in 20 or 30 years. I don't think it will ever be bettered. Obviously we can win this trophy again but I think it's the way we've won it that makes it so special'

– Jamie Carragher

CARRAGHER
23
STEWARD
MAJOR TROPHIES
M'GLADBACH
77
BRUGGE
78
1981 1984

istanbul
The Final 2005

Contents

THE MEN WHO CONQUERED

EUROPE >

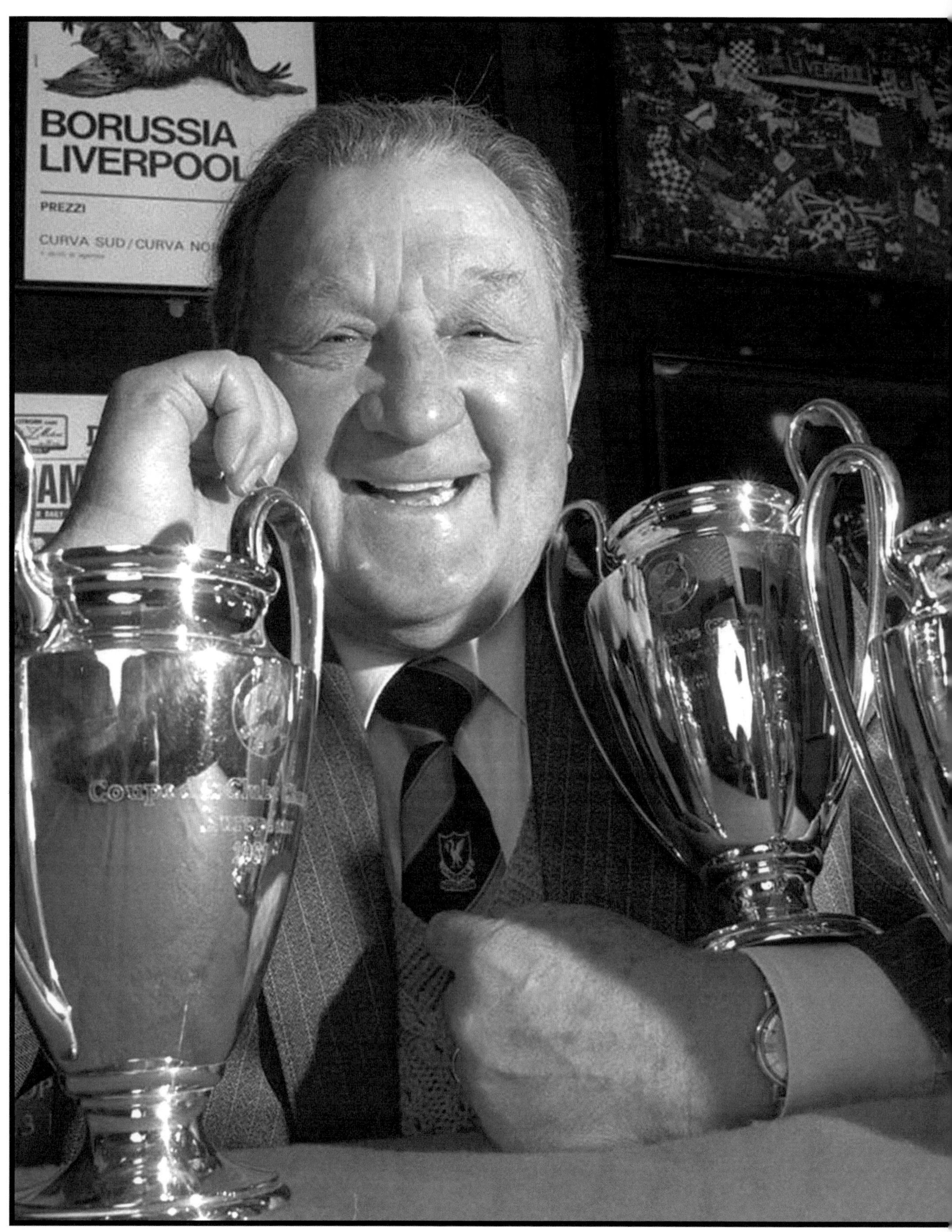
BORUSSIA
LIVERPOOL
PREZZI
CURVA SUD/CURVA NO

Bob **Paisley**

Behind the scenes he was the quiet man of Anfield and would sit in the Boot Room in his favourite flat cap and cardigan. But to Liverpool fans Bob Paisley was the man who brought the club an unprecedented and since unmatched haul of silverware that included our first three European Cups

THEY say that as one door closes, another one opens. On April 20, 1977, Liverpool's Exchange Station on Tithebarn Street was closed down to make way for the new underground link line.

On the same night, Bob Paisley led Liverpool Football Club to their first ever European Cup final with a 3-0 semi-final second-leg win over FC Zurich at Anfield.

The irony of both events occurring on the same evening was deep, as on May 6, 1939, a 20-year-old Paisley had stepped off a train at Exchange Station to sign for Liverpool.

No-one could have then foreseen the glory he would lead Liverpool to 38 years down the line.

It cost Liverpool a £25 signing-on fee and £8-a-week (£6 in the summer) wages to sign Paisley from non-league Bishop Auckland.

Born in Hetton-le-Hole in 1939, he'd starred for the Bishops in their treble-winning campaign of 1938/39 and Liverpool boss George Kay beat off competition from Sunderland to take him to Anfield.

The Second World War interrupted his Liverpool playing career and he was posted abroad in 1941. He joined the 73rd regiment of the Royal Artillery and served with Montgomery's Eighth Army as an anti-tank gunner.

In 1944 he was on a tank as the Allies liberated Rome, a city that would play a significant part in his life in the future.

His Liverpool career resumed in 1945/46 - he met wife Jessie on a train in 1945 before getting married the following year - and by the end of the following season he had a league championship medal to his name.

But that was to be Bob's only major honour as a Liverpool player. Paisley retired in 1954, after making 278 appearances and scoring 13 goals for Liverpool, and was offered a place on the coaching staff by the Anfield board.

He was appointed as reserve team manager (where he guided the club to their first ever reserve title in 1956) and trained as a physiotherapist.

Liverpool were still struggling in the second division but that all changed when a certain William Shankly was appointed as Liverpool manager in December 1959.

Bob became a key-part of Shankly's backroom staff as he built the Anfield empire. Shanks' motivational skills and Bob's tactical awareness were a match made in heaven and Liverpool embarked on an era of success after success.

When Shankly stunned the football world and quit Anfield after the 1974 FA Cup final, there was only one man who could step into his shoes and although Paisley didn't want the job he was talked into it by Liverpool chief-executive Peter Robinson. Typically, he took it for the good of his friends and the club.

"I thought that if I accepted it would prevent the whole backroom set-up being disturbed but I looked on myself as a buffer until they appointed a new manager and I told the players that."

He was so good at the job that Liverpool had to buy a buffer to shine all the silverware.

Paisley remained the same quiet, understated character when he took the manager's job.

Phil Neal recalls that the morning after Bob won his first European Cup in Rome, 1977, he turned up for breakfast carrying the famous trophy, wearing a cardigan and carpet slippers and with a newspaper tucked under his arm.

Bob shunned all publicity and even his players often found his North-East accent difficult to understand but, with the help of Joe Fagan, Ronnie Moran, Roy Evans and Tom Saunders, he always got his message across.

He was brilliant in the transfer market - how else could you describe the man who signed Kenny Dalglish, Graeme Souness and Alan Hansen? - and as a man-manager he excelled. Converting Ray Kennedy from a decent striker to a world-class left-sided midfielder was a stroke of genius.

Even though he had simple tastes and was as down to earth as they come, he was a shrewd operator and in nine seasons he led Liverpool to an amazing 19 trophies.

That, in itself, was a remarkable achievement but it's the three European Cups that he landed in five seasons that sets him apart from every other British manager.

When Bob arrived in Rome for the 1977 final against Borussia Moenchengladbach he joked that 'The last time I was in Rome I helped to capture it' and by full-time he'd captured Liverpool's first European Cup.

A year later and the Reds beat Bruges at Wembley to retain the trophy and in 1981, despite Liverpool finishing fifth in the league, he lead his side to a third European Cup with a 1-0 win over Real Madrid in Paris.

He retired as Liverpool manager at the end of the 1982/83 season and passed away on February 14, 1996.

Paisley's success record makes him the greatest British manager of all time but sadly that was never recognised with the knighthood he fully deserved.

But his legendary status at Liverpool will never be forgotten and to Kopites he will always be Sir Bob - the quiet man who gave us so much to shout about.

Joe **Fagan**

'Fagan's Treble Was No Trouble' announced the famous Kop banner. The modest Liverpool boss who masterminded the Reds' European Cup triumph in Rome would no doubt have told you a different story. On the spot to beat the favourites in their own back yard, smokin' Joe gave us number four in '84

JOE FAGAN managed Liverpool for just two years but won more honours during that spell than most achieve in a lifetime.

Fagan became Bob Paisley's number two when Bill Shankly retired and in famous Boot Room tradition the apprentice succeeded the master once more when he was handed the managerial reins once Paisley stepped down in 1983.

After a playing career that started as a 17-year-old centre-half with Manchester City, Fagan played for several non-league clubs and had a brief spell as a coach at Rochdale before moving to Anfield just 18 months before Shankly arrived.

As part of the backroom staff, it was under Shankly and then Paisley that Fagan played a key role in laying the foundations that would make Liverpool the most successful club in the country.

"You may have found me mean and thirsty in my search for trophies, but the bad news is the man who is taking my place is hungrier than me," said Paisley as he handed responsibility to Fagan.

Still, his elevation to manager raised a few eyebrows, but to those in and around the club it was simply inevitable.

Within 12 months, Fagan was being hailed as Manager-of-the-Year after presiding over what remains the club's most successful season ever while ensuring his place in history as the first British boss to win a treble.

This was the pinnacle of a 27-year Anfield career in which he worked his way through the coaching ranks to lift the League Cup and League Championship before entering the lion's den to mastermind victory over AS Roma in Rome to give Liverpool a fourth European Cup triumph.

Only Sir Alex Ferguson has completed a European Cup, domestic trophy treble since, an achievement that earned him a knighthood. In contrast, the modest and unassuming Scouser rarely received the widespread credit he so richly deserved.

Following Fagan's death after a long illness in July 2001, Kenny Dalglish, who succeeded him in 1985, recognised this. He said: "Joe's contribution to Liverpool was immense.

"I don't think he ever got the recognition he deserved for winning the European Cup, the Championship and the League Cup in 1984. It was a marvellous achievement.

"He was a different character to Bill Shankly and Bob Paisley, but his impact on the club was immense."

Alan Hansen echoed Kenny's sentiments and, like most people who worked with Fagan, holds him in the highest regard:

"When you look at the all-time greats of Liverpool, Bill Shankly and Bob Paisley, you have to have Joe up there.

"The players regarded him as one of the greats and his contribution to the success of Liverpool Football Club was as big as anyone's.

"Joe was a great man, a great coach and a great manager."

Ever the reluctant hero, Fagan's affable approach earned him the nickname 'Uncle Joe'. It was a name said with affection but never to his face. While he cast a placid persona he was certainly no pushover. He operated on a no-nonsense basis and with one knowing look, be it to journalists, his players or staff, made certain nobody messed with him.

He was a private and honest man. What you saw was what you got and he commanded the respect of all who dealt with him. Jim Beglin recalls: "He was just a very genuine nice man. He was a very humble, down to earth person.

"He had a lovely way about him and was very gentlemanly.

"Underneath that soft exterior, there was also a hardened professionalism. Joe had authority and when strong words were needed, Joe could produce them."

Fagan brought in Jan Molby to replace the likes of Graeme Souness and Sammy Lee as he put his own stamp on the team he inherited from Paisley.

He slotted into the mould of his predecessors perfectly and provided the continuity of success that made him an instant managerial hit at Anfield.

It was a terrible shame then, when just two years into his reign, tragedy struck. After guiding Liverpool to consecutive European Cup finals, what should have been another great night for Fagan turned to disaster as 39 Juventus fans died in a crush as crowd trouble flared at the Heysel Stadium.

These events clearly affected Fagan and he announced his retirement from football soon after.

In a year when some of the ghosts of Heysel were laid to rest as Liverpool and Juventus faced each other for the first time in 20 years, it was a fitting tribute to Fagan's memory that Rafa Benitez, a man with many similar qualities to 'Uncle Joe', also guided the Reds to European Cup glory in his first season in charge.

istanbul
istanbul

Rafael **Benitez**

To the singing Kopites he is the legend they call Ra-fa, Ra-fa-el! To history he will always be known as the tactical genius who conquered Europe in his first season at Liverpool. The man who somehow turned back time at Anfield and inspired his players to pull back a 3-0 half-time deficit against the mighty Milan

HOURS before Liverpool played Juventus in Turin, Rafael Benitez was seen shopping for Lego. Benitez must be good at it, given the way he created a European Cup-winning team without having all the pieces he would want in place.

He has a weakness for puzzles that require careful planning. An ability to plan tactics and understand every detail was first demonstrated when playing the board game 'Stratego' as a 12-year-old in Madrid.

The aim of the game is to get your military commanders to capture the opponents' flags. Rafa was most upset when he lost to a friend and set about ensuring he never did so again, as he explained to bemused English journalists in March 2005.

"I stayed up all night thinking about why I'd lost and how I could prevent it happening again," he revealed.

"Once I'd learned the rules and understood the strategies, I didn't lose again. I worked out a way to win no matter who I played."

Even as a child, Benitez was fascinated by planning and analysing. Aged 13, "I would write in a book the names of the [Real] Madrid players and give them all marks". He would soon do the same in matches in which he was taking part.

By 18 he was player-manager of a university side. He oversaw them at a tournament and while the opposition teams partied until daybreak, Benitez ensured his squad went home early. They won.

His own playing career was never more than an extended warm-up for what he really wanted to do: coach.

Benitez was at Real Madrid between 1974 and 1981 but never broke into the first team. After five unremarkable years at clubs in the lower divisions, a knee injury forced his retirement in 1986.

Aged 26, he began coaching the Castilla 'B' youth team, returning to Real Madrid in 1989 as coach of their Under-19 side. He made his way up the ladder, taking charge of their reserve side before being appointed assistant manager in 1994.

During this period, he also worked at the Abasota gymnasium in Madrid, utilising a degree in physical education. Here he met his future wife, Montse.

By the time he reached his mid-thirties, Benitez was ready to become a fully-fledged coach of a professional team.

He began his managerial apprenticeship at Valladolid and Osasuna.

Circumstances were not in his favour at either club, however, and when he was given time he was able to shape winning teams.

Benitez took Extremadura and Tenerife into the Spanish Primera Liga, spending a year's sabbatical between the two jobs studying coaching methods at leading clubs throughout Europe, including AC Milan. Perhaps the Italians regret their hospitality now.

Valencia offered Benitez his first major managerial job, where he took over from Hector Cuper in 2001. He broke the Real Madrid-Barcelona duopoly that reigned in Spain, winning two league titles and one UEFA Cup in his three seasons at the Mestalla.

A deteriorating relationship with chief executive Manuel LLorente hastened his departure from Valencia and within a fortnight Benitez was unveiled as Liverpool's new manager.

He soon found a way into the affections of the club's supporters, signing exciting players and making Anfield on match-day a fun day out again.

His low-key but charming manner further endeared him to a foreign public. The ingenious re-working of the 'La Bamba' lyrics to honour Benitez and his Spanish signings is just one example of the instant adoration he has inspired. Joining supporters in an Irish bar in Cologne the night before Liverpool played Leverkusen added to a burgeoning legend.

Behind the warm smile lies a man fixated with winning football matches. He is obsessed with the sport and the small details that can separate the best from the rest. In training sessions, the various aspects of the game are broken down for intense preparation, and these drills are frequently stopped so he can make a tactical point. Video analysis of his team and opponents is conducted to an exhausting degree. Anyone who watched a Liverpool game in 2004/05 is well aware of how animated he is on the touchline, instructing almost constantly while the match is in progress.

Benitez is always thinking, always working. On the rare occasions he switches off from football, he will engross himself in another game of strategy: chess. Even when the opponent has him virtually at checkmate, Rafa can still find a way to prevail, as any supporter of AC Milan will testify.

Carlsberg
the final 2005
CHAMPIONS LEAGUE
the final 2005
Carlsberg

2005

★★★★★

The road to Istanbul

From the Arnold Schwarzenegger stadium in Austria to the Ataturk. It's been an epic crusade. Rafa's red and white army returned from the principality of kings and the land of the gods with battle scars. But a fortress was built on the fields of Anfield Road. Our troops regrouped, we crossed the Rhine, scaled the Italian Alps and the Bridge was finally taken

Qualifying round - 1st leg

UEFA Champions League
Third qualifying round, 1st leg
August 10 2004

Grazer AK 0

Liverpool 2
(Gerrard 23, 79)

Att: 15,000

Team: Dudek, Josemi, Hyypia, Carragher, Riise, Finnan (Potter), Gerrard (Warnock), Hamann, Kewell, Baros (Diao), Cisse.

LIVERPOOL'S first competitive match under the management of Rafa Benitez ended in a comfortable 2-0 win in the Arnold Schwarzenegger stadium.

Skipper Steven Gerrard was the destroyer with a long-range effort before the break and a predator like strike before the end. Stevie also got a raw deal when he had another spectacular effort disallowed.

Rafa introduced his Kindergarten Kop with Stephen Warnock and Darren Potter handed their Liverpool debuts as substitutes and by the end it looked like Grazer had been well and truly terminated.

Qualifying round - 2nd leg

UEFA Champions League
Third qualifying round, 2nd leg
August 24 2004

Liverpool 0

Grazer AK 1
(Tokic 55)

Att: 42,950

Team: Dudek, Henchoz, Hyypia, Carragher, Riise, Diao, Potter, Gerrard, Kewell (Warnock), Baros (Hamann), Cisse (Pongolle).

GRAZER recorded a shock win at Anfield but it wasn't enough to stop Rafa's Reds progressing to the Champions League group stage.

Liverpool were poor on the night and a powerful 55th minute strike from Mario Tokic made for an uncomfortable last half-hour for Kopites.

The Reds created little and didn't deserve to win although they should have been up against 10 men when Rene Aufhauser was booked twice but the referee failed to send him off.

Group stage - game 1

UEFA Champions League
Group A, matchday 1
September 15 2004

Liverpool 2
(Cisse 22, Baros 84)

Monaco 0

Att: 33,517

Team: Dudek, Josemi, Hyypia, Carragher, Riise, Finnan, Gerrard, Alonso, Kewell (Warnock), Garcia (Biscan), Cisse (Baros).

DJIBRIL Cisse slammed home his first goal at Anfield as Liverpool got their Champions League group campaign off to a flying start against the previous season's beaten finalists.

The French international striker fired home before the break after a neat passing move between Luis Garcia and Steven Gerrard as the Reds dominated the game.

Cisse should have scored a second after the break but it was substitute Milan Baros who finished Monaco off with an individual effort six minutes from time.

Group stage - game 2

UEFA Champions League
Group A, matchday 2
September 28 2004

Olympiakos 1
(Stoltidis 17)

Liverpool 0

Att: 33,000

Team: Dudek, Josemi (Cisse), Hyypia, Carragher, Riise, Finnan, Hamann (Diao), Alonso, Warnock (Kewell), Garcia, Baros.

LIVERPOOL turned in a particularly poor display in Greece and were lucky to get away with a one goal defeat.

Ieroklis Stoltidis headed home the winner in the first half and Olmypiakos were unlucky not to score more despite having Anastasios Pantos dismissed.

Group stage - game 3

UEFA Champions League
Group A, matchday 3
October 19 2004

Liverpool 0

Deportivo 0

Att: 40,236

Team: Kirkland, Josemi, Hyypia, Carragher, Traore, Riise (Kewell), Hamann, Alonso, Garcia (Pongolle), Baros, Cisse (Finnan).

IT was to be a night of frustration at Anfield as Liverpool threw everything but the kitchen sink at Deportivo but just couldn't break their resolute defence down.

The Spaniards arrived at Anfield intent on keeping a clean sheet and as a result it was Liverpool who made all the running.

Liverpool, missing Steven Gerrard through injury, were sent out to attack although they survived an early scare when John Arne Riise was forced to clear Cesar Martin's header off the line.

Djibril Cisse, Milan Baros and Luis Garcia should all have scored before the break.

Cisse was denied in the 18th minute by Manuel Pablo and when Baros rounded keeper Jose Molina nine minutes later he seemed certain to score until Pablo appeared from nowhere to make another goal-saving tackle.

Garcia was then denied by an extraordinary save from Molina.

Xabi Alonso's shot had deflected into Garcia's path and he smashed a first-time effort goalwards only to see the Depor keeper instictively thrust his arms upwards and somehow deflect the ball over the bar.

Chances were at a premium in the second half and substitute Harry Kewell came closest to breaking the deadlock when his 91st minute free-kick flashed just wide of Molina's goal but it wasn't to be Liverpool's night.

Group stage - game 4

UEFA Champions League
Group A, matchday 4
November 3 2004

Deportivo 0

Liverpool 1
(Andrade, og 14)

Att: 32,000

Team: Kirkland, Josemi, Hyypia, Carragher, Traore, Riise, Hamann, Biscan, Garcia (Alonso), Baros (Pongolle), Kewell (Finnan).

IGOR Biscan was the unlikely star of the show as Liverpool recorded a vital 1-0 win at The Riazor on Rafa's return to Spain.

With Xabi Alonso struggling with a calf injury and Steven Gerrard nursing a broken metatarsal, midfield responsibility was handed to Biscan and Didi Hamann.

It took Biscan less than a minute to show he meant business when he played Milan Baros clean through but the Czech failed to go round keeper Jose Molina and the opportunity was wasted.

The Croatian midfielder was in top form and in the 14th minute was the architect of Liverpool's winner.

Picking up the ball in the centre of midfield, Biscan made a clever feint to avoid one challenge before going on a driving run forward and spreading the ball out wide to John Arne Riise.

The Norwegian crossed towards Baros but defender Jorge Andrade got to the ball first and could only look in horror as he sent it past Molina and into his own net.

Riise almost doubled the lead before the break but Andrade cleared off the line and with Josemi and Djimi Traore outstanding at full-back, Depor's dangerous wide men had little influence on the game.

The win put Liverpool joint top of Group A.

Group stage - game 5

UEFA Champions League
Group A, matchday 5
November 23 2004

Monaco 1
(Saviola 56)

Liverpool 0

Att: 15,000

Team: Kirkland, Traore (Kewell), Hyypia, Carragher, Riise, Finnan, Hamann Gerrard, Biscan, Garcia (Josemi, (Warnock)), Mellor.

NOTHING went right for Liverpool who lost Luis Garcia, Josemi and Djimi Traore through injury and saw Javier Saviola score the winner after controlling the ball with his hand.

Neil Mellor had a goal disallowed but defeat left the Reds needing to win their final game against Olympiakos by two goals to progress.

Carlsberg

Carlsberg

Group stage - game 6

UEFA Champions League
Group A, matchday 6
December 8 2004

Liverpool 3
(Pongolle 47, Mellor 81, Gerrard 86)

Olympiakos 1
(Rivaldo 26)

Att: 42,045

Team: Kirkland, Traore (Pongolle), Hyypia, Carragher, Riise, Finnan (Josemi), Alonso, Gerrard, Nunez, Kewell, Baros (Mellor).

ON one of Anfield's greatest European nights, Liverpool booked their place in the last 16 of the Champions League with a heroic second-half display.

Rivaldo's first half free-kick looked to have ended the Reds' interest in the competition but inspired performances from second half substitutes Florent Sinama-Pongolle and Neil Mellor turned the game on its head before Steven Gerrard smashed home a glorious late winner that will forever remain part of Anfied folklore.

It was mathematics rather than tactics that Kopites had on their minds when they arrived at the ground before kick-off.

A 1-0 win would be enough to send Liverpool through but if Olympiakos scored, the Reds needed to win by two clear goals, although they could sneak through with a 2-1 win if Monaco lost in La Coruna.

Anything other than a win and Liverpool were definitely out.

Benitez had selection problems. In addition to long-term casualties Djibril Cisse and Vladimir Smicer, Didi Hamann was suspended, Luis Garcia was ruled out with the hamstring he pulled in Monaco and Igor Biscan wasn't allowed to play because he'd suffered concussion a week earlier in a Carling Cup tie at Spurs.

It meant that Antonio Nunez was handed his first Champions League start on the right with Harry Kewell playing in the hole behind Milan Baros who himself was back after missing the previous five games with a hamstring injury.

With a highly-charged Anfield backing them all the way, Liverpool started like a house on fire and forced three corners in the opening minute, the third of which Baros headed goalwards only to see the ball cleared off the line.

Sami Hyppia headed a good chance wide and Gerrard struck a post but in the 27th minute Rivaldo won himself a free-kick on the edge of the box and curled it past Chris Kirkland.

The Greeks went in at half-time a goal up and with the news from Spain that Monaco were several goals to the good, Benitez knew his team had to score three times if they were to progress.

He responded by replacing Djimi Traore with Sinama-Pongolle at the interval and the change paid dividends straight away.

Two minutes into the second half and Kewell got to the byeline and crossed for Sinama-Pongolle to score from close range. Liverpool were back in it.

Gerrard then got booked - which would keep him out of Liverpool's next European game - and saw a brilliant long-range strike in the 62nd minute disallowed after erratic Spanish referee Manuel Gonzalez adjudged Baros to have committed an offence earlier in the move.

With the clock ticking down Rafa made his last throw of the dice, replacing the tiring Baros with Neil Mellor.

Three minutes later Mellor poached a goal in typical fashion, tapping home after Nunez's header was saved by Antonios Nikopolidis.

Now the Kop were trying to suck the ball into the net and, with just four minutes left, came a moment of sheer exhilaration.

Jamie Carragher played a high ball forward that Mellor brilliantly steered into the path of Gerrard who let it bounce once before striking a thunderbolt from just outside the box that flew past the Greek international keeper and into the net.

Anfield erupted. The Olympiakos players looked stunned and had no answer. Against all odds, Liverpool were through to the last 16.

1st knockout round

UEFA Champions League
Last 16, first leg
February 22 2005

Liverpool 3
(Garcia 15, Riise 35, Hamann 90)

Bayer Leverkusen 1
(Franca 90)

Att: 40,942

Team: Dudek, Hyypia, Carragher, Finnan, Riise (Smicer), Biscan, Hamann, Garcia, Kewell (Le Tallec), Baros (Potter).

WITH Steven Gerrard suspended it was Igor Biscan who stepped into his shoes and the Anfield cult-figure was in inspirational form again.

Right from the start of the game the pace of Liverpool's passing and movement unsettled Bayer and the in-form Germans were on the back-foot.

Luis Garcia opened the scoring in the 15th minute after Biscan stormed through the Leverkusen midfield and played an inch-perfect pass for the Spaniard to run on to and slip under the body of keeper Jorg Butt.

Leverkusen responded by looking for an away goal and striker Dimitar Berbatov, who had scored one of the goals that helped to eliminate Liverpool in the 2002 Champions League quarter-final between the two sides, should have equalised in the 29th minute.

Steve Finnan's attempted back-header hit Sami Hyypia and the Bulgarian raced clean through but rolled the ball wide of Jerzy Dudek's post. He was punished moments later when John Arne Riise smashed home a powerful free-kick that beat Butt at his near post.

Didi Hamann appeared to have ended the tie in the 90th minute with another free-kick.

However, an injury-time fumble by Jerzy Dudek allowed Franca to steal a precious away goal to silence Anfield and give the Germans renewed hope of repeating their success against the Reds of three years earlier.

1st knockout round

UEFA Champions League
Last 16, second leg
March 9 2005

Bayer Leverkusen 1
(Krzynowek 88)

Liverpool 3
(Garcia 28, 32, Baros 67)

Att: 23,000

Team: Dudek, Finnan (Nunez), Warnock, Hyypia, Carragher (Welsh), Riise, Biscan, Hamann (Smicer), Garcia, Gerrard, Baros.

ALL the talk before the game had been about Leverkusen's exceptional European form in the BayArena but Liverpool turned in an accomplished display in Germany.

After a minute's silence in honour of the late, great Rinus Michels, Liverpool were in control of the game from the start and Luis Garcia killed the tie off with a double strike in the space of four minutes.

The little Spaniard cancelled out Leverkusen's away goal in the 28th minute when he headed home Steven Gerrard's pin-point cross from the right.

He then finished the home side off completely when Igor Biscan powerfully headed a Gerrard corner goalwards and Garcia cleverly touched the ball past the diving Butt from close range.

Liverpool were in cruise control after that and Milan Baros added a third in the 67th minute after good work from Gerrard again.

Benitez then had the luxury of resting players and ended up fielding an unlikely back four of Hyypia, Biscan, Warnock and Nunez with a late consolation from Jacek Kryznowek in no way taking the gloss off the night.

Quarter-final - 1st leg

UEFA Champions League
Quarter-final, 1st leg
April 5 2005

Liverpool 2
(Hyypia 10, Garcia 25)

Juventus 1
(Cannavaro 63)

Att: 41,216

Team: Carson, Hyypia, Carragher, Finnan, Traore, Riise, Biscan, Gerrard, Garcia, Le Tallec (Smicer), Baros (Nunez).

TWENTY years after the horror of Heysel, Liverpool and Juventus met again for the first time.

Inevitibly the events of the 1985 European Cup final, at which 39 people lost their lives, dominated the headlines and before kick-off the message was 'memoria e amicizia' - in memory and friendship.

The Kop held up a mosaic that simply said 'amicizia' while Ian Rush, Phil Neal and Michel Platini presented a specially crafted plaque to the travelling Juve fans.

On the pitch Rafa had sprung a surprise by starting youngsters Scott Carson and Anthony Le Tallec.

With the noise levels high Liverpool attacked from the start and within 10 seconds of Juventus kicking off Milan Baros had a shot that was deflected wide for a corner.

Juve had only conceded two Champions League goals all season but it took Sami Hyypia just 10 minutes to get his name on the scoresheet when he cracked home a wonderful left-footed volley after Luis Garcia flicked Steven Gerrard's corner on.

Garcia then added a stunning second 15 minutes later with a left-footed half-volley from 30 yards out that dipped over the stranded Gianluigi Buffon.

Zlatan Ibrahimovic hit a post and Carson saved from Alessandro Del Piero as Juve pushed for an away goal and they got one in the second half when Fabio Cannavaro's header squirmed past Carson to leave Liverpool facing a tricky trip to Turin.

Quarter-final - 2nd leg

UEFA Champions League
Quarter-final, 2nd leg
April 13 2005

Liverpool 0

Juventus 0

Att: 59,400

Team: Dudek, Hyypia, Carragher, Finnan, Traore, Riise, Biscan, Alonso, Garcia (Le Tallec), Nunez (Smicer), Baros (Cisse).

AS expected, Liverpool received a hostile reception in Turin with many Juventus fans taking the opportunity to make their feelings known about events in Brussels in 1985.

Rafa's Reds needed a draw to progress but with Steven Gerrard and Didi Hamann both ruled out through injury, the task was made more difficult.

Igor Biscan stepped in again and Xabi Alonso returned to play his first game since breaking his ankle against Chelsea on New Year's Day.

Five of the Liverpool team that started in Turin had also started in the ignominious FA Cup defeat at Burnley just three months earlier.

They more than made up for that in Italy with a display of defiance and courage to secure a 0-0 draw that was likened to Liverpool's 1-1 result in Munich in 1981.

Juventus, who would later go on to win Serie A, were limited to just two clear-cut chances all night.

Zlatan Ibrahimovic headed over in the first half and after the break Jerzy Dudek managed to claw the ball off the line after Fabio Cannavaro's header had hit the post and deflected goalwards off Djimi Traore. At the other end Milan Baros missed a gilt-edged chance when he forced his way through only to shoot wide. The sight of the night though was Djibril Cisse's substitute appearance just six months after he had suffered an horrific double leg fracture at Blackburn which almost left him needing an amputation.

It was a night and a return that the word 'heroic' was invented for.

Semi-final - 1st leg

UEFA Champions League
Semi-final, 1st leg
April 27 2005

Chelsea 0

Liverpool 0

Att: 40,497

Team: Dudek, Hyypia, Carragher, Finnan, Traore, Riise, Biscan (Kewell), Alonso, Garcia (Smicer), Gerrard, Baros (Cisse).

UNBEATEN at home under Jose Mourinho and having scored four goals apiece in their previous two Champions League home games against Barcelona and Bayern Munich, Chelsea looked like being formidable semi-final opponents.

They'd already beaten Liverpool three times - including the Carling Cup final in Cardiff - although had been incredibly lucky to win two of those games.

With Didi Hamann still out injured, Igor Biscan sat alongside Xabi Alonso in front of the back four with Steven Gerrard - who was playing despite having an operation to remove an abscess from his mouth on the morning of the game, asked to play behind Milan Baros.

The system worked well and Chelsea only created two clear chances of note in the whole game with Didier Drogba firing wide and Frank Lampard blasting over.

Baros was unlucky not to give Liverpool the lead, and a vital away goal, when he headed Gerrard's cross goalwards only for Petr Cech to somehow claw it away.

Chelsea got more anxious as the second half went on but with Jamie Carragher in imperious form at the heart of the defence and Sami Hyypia, Djimi Traore and Steve Finnan all excelling, Jerzy Dudek didn't have a single save to make all night and the game finished goalless.

Not even Mourinho's post-match confidence could dissuade Kopites now that Liverpool were on the verge of something special.

Semi-final - 2nd leg

UEFA Champions League
Semi-final, 2nd leg
May 3 2005

Liverpool 1
(Garcia 4)

Chelsea 0

Att: 42,529

Team: Dudek, Hyypia, Carragher, Finnan, Traore, Riise, Biscan, Hamann (Kewell), Garcia (Nunez), Gerrard, Baros (Cisse).

AFTER winning the Premiership title just three days earlier and having scored in every away European game they'd played for the last two seasons, Chelsea arrived on Merseyside full of confidence.

They didn't just come up against Liverpool though - they faced arguably the most partisan, awesome atmopshere that Anfield had ever produced.

At times the noise was spine-tingling as the sight of thousands of scarves being twirled around heads all around the ground inspired the players, and within four minutes, Liverpool - who were missing the suspended Xabi Alonso - were ahead.

Milan Baros latched on to Gerrard's incisive through-ball and was brought down by Petr Cech as he chipped the ball over him but as the Liverpool fans screamed for a penalty Luis Garcia flicked the ball goalwards and although William Gallas cleared it, the Slovakian linesman adjudged it to have crossed the line. 1-0 Liverpool.

Chelsea now had to attack but couldn't find a way through a resilient Liverpool defence which was superbly marshalled by the outstanding Jamie Carragher with Didi Hamann, who had just returned from injury, protecting his back four superbly.

Chelsea's best chance fell to Eidur Gudjohnsen deep into the ludicrous six minutes of injury time but he fired wide and moments later the celebrations began. They continued all the way to Istanbul where Liverpool would take on AC Milan in their sixth European Cup final.

★★★★★

TELL ME MA, ME MA, THE CABINET IS NOT QUITE FULL, WE'RE GOING TO ISTANBUL...

It wasn't the most accessible place in the world but nothing was going to stop Liverpool supporters from travelling to Turkey. They turned Taksim Square into Concert Square before watching Rafa's Reds try to land the European Cup for keeps.

The match involved the biggest-ever security operation mounted by UEFA in 49 years of European club competition. This was due partly in the wake of the death of two Leeds fans following violence in Istanbul in 2000, and the problems caused when England and Turkey had met in the qualifiers for the 2004 European Championship.

Indeed, at a news conference to promote the game eight days before the match, there were warnings that anybody travelling to the city without a ticket may be denied entry to Turkey.

"If police don't like their face, they will be sent back," claimed Sami Colgecen, the Istanbul mayor's chief adviser for the final.

Both sets of supporters boarded buses from different parts of the city; Reds fans from central Taksim square, while Milan followers were transported from the historic Sultanahmet district several miles away.

UEFA spokesman William Gaillard said beforehand: "There will be minimum contact with the Turkish crowd and minimum contact between the two sets of supporters."

Reds fan and academic Dr Rogan Taylor of the Football Research Unit at Liverpool University believed there would be few problems in the Turkish capital. As the game approached he said: "The key is that a Turkish club is not involved, and there will be no particular history between Liverpool and their opponents in the final, and that Liverpool are quite a popular club in Istanbul.

"It will be like Celtic in the UEFA Cup final in Seville a couple of seasons ago - thousands will go hoping to pick up a ticket there or just to be part of the event.

"I think the people of Istanbul are in for a great party. Liverpool fans will be going on cheap package holidays to Turkey, getting a bus to Istanbul, and having a ball."

A week before the game a spokesperson for Merseyside Police said: "We would advise all Liverpool fans travelling to Istanbul to take notice of any advice given to them by the local police and authorities in Turkey.

"I'm sure the Liverpool fans are looking forward to the match and their trip to Istanbul and are hoping to enjoy a good spectacle of football as well as the local sights in Turkey.

"Throughout all of the Liverpool games in the European Cup the fans have behaved impeccably and have really entered into the spirit of the competition and I'm sure it will be the same in Istanbul."

FIRST IN LINE

The first tickets went on sale on May 10, with the ticket office opening an hour earlier than normal to meet expected demand – with many fans arriving before 6am. The first batch of Liverpool's 20,000-ticket allocation was made available to supporters who had been to eight or more European games. Engineer Joe Caddick (63) from Formby said: "I queued for half-an-hour to get this ticket and I have no idea how I'll get to Istanbul – I'll work it out later! I'm on cloud nine."

NO SPOILING THE FUN

Organisers of the St Helens Corporate Cup were left with a dilemma following Liverpool's run all the way to the final. The event, which is a series of 5km team runs or walks open to teams of four, was scheduled to start at 7pm on the night of the showpiece, a 7.45pm kick-off. But the run was brought forward to 6.30pm so Reds fans wishing to compete would not miss out on the game.

Series director Alison Abbott said: "This is definitely one occasion when another sport takes precedence and we wish Liverpool every success in Istanbul.

"It is going to take a fair bit of ringing around to inform everyone of the new start time. We have tried to find an alternative date for the run, but nothing is available."

WISHFUL THINKING

Welsh League champions TNS offered Liverpool a potential Champions League place should they be victorious in Turkey – a potential qualifier in the first round.

Managing director Mike Harris said: "If it was done properly, I think I would be in favour of it. It would have to be in the form of one 90-minute match, decided by penalties if it was a draw.

"We would get the benefit of the gate, and should we be unfortunate enough not to get through, we would want a percentage of Liverpool's income from the competition.

"We would want it covered by a national television station, and from a personal point of view, it would be nice to stage it at the Millennium Stadium."

But Richard Pedder, chairman of the Liverpool Supporters' Club in Lower Breck Road, was among those who did not support the idea. He said: "This idea is completely out of order. TNS are champions of Wales and as such should take up their place in the Champions League.
"Their offer shouldn't even be considered. If Liverpool do go on to win the Champions League then it's up to UEFA to find us a place and no-one else."

THE FINAL WORD:

Ian Rush:
"Forget what you might have read about Milan not being as good as people think. This is going to be as tough a test as Liverpool have had in the competition.
On paper, everyone can see AC Milan are the strongest of the two teams. The players will have to be properly drilled and the tactical side of the game will be far more important to the current side than it was for us (in 1984)."

Steven Gerrard:
"As a Liverpool lad, I'm not only proud to be leading the team out, but also to be following in a great tradition. There aren't many lads from Liverpool who have had the honour of being captain in a European Cup final.
If we win it, and I can get the permission I need from the club, I'll take the cup to Huyton to show all my friends and family."

Sami Hyypia:
"Learning the history is good and a lot of the old players are giving us their support.
Now I believe that when we win this trophy it will be the start of a good era and all the players here will be in the history books.
Everyone is always remembering the good days when Liverpool were dominant in Europe. This game is the opportunity to bring the cup home and to write our names into that history."

★★★★★

But Thomas Constantinou, 20, of Liverpool city centre, who travelled with friends to the Istanbul final in a motor home, disagreed, saying: "It's a feasible option, but I still don't think Liverpool should have to do something like that to defend the title. It sounds a bit ridiculous and far-fetched, but it's been that sort of season for Liverpool fans."

Of course, Liverpool would ultimately play TNS, but only when they drew the Welsh double winners in the first qualifying round of the 2005/06 tournament.

TICKET TOUTS

Less than two weeks before the final, tickets were reportedly changing hands for up to 20 times their face value. Prices as much as £750 were being quoted, as touts and ticketing agencies flout laws that are supposed to prevent them cashing in on the occasion.

Richard Pedder said: "If you look at the number of fans both Liverpool and AC Milan have, then common sense would suggest they should have been given a minimum of 30,000 tickets each.

"The fact that they weren't given anything like this just played into the hands of touts, who can now demand pretty much what they like for tickets.

"I can understand UEFA giving a certain amount of tickets to various associations, just as the FA do for the FA Cup final.

"But in this case, it looks like they've given far too many tickets to people who've got nothing to do with the final and this is a major problem that needs addressing."

Riverside MP Louise Ellman said: "It seems very unfair that genuine fans who have missed out on tickets are being forced into paying vastly inflated sums simply to watch their team play.

"This is something that UEFA and the football authorities in general need to look at and they should do so with utmost urgency."

Liverpool Wavertree MP Jane Kennedy agreed with her colleague, adding: "It's a disgrace when genuine fans who go to game after game in the hope of eventually making it to an occasion like this have to miss out.

"It's time UEFA sorted this out once and for all so that situations like this can never arise again in the future."

A UEFA spokesman insisted the body was already aware of the problem of tickets being sold at hugely inflated prices and had placed the matter in the hands of its legal department.

"Our ticketing policies were established many months before the final and would be exactly the same regardless of which clubs were in the final.

"We'd urge fans not to buy tickets from bodies and individuals not officially recognised by UEFA, mainly because in some cases we aren't convinced the tickets even exist.

"But whenever we spot cases like this we take action. We're aware of tickets being offered for sale on the internet, and not only on eBay, and the matter is now in the hands of our legal team."

Incidentally, four tickets on eBay were being advertised for £1,500 with an 'information leaflet' (eight days before the final); two tickets were available for £1000 and £911. As it turned out, the most expensive tickets bidded for were £260 each for a pair.

NIGHT MAYOR

Fans attending the appointment of the next Lord Mayor of Liverpool were able to keep up with on-field events via a big screen.
Staff set up a TV in the town hall ballroom so guests at Cllr Alan Dean's mayor-making ceremony could catch updates.

The civic event, which saw committed Evertonian Cllr Dean take over the mayoral chain, clashed with Liverpool's showdown against AC Milan.

Cllr Dean would not consider changing the date of his big night because he had guests travelling from across the UK. He also said the ceremony and subsequent dinner were originally due to take place a week earlier, but were moved at the request of council officers.

Cllr Dean said: "The final is a massive event for Liverpool fans, but it's also a massive night for me and a proud moment in my life.

"A year ago, I was told the mayor-making would take place on May 18, but a few weeks ago - before Liverpool reached the final - it was changed to May 25.

"It wasn't my decision and I was against it at the time, but now it would be impractical to change it again. If I did, I would lose 80% or 90% of my guests."

TIPS AND ADVICE

- A Visa is required for British nationals to enter Turkey - £10 at the port of entry.
- A pint of beer in some establishments costs less than £1, and a three-course meal is available for £5. Like in Liverpool, club prices tend to rise.

Hernan Crespo
(AC Milan striker):

"They (Liverpool) are a really strong side and it won't be easy to beat them. Considering Liverpool's capabilities in defence, against Juve and Chelsea, we will have to manage the match. We need to be attentive, not to be surprised by them because they have dangerous players."

Carlo Ancelotti
(AC Milan coach):

"I think a team that wins should have the right to defend it but we may just do the English federation a favour and solve this. Liverpool is a team I like. They are organised and they have ideas.
Liverpool have had problems in their own competition, they've had many players out injured and they haven't been able to combine both competitions. But, just like Milan, they are very happy to have reached the European final.
Benitez has done a very good job with Liverpool. In his first year with the club he has taken them to the Champions League final. He has won the tactical battle against Chelsea and Juventus so I have a lot of respect for him."

EURO '05 SEND-OFF

GETTING THERE

Sunny Beach resort near Borghas in Bulgaria became a popular destination due to its proximity to Istanbul. With a week's stay under £300 and with fans struggling to find affordable places to stay in the Turkish capital, the country was ideal for fans – and only four hours from Istanbul by ferry.

The official club tour operator Lonsdale Travel was also struggling to cope with demand. Sports division spokeswoman Laura Thwaites said: "It's been completely mad. We had to close the phone system down we were so busy.

"We've put together 24 different packages and the workload has been huge – a total nightmare."

AMBASSADORS

Chief superintendent Dave Lewis of Merseyside Police: "It's up to the Liverpool supporters to behave respectably and act as great ambassadors for the city."

DREAM COMES TRUE?

Bookmaker Victor Chandler faced a six-figure pay-out should one punter's premonitions turn into reality on May 25. The anonymous gambler laid £1000 on Liverpool claiming a 4-2 victory over AC Milan – after dreaming of the scoreline.

Nick Gray of Victor Chandler Bet said before the game: "He'll be returning to dreamland for some time to come if that one kops. Everyone has their own way of finding a winner and good luck to the guy.

"I've backed a few premonitions myself without much success. Considering both sides have pretty awesome defences the formbook might suggest it's too much to expect six goals in the Istanbul final.

"We had a punter who confessed to seeing the initials of a player in the condensation of his shaving mirror in the past."

Indeed, a Reds win was good news for punters – particularly on Merseyside. Bookmakers were deluged with bets on Liverpool to win the trophy for a fifth time when their odds stood at 80-1.

William Hill took one bet of £500 at 80-1 – which netted the punter £40,000, and a spokeswoman for the company said: "There was quite a bit of interest in Liverpool all the way through the competition.

"Even when they were among the outsiders people from Merseyside were supporting them in our shops.

"We had several bets of £100 when the odds were 80-1 and one at £500."

Ladbrokes' Phil Cavanagh added before the action got underway in Turkey: "We are facing a payout of around £500,000 if Liverpool win and industry-wide the figure is much higher.

"Early in the competition most of the money was going

On the Box

The Apprentice (Former Spurs chairman Alan Sugar chooses one of 14 desperate hopefuls competing to win a £100,000 job with his Amstrad company).

- **24**
- **Ramsay's Kitchen Nightmares**
- **Celebrity Love Island**
- **Chubby Chasers**
- **Murphy's Law**
- **Kath and Kim**

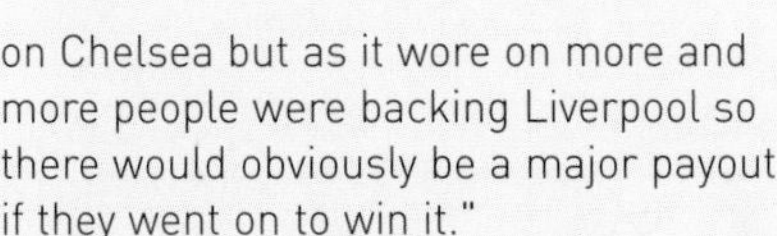

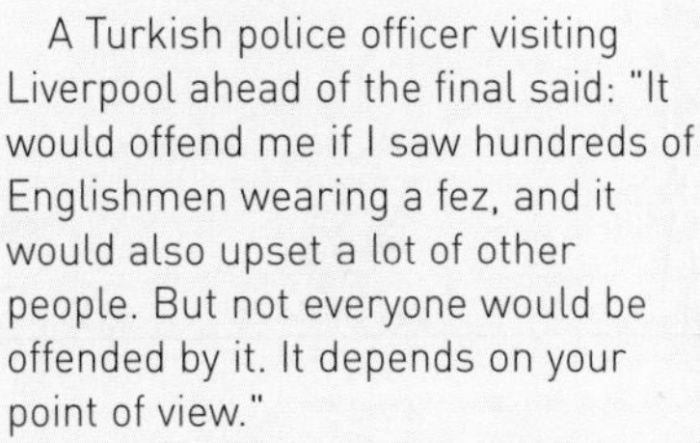

on Chelsea but as it wore on more and more people were backing Liverpool so there would obviously be a major payout if they went on to win it."

FEZ WARNING

Supporters planning to don a fez in Turkey were warned that it could cause offence to their hosts.

Wearing a fez is seen as insulting by many Turks, and remains a controversial issue in the country. The founder of modern Turkey Kamal Ataturk banned them in 1925, and since then opinion has been divided between those who view the fez as harmless headwear and those who view it as an afront to their revered former leader.

A Turkish police officer visiting Liverpool ahead of the final said: "It would offend me if I saw hundreds of Englishmen wearing a fez, and it would also upset a lot of other people. But not everyone would be offended by it. It depends on your point of view."

Alan Greaves, a lecturer in archaeology at Liverpool University added: "Ataturk is very highly revered in Turkey. To wear a fez would indicate that the wearer wished Turkey, which is a proud republic, to revert to the Ottoman Empire.

This would be offensive to most Turkish people."

The Top 10 Singles

May 25th, 2005

1	**OASIS** Lyla
2	**AKON** Lonely
3	**THE BLACK EYED PEAS** Don't Phunk with my heart
4	**GORILLAZ** Feel Good Inc
5	**TONY CHRISTIE FEAT. PETER KAY** (is this the way to) Amarillo
6	**JENNIFER LOPEZ FEAT. FAT JOE** Hold you Down
7	**THE GAME FEAT. 50 CENT** Hate it or love it
8	**SNOOP DOGG FEAT. C WILSON/J TIMBERLAKE** Signs
9	**MAX GRAHAM VS YES** Owner of a lonely heart
10	**KAISER CHIEFS** Every day I love you less and less

Greatest comeback in Reds' history

CUP RETURNS TO SPIRITUAL HOME

Liverpool 3
AC Milan 3 **(Liverpool win 3-2 on penalties aet)**

by Chris Bascombe in Istanbul
Liverpool Echo, Thursday, May 26 2005

WHEN you get homesick nothing will stop you returning to the arms of those you love. AC Milan had a few tricks up their sleeves to keep the European Cup away from her spiritual base.

They tempted her with sublime skills, destructive finishing and a fairytale script, courtesy of their legendary captain.

Paolo Maldini wasn't just holding the trophy at half-time, he was planning his fifth acceptance speech.

What he never foresaw was the homing device triggered by 35,000 Liverpool fans in the Ataturk Stadium who inspired their side to transform the most humiliating night in their history to the most triumphant.

The European Cup didn't fancy Paolo. She wanted Steven but it took a series of remarkable chat-up lines from the Liverpool manager to ensure his skipper got his wicked way.

The only reason Liverpool weren't fatally wounded by a first-half blitz is the fortunate fact immortals can't be destroyed.

Gerrard and company have rewritten football "possibilities" throughout this campaign but even the heroic

istanbul
The Final 2005
Rbk
OPEL

efforts of Olympiakos, Juventus and Chelsea were rendered insignificant compared to this.

It shouldn't have happened. Some of us aren't convinced it did. Only the pinch marks confirm it. We thought it was all over. It wasn't.

Liverpool fans faced a sickening dilemma. What do you do when your side is 3-0 down in the Champions League final to a side superior in every position?

Praying was one option. Another, which was rather attractive at half-time last night, was to grab the nearest taxi back to Taksim Square and drink the night away trying to forget the embarrassment they had just suffered.

The other alternative, which one red-shirted gent decided was more favourable, was to start an impromptu rendition of You'll Never Walk Alone, drowned in the kind of sentimentality Liverpool's opponents find repulsive.

But the 35,000 didn't sing it with hope in their hearts, nor with fire in their bellies. It was poignant rather than passionate.

The tear in the eye wasn't one of joy but despair. A mere 45 minutes into a ceremony 21 years in preparation and a dream had died.

As the second chorus faded Liverpool's players ran back onto the pitch to an astonishing ovation.

The cresendo of noise somehow injected volumes of self-belief into the hitherto drained souls.

The inspirational orchestrator of the famous anthem had perfectly complimented Rafa Benitez's team talk.

He had inadvertently inspired the greatest fightback ever witnessed in any football stadium in any decade by any team ever.

Okay, a few belated but painfully necessary tactical changes helped.

The previous manager's fatal mistake in this competition was subbing Didi Hamann during a crucial European clash three years ago.

Far more serious was the decision to omit him completely.

Benitez made an astonishing gamble, abandoning caution for an attacking formation which backfired so hideously the away end resembled a series of portraits of Edward Munch's The Scream.

Everything which could go wrong did, until Harry Kewell was injured.

Djimi Traore endured a nightmare start, conceding possession and then a free-kick which allowed Maldini to score in his seventh final.

Then Kewell, a surprising choice, pulled a muscle and limped out of his second showpiece of the season.

Whether this was a blow or a blessing was debatable. The choice of Vladimir Smicer ahead of the overlooked anchorman, however, ensured the only immediate change was to Liverpool's detriment.

Not because of Smicer who gave the performance of a player who should be signing a new deal rather than waving goodbye, rather Liverpool's defence remained exposed.

The Reds pushed for an equaliser as if eight minutes remained, not 89. And they were duly punished.

With no riot gear to protect them the defence was left bruised by the combined force of Kaka, Crespo and Shevchenko.

Three-nil could have been five but for Luis Garcia's goal line clearance and a generous offside flag when Gerrard's tackle sent Shevchenko clean through.

"It was embarrassing," admitted Jamie Carragher later.

If a black hole had appeared in the centre circle some of the players would have dived into it, swiftly followed by the fans.

Half-time was a painkiller. Not losing by more than three represented a triumph.

What followed defied logic. If Elvis rose from the grave, brushed off his white suit and announced plans for a world tour we'd still say it wasn't as good a comeback as Liverpool's in Istanbul.

Freed by the essentially restored Didi Hamann, Gerrard started to advance. The most important cross of John Arne Riise's life found the skipper's head.

Then Smicer matched his former nemesis thanks to Dida's careless dive. Yes, Smithy, Vlad has now scored a crucial European Cup goal just as you did!

The improbable was suddenly possible. By the time

Gennaro Gattuso (the biggest culprit when it came to counting chickens at half-time) tripped Gerrard, Liverpool were rampant.

Gattuso should have seen red. Liverpool's equaliser at the second attempt from Xabi Alonso was an acceptable consolation.

But the momentum shifted back to Milan. The Reds looked like they had punched above their weight once too often. The only winner seemed destined to come from a white shirt with Shevchenko and the increasingly confident Dudek engaging in a personal duel.

When the Pole made an astonishing double save with two minutes of extra time remaining rumour had it the engraver started with an L on the famous trophy.

Penalties were still Liverpool's only hope. The spirit of 1984 was enacted. Dudek was the hero. What's likely to be his final appearance for Liverpool will sit comfortably alongside the images of Bruce Grobbelaar - although the Pole's weren't the only knees wobbling by this stage.

All that remained was for Gerrard to grab his prize.

The European Cup seemed to radiate a smile which beamed as broad as the skipper's face.

The dreams of the captain, the manager, the squad and fans were realised in a way the most elaborate fantasist couldn't have imagined.

Finally a new generation of Liverpool fans and players know how it feels to be no games from greatness.

And the European Cup is coming home.

MATCH FACTS

Liverpool (4-4-1-1): Dudek, Finnan (Hamann), Traore, Hyypia, Carragher, Riise, Gerrard, Luis Garcia, Alonso, Kewell (Smicer), Baros (Cisse)
Subs unused: Carson, Josemi, Nunez, Biscan.

AC Milan (4-3-1-2): Dida, Cafu, Maldini, Stam, Nesta, Gattuso (Rui Costa), Seedorf (Serginho), Pirlo, Kaka, Shevchenko, Crespo (Tomasson)
Subs unused: Abbiati, Kaladze, Costacurta, Dhorasoo.

Goals: Maldini (1), Crespo (39, 44), Gerrard (54), Smicer (56), Alonso (60)
Penalties: Serginho (0-0), Hamann (0-1), Pirlo (0-1), Cisse (0-2), Tomasson (1-2), Riise (1-2), Kaka (2-2), Smicer (2-3), Shevchenko (2-3)

Bookings: Carragher, Baros

Conditions: Cool, dry, good playing surface

Referee: Manuel Gonzalez (Spain)

Attendance: 69,000

Rafael Benitez

RAFAEL Benitez admitted he faced the toughest job of his footballing life when he walked into the Liverpool dressing room at half-time with his team 3-0 down.

He may have been the only man in the Ataturk stadium who believed the Reds were not a condemned team, but he was able to rouse his men for the comeback of all comebacks.

"It was very difficult to go into that dressing room and see the players with their heads down," said Benitez. "We talked about different things. We had worked very hard for ten days and we needed to fight to the end. You have to keep believing in yourself.

"We had fought hard to be in the final. I was thinking about what to say and what to change. I needed to change the system and we needed to be more aggressive. I had to give confidence to the players.

"The first thing I did was explain the plan to Didi [Hamann]. I wasn't thinking about winning then, only about scoring. If we did that then Milan's reaction could be very different. They were afraid and everything changed when we scored."

Immediately after the game, Rafa was still trying to absorb the magnitude of the achievement.

"I don't have words to express what I feel at the moment. You concede in the first minute, you lose Harry Kewell, players go down with cramp and it's very difficult. We tried to change things at half-time and said it would be different if we scored - and it was. But the players believed and we won. Steven Gerrard is a key player for us, he has the mentality."

Benitez, who stood unobtrusively to the side of the Liverpool squad on the podium as the trophy was handed over, tried to play down his own role in the achievement.

"As a manager you are important sometimes and you make mistakes, but the most important people are your staff and your players. Never call me the special one!

"I am one step closer to what the other [Liverpool] managers achieved, that's all. I have to do a lot more before I am considered on the same level."

Steven Gerrard

"LIFTING the trophy has to be the best feeling ever. How can I think of leaving Liverpool after a night like this?

The supporters have saved up for weeks and months to come here. I am so happy to lift the cup for the fans.

This is the greatest game I have played in. There can never have been anything like it before. Lifting the cup as Liverpool captain was just the best moment of my life.

We were massive underdogs at the beginning of the competition and I'll put my hands up and say I didn't think we were going to go all the way. But, as you can see, we are never beaten.

The manager told us to keep our chins up, to try and score early in the second half and give some respect for the fans.

Milan had played the ball so quickly and so fluently and cleverly during that first half that it took a lot out of us chasing their shadows because we could not get near them. We were lucky to be only 3-0 down. Milan's football was world class.

When I scored it started to change. That goal gave us a bit of belief. What happened next was amazing. How do you find words to describe it?

When Jerzy made that double save from Shevchenko deep into extra time, just before he hit it, I thought 'goal', and I knew that would be the end of it but then when it went over the bar, I thought maybe it was going to be our day.

In extra time, I spoke to a few of the lads on the pitch and we were all tired. I was running on empty even with 10 or 12 minutes of normal time still to go and admit I was thinking of penalties.

Then when Serginho missed their first one I thought to myself again 'we are meant to win this'.

I was down to take the fifth penalty so I was especially delighted when Jerzy saved from Shevchenko. The manager had asked me whether I wanted to take one and I said 'yes'. When he told me he had put me on the last one, I thought 'cheers'.

How can anything follow a game like that? But we must. Liverpool have got to improve and I have got to get better."

David Moores

LIVERPOOL chairman David Moores revealed that football legend Michel Platini commiserated with him at half-time, believing Liverpool's only target in the second half would be to maintain respectability.

He said: "I was sitting near Platini and he came up to me at half-time and said 'I'm sorry, Mr Chairman, but your manager is going to have to do some damage limitation from this point.'

"Then he came up to me at full-time and said 'I must apologise. Your club has shown great courage. You should be proud of them.'

"I am. I'm proud of every player and supporter.

"No one thought we'd get this far at half-time against Olympiakos. Even when we were losing to Grazer in the qualifier things didn't look good. We've been underdogs all the way."

Moores, who had been on the brink of standing down as chairman admitted the uncertainty surrounding his position had strained him.

"Everyone has difficult times and you just have to believe you're right and battle on.

"This club means the world to me and I'm not going to let it go easily.

"I admit the pressure was telling on me, but my wife had said to me 'What else would you do? This is your life.' It is.

"The grass-roots support has helped me through it all. You've got to keep going in life and a night like this is what this club is all about as far as I'm concerned."

Rick Parry

"OUR sensational victory in the Ataturk Stadium in Istanbul provided me with the greatest moment of my football life.

I was delighted for the fans, the players and our manager Rafa Benitez who deserved this moment of glory after coming through a challenging first season at Anfield.

Debate will continue as to whether this was the greatest European Cup final of all-time. What an achievement for the boys. For me, this success is up there with any of our previous glory days and that includes 1977, 1978, 1981 and 1984. The fact that our fifth triumph enables us to keep that most famous of trophies adds to it.

I'm sure many thousands of you will have great pleasure in looking at it in future, be it displayed in our famous trophy room or in the Anfield Visitors' Centre. It certainly won't be in the boardroom. It will be out on public display as a symbol of the part our supporters played in an incredible night in Turkey.

I'm still in a state of shock. No one could believe the way we stared defeat in the face and came back so powerfully to force a penalty shoot-out.

I'm still trying to take it all in. Like many of you, I didn't want to leave the stadium. At the same time I was aware of the scenes that were going on back in Liverpool as those who couldn't be with us began a very special city centre party that continued when we returned with the cup on Thursday.

Once again our fans did us proud. Magnificent in Istanbul, majestic on Merseyside, they helped everyone believe that anything is possible at LFC. We wanted to win that trophy for them. Let's just say it's 20 years overdue."

Michael Owen

"WHO knows if they would have got to the final if I was leading the attack or if I would have done things differently from Milan Baros.

People will say my timing for leaving Anfield was suspect but how was I, or anyone else, to know that Liverpool were about to go on the most incredible run to the final?

A few months ago when they had been knocked out of the FA Cup at Burnley and were struggling outside the Champions League places, people were speculating that it might be a disastrous season for Liverpool.

There are so many turning points but now that they have come good I am thrilled for some of my old colleagues such as Stevie Gerrard, Didi Hamann and Jamie Carragher.

I hope it does kick-start a great new era for Liverpool."

Xabi Alonso

"There was real suspense surrounding my penalty - it was like something out of a Hitchcock movie!"

Jerzy Dudek

"I DON'T know how I did it. With that last save in the last three minutes, someone up there saved us," (regarding his double save to deny Andriy Shevchenko what would have been the winner at the end of extra-time).

I'm so glad I made that save. I feel he got between the defenders and nobody could stop him. All I could do was prepare myself or make a save from his header and I managed to do that. Then he was straight up and it was obvious he was going to get the rebound. I jumped up as quickly as I could and made myself as big as possible and fortunately the ball hit my arm and went over the bar.

It was fortunate for myself that I did it. Fantastic for me. I was waiting for this moment. I had difficult moments in this game but this is fantastic.

That was by far the best and most important save I have ever made in my life.

Before the penalties Carragher came up to me like he was crazy, as always. He grabbed me and said 'Jerzy, Jerzy, Jerzy remember Bruce (Grobbelaar). He did crazy things to put them off and you have to do the same. Just put them off all the time'.

He told me I would be the hero. I said: 'Okay, calm down. I've seen the video of Bruce and the penalty shoot-out loads of times.'

The first one was missed and I tried the crazy legs for the next one but he scored. But a lot of other things worked out and I was very happy.

It was the most fantastic and biggest game of all of our lives.

We are in heaven now."

Bruce Grobbelaar

"I'VE got a big hangover. Jerzy Dudek was fantastic, he was like a starfish with jelly legs. I heard he was told to remember what I did in 1984 and he did it – I think he did better! He put the first one off and saved two penalties.

That must be the most magnificent comeback in the history of the Champions League and hopefully they'll be able to defend it next year.

I think the side now is much better than ours was then, in the way they came back.

It was a beautiful moment, and I wish everyone all the best."

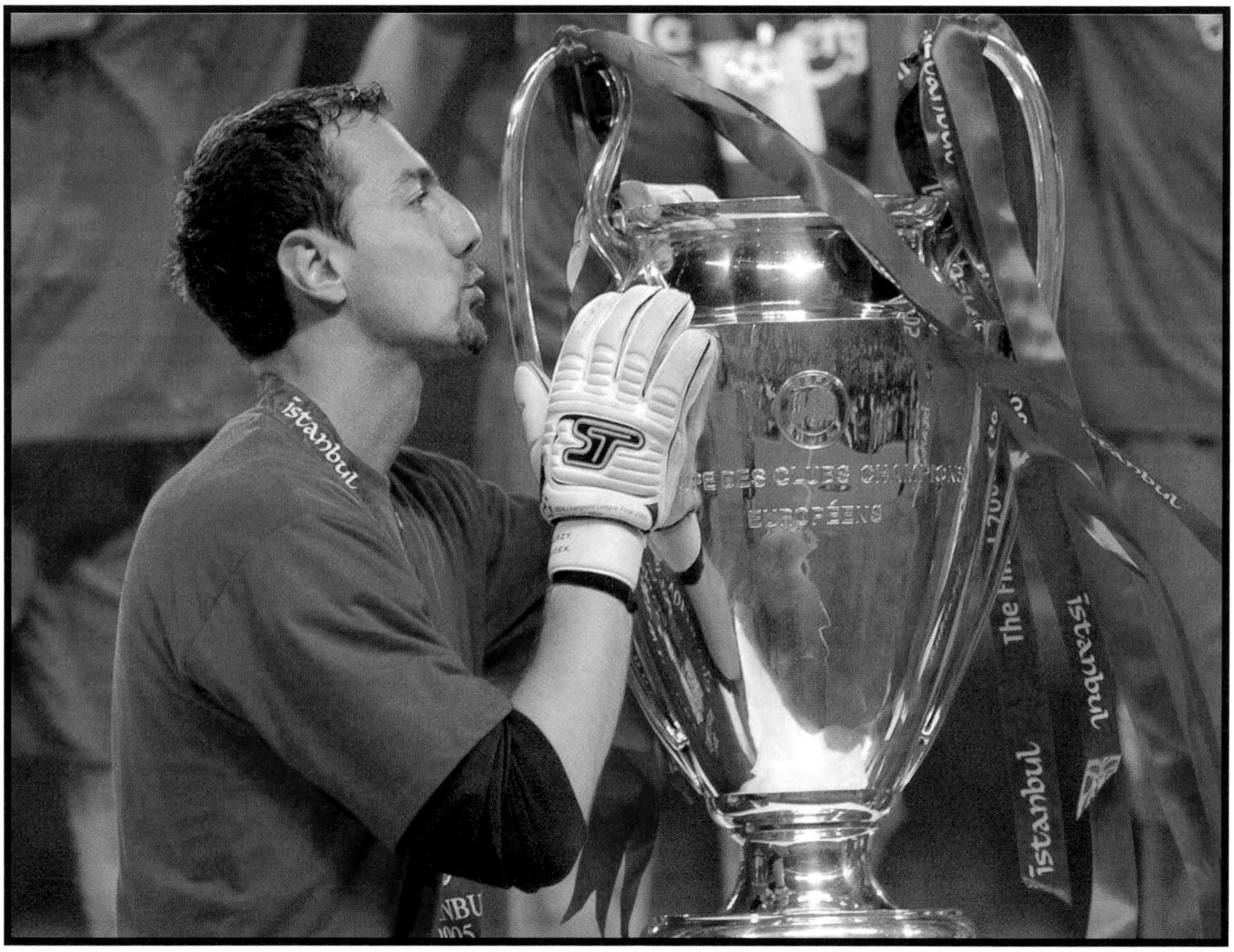

Vladimir Smicer

"I ALWAYS felt I owed a bit to Liverpool because I have had plenty of injuries and wanted to show the fans I am a good player.

I wanted to show I could help the team, so I am so proud.

It is a long time since I scored a goal like that and, unbelievably, it was the first of my season so it was good timing.

Going around the ground was very sad and emotional. I can say I will never forget that, not just because I am leaving either, because all the players will feel the same. We will never forget it.

When I got back to the hotel I lit a huge cigar. It is the tradition in America when you've won a trophy. It was huge.

I had it all night and I kept puffing and lighting it up and it never went out. I did not get any sleep at all.

I'm so glad I scored.

This is my seventh trophy with Liverpool. That's not bad is it?"

Phil Thompson

"I NEVER thought that Rome 77 would be beaten but, for me, this has eclipsed it.

The passion, commitment, never-say-die attitude...Bill Shankly, Bob Pailey and Joe Fagan will be up there watching these lads now and they'd be so proud.

Nobody could have thought this at half-time, no way. And that's why it's the best.

I know some of the former players might be out there saying: "No, Thommo, you've got it wrong.' I don't think so. I think we've seen something incredible today. This was against all the odds. They've pulled it off.

I was down at half-time but I believed. It just needed that first goal. I can't believe what I've witnessed but then it's Liverpool Football Club and the trophy's coming home."

Alan Kennedy

"WE had a fantastic time. It is the best atmosphere I've ever experienced.

We were lethargic at the start, and I couldn't see us recovering. But Liverpool took the game to Milan.

Dudek's antics reminded me of Bruce Grobbelaar.

Rafa was bold and brave at half-time. He wasn't happy but turned it around.

This victory has got to top the lot (in comparison to their other European triumphs), they showed their spirit."

★★★★★

Luis Garcia

LUIS Garcia didn't score the goal he dreamed of in the build-up to the Champions League final but that didn't take away from the feelings of euphoria he experienced after the game.

He said: "We were all a little worried at half-time when we were 3-0 down because it didn't look as if there was any way back for us. But we kept believing in ourselves and I think we deserved to win.

"We have showed our strengths many times this season and this is a fantastic moment for us all now.

"It's reward for the hard work we've put in this season.

"The support we have had throughout has been magnificent but the way the fans stayed with us in Istanbul, even when we looked out of it, is something that will live with me for a very long time. We are lucky to have such an excellent twelfth man."

Alan Hansen

"THE second half was just unbelievable. What this Liverpool team have shown, time and time again in the Champions League, is that when they've had a mountain to climb they've climbed it.

You go back to Olympiakos when they needed to score three in the second half to get through the group stage and they did it.

But this time they were 3-0 down against AC Milan. They had been made to look like second-raters with the Italians flooding all over the top of them.

I don't know what Rafael Benitez said at half-time but I'd love to get a tape of it.

The second half was the most incredible turn-around I've seen in any sport at any time.

You've got to give credit to the players and the manager because they were the ones that did it and to the supporters who were again their twelfth man.

This has been without a shadow of a doubt the greatest night of them all.

Rome in '77 was great and then the finals against Bruges, Real Madrid were dull affairs but this one was just unbelievable.

It's difficult to describe. You could not have written this.

Somebody said to me after half-an-hour that it's a big game and we haven't seen much of Gerrard. He wasn't saying that to me after 65 minutes!

The captain lifted the game by the scruff of the neck. He scored the goal that got us back into it, won the penalty for Xabi Alonso's equaliser and then turned in an exceptional performance at right-back. He was unbelievable.

But it wasn't about one player. It was about the lot of them."

Gary McAllister

"RAFA must really have inspired the team at half-time, they were totally outclassed in the first half. He is a very humble manager, and I am delighted for the players.

I hoped Liverpool would be offensive, and they were in starting with Harry Kewell. But losing that early goal didn't help them, and Didi Hamann made such a difference when he came on.

They are a super club, with a very special set of fans.

It has got to be their greatest-ever European triumph, all their previous European Cup wins were when they were champions of England. This time they had only finished 5th, about 40 points behind Chelsea."

Jamie Carragher

"IT is one of the greatest finals of all time. People will be talking about that game in 20 or 30 years time. And the save Jerzy made from Shevchenko at the end was just unbelievable.

It sounds strange but I've not really been celebrating in the changing room. I just can't believe it.

I cannot believe how we've won that cup. We had a similar scenario a few years ago in the FA Cup final against Arsenal when we were dead and buried but ended up coming back and we've done it again tonight. That makes it that much sweeter.

I didn't believe we could turn it around at half-time. I was going out there in the second half hoping that we weren't really going to embarrass ourselves more by letting in four or five.

We didn't want it to be remembered as a final where there was a bit of an embarrassment.

They got the early goal and we seemed to be pushing for the equaliser too early and they kept hitting us on the break.

They're a good side. Kaka was causing us a lot of problems. But to do what we've done in the second half - I think that final will go down as one of the greatest European finals.

It was very important that we got that goal early in the second half because that gave belief to our supporters.

Milan seemed to go down a notch when we got that goal and we really put them under pressure after that with our tackling and winning the second balls. It was just a great night.

We'd gone in extra-time. We put that much effort into the second half and I'd gone with cramp. I was feeling it right up my leg.

To be honest, in extra-time I think we were playing for penalties because we were that tired. Jerzy's save from Shevchenko was unbelievable.

I was just waiting for it to hit the net and it being game up.

I couldn't believe it never went in and I think that was the moment that I thought our name was on the cup.

I don't think tonight will ever be bettered.

We can win this trophy again but I think it's the way we won it this time that makes it so special."

ISTANBUL UNCUT

The images of Liverpool winning the European Cup for the fifth time will last forever! Here are some of the greatest pictures from an incredible night, including many UNSEEN images...

Pictures John Cocks and Colin Lane

CHAMPIONS LEAGUE WINNERS
ISTANBUL
2005
TANDBERG
Istanbul
The Final 2005

The Reds train in the Ataturk Stadium on the eve of the big game and the two skippers meet ahead of kick-off (bottom right)

The Final 2005
AMSTEL
AMSTEL

Rafa's red and white army in Taksim Square

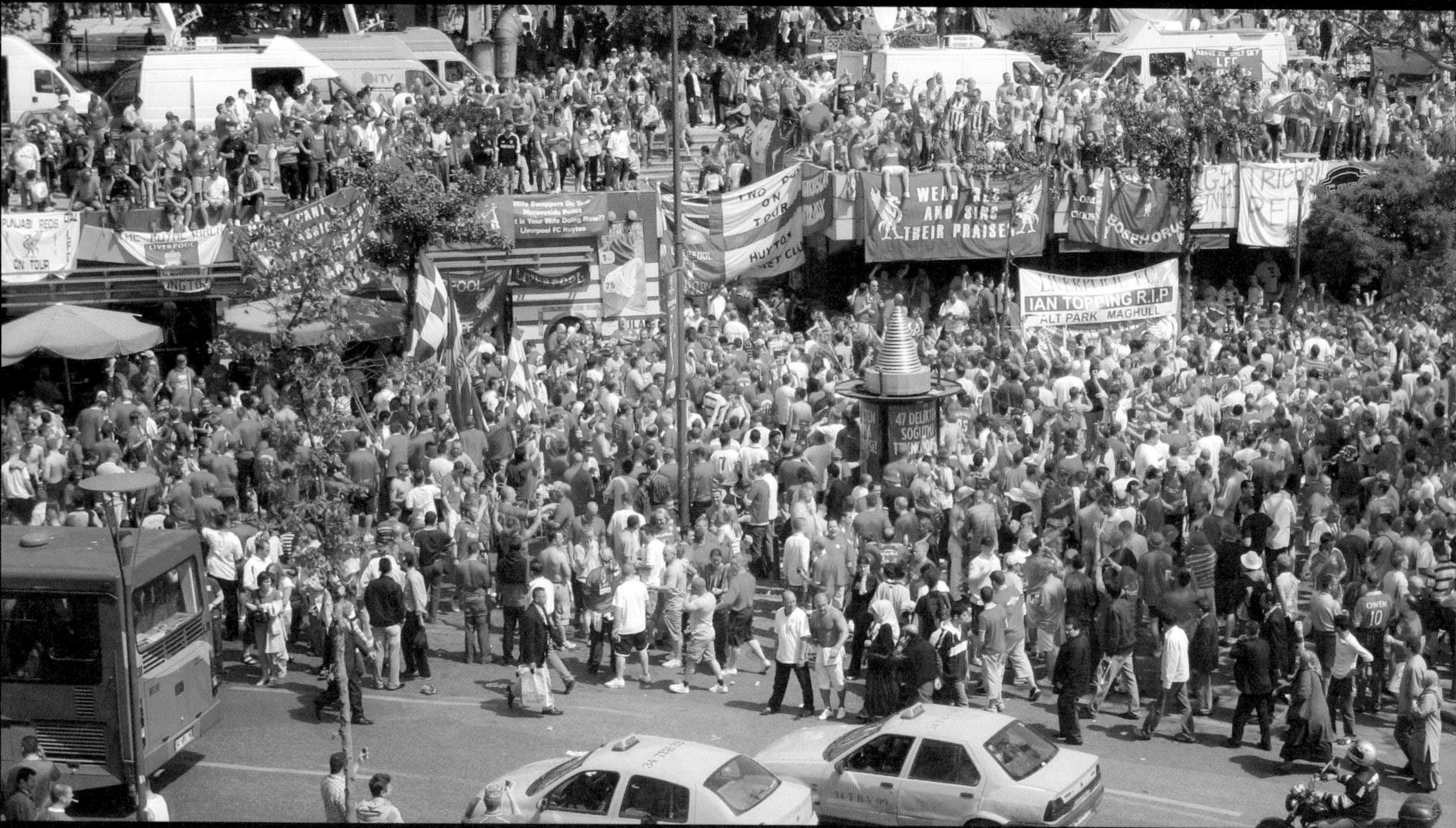

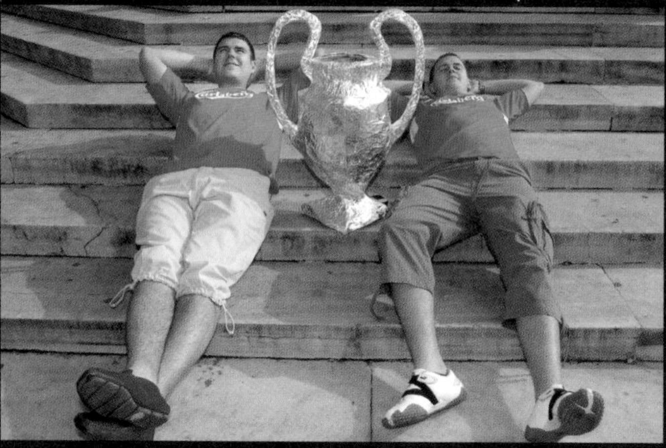

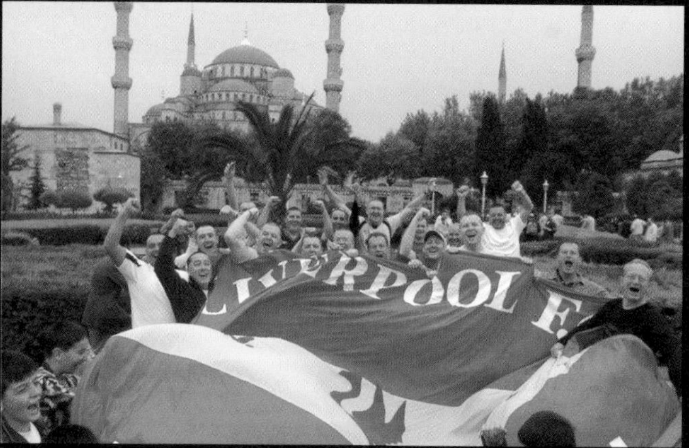

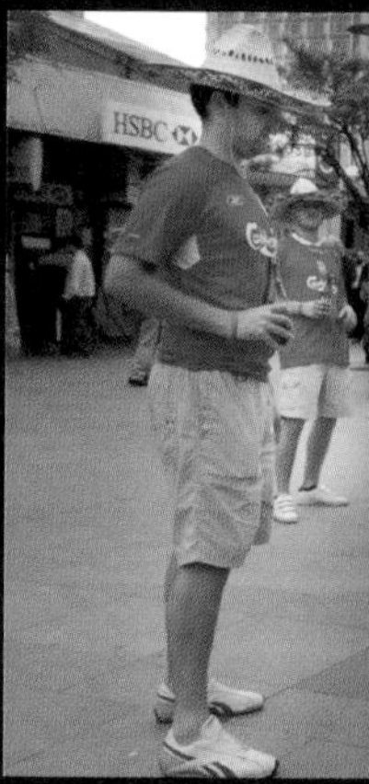

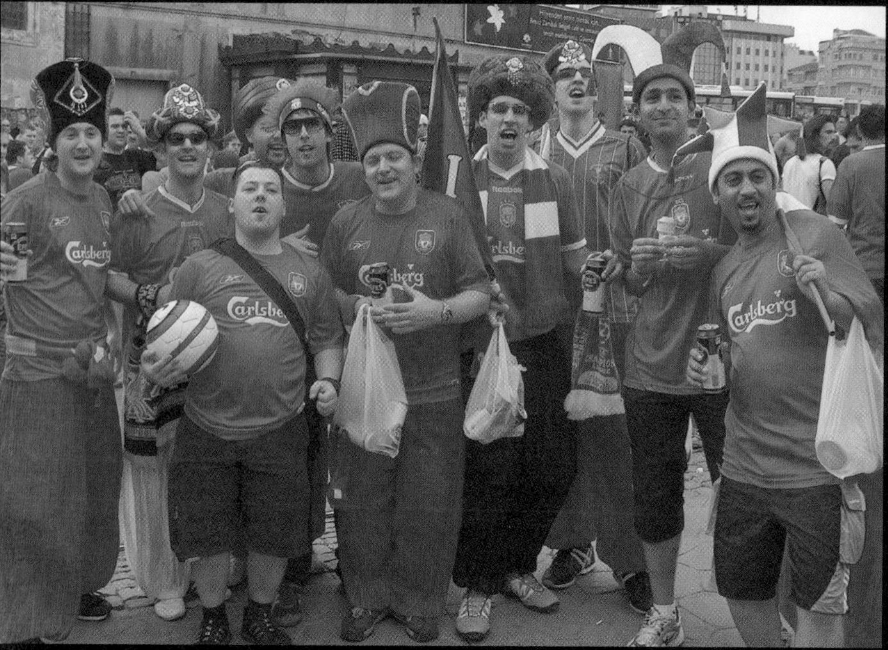

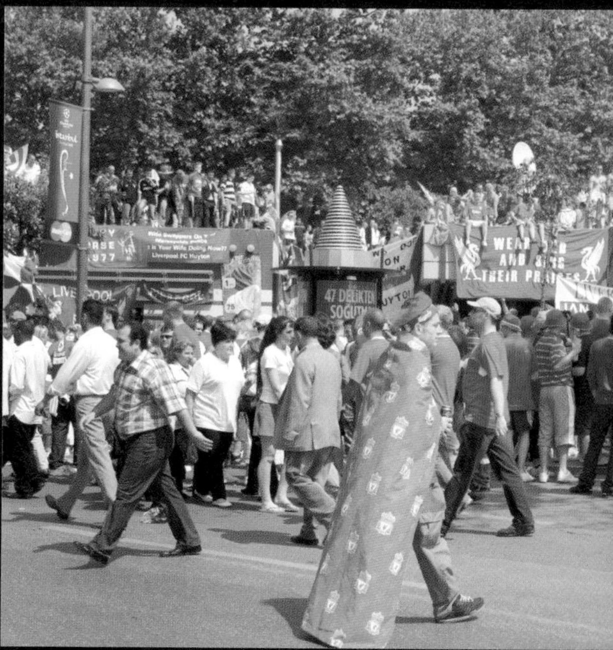

LI ERPOOL
FOOTBALL CLUB
EUR PES FINEST

OWEN
10

ISTANBUL UNCUT

The travelling Kop arrives on the big stage
Picture: Tony Woolliscroft

LIVERPOOL F.C.
ITALIAN JOB
LIVERPOOL

WINNER
LIVERPOOL F.C.
LIVERPOOL
LIVERPOOL FC

High drama on the field of play

TRAORE
21
14
10
Carlsberg
İstanbul
The Final 2005

ISTANBUL UNCUT

Celebration time for our heroes

istanbul
The Final 2005
UEFA

One of us: Carra runs to celebrate with the fans

WINNER
Carlsberg

The chairman and his staff share a moment with the European Cup by the pool at the team hotel in Istanbul

Below: Steven Gerrard leaves the stadium with the European Cup for company and the fans wait for their first glimpse of the trophy back home on Merseyside

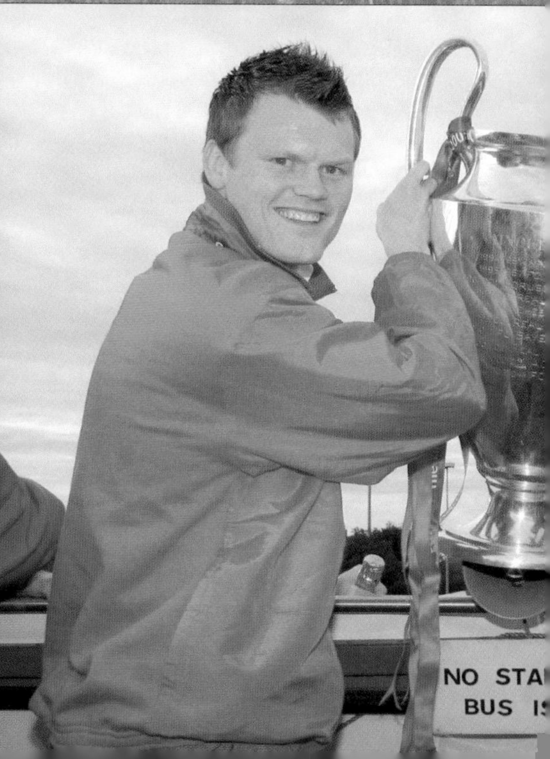

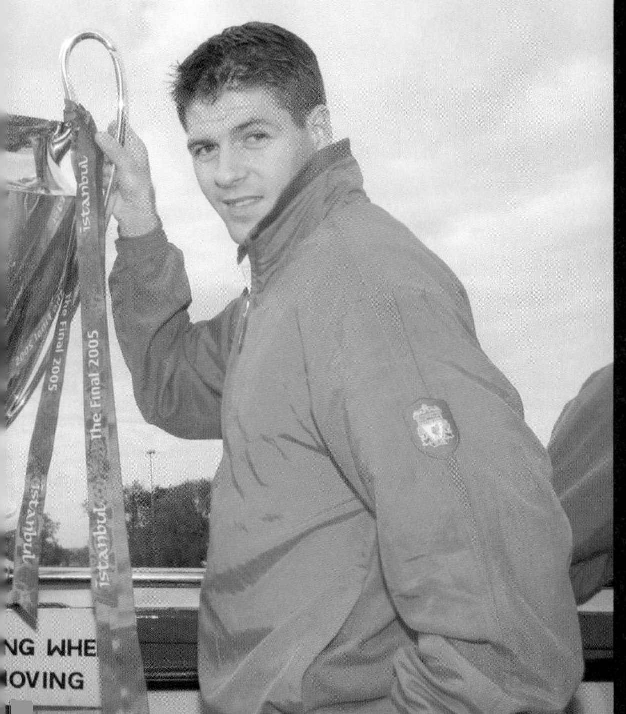

The morning after the night before: The players relax with the trophy before bringing it home for keeps

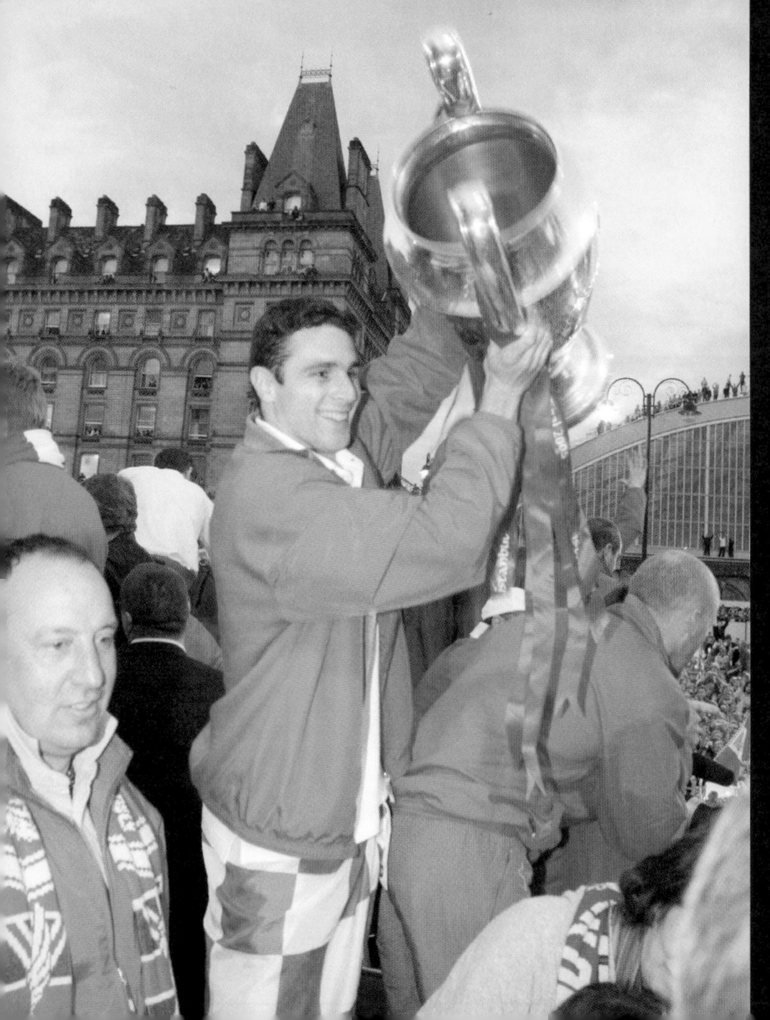

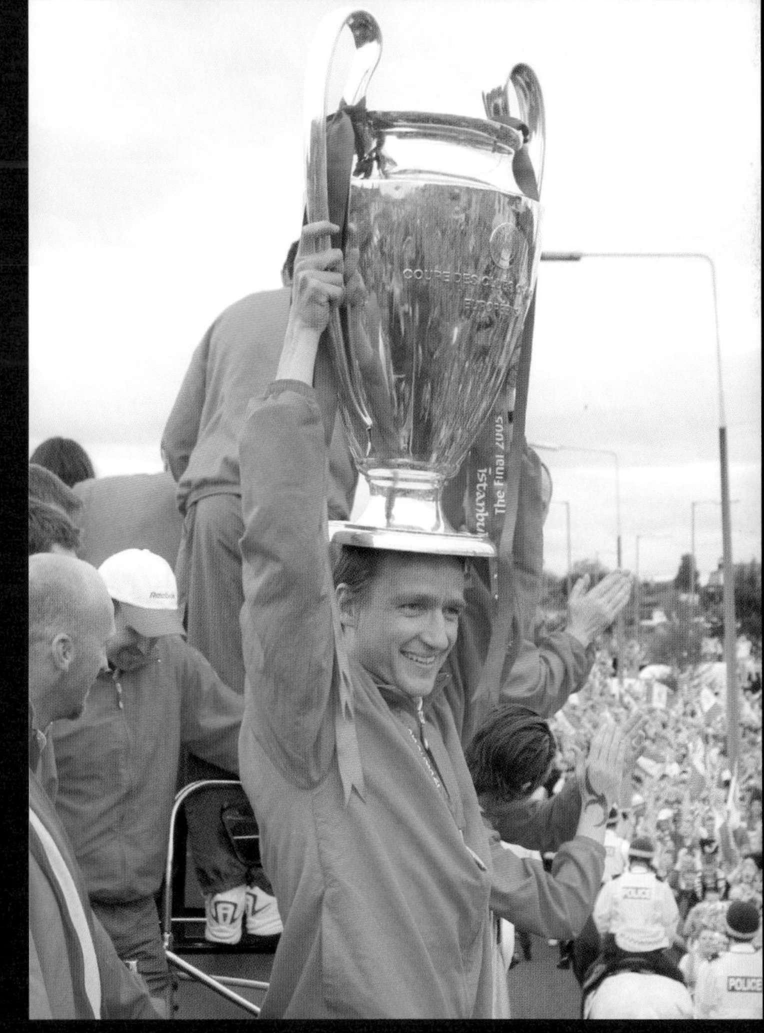

LIVERPOOL

Early delivery: Rafael Benitez with the European Cup in his first season in charge

It's ours to **keep**

'Ol' Big Ears' is back in town. After 21 years away from Anfield, this time he's here to stay. Lifted by Emlyn Hughes (twice), Phil Thompson, Graeme Souness, Steven Gerrard and dropped by Milan Baros. At the end of the storm there'll always be a sweet silver cup...

THE European Cup that now takes pride of place in the Liverpool Football Club Museum at Anfield is the fourth incarnation of the current, modern trophy.

Liverpool have become the fifth club in an elite band who own an original of the Swiss designed silverware, and will do for all eternity.

The others are Real Madrid, AC Milan, AFC Ajax and Bayern Munich.

Real Madrid (9) and Milan (6) have both won the trophy more than the required five times in order to keep it while Ajax (1970-72) and Bayern Munich (1974-76) filled the other criteria by winning it three times in a row.

The trophy that Liverpool won, thanks to the most famous comeback in the history of the European Cup, is much larger than the original trophy handed to Real Madrid captain Francisco Gento in 1966 after the Spaniards' sixth win in 11 years.

Back then, the trophy could be held in just one hand. It was decided a new design was required and UEFA'S general secretary Hans Bargeter turned to a Swiss expert in the field.

Father and son, Hans and Jurg Stadelmann, were charged with the responsibility but they had a problem. Each competing country had its own particular taste and design for the trophy so it was put together in sections. It was, in the makers' own words a "bastardised design".

It took Liverpool 9,860 minutes of competition to win the trophy but it took its makers more than twice that time - 20,400 minutes to be precise - to construct their masterpiece. We're sure they'd be heartened to hear that it took Milan Baros just two seconds to change its design forever when he dropped it on the floor and dented the handle.

A total of 38 different pairs of hands had lifted the Champion Club's Cup before Steven Gerrard became the 39th skipper to hold it high above his head.

Only one man has ever had his hands on the trophy three times, and that man was Bayern Munich and Germany legend Franz Beckenbauer between 1974 and 1976 - so therein lies a challenge for Steven Gerrard and Liverpool.

The last man to lift it twice in consecutive seasons was, ironically, for our vanquished opponents this season, AC Milan captain Franco Baresi who stood proudly on the winners' rostrum in 1989 and 1990 after victories over Steaua Bucharest and Benfica.

THE OMENS

SO the omens were true then. The spooky coincidences with previous years when Liverpool won the European Cup may have been more than coincidence. At least that's what the mystics are telling us.

In case you require a reminder about parallels with past triumphant years:

In 1978, the Pope died, Wales won the rugby union Grand Slam and Liverpool lost the League Cup final to the eventual league champions.

In 1981, Prince Charles got married, there was a new Doctor Who, Ken married Deirdre in Coronation Street and Liverpool finished fifth in the league, winning 17 games, while Norwich and Crystal Palace were relegated.

Mathematics was also on the Reds' side. They had won the competition on four previous occasions: 77, 78, 81 and 84. Add each of those digits together and you get 50. May 25 was the date of the 50th European Cup final. Turn 50 around and you get '05'.

1984

The road to Rome

After dismissing Odense it was something of an odd European campaign for Liverpool - indifferent at Anfield, outstanding away. Joe Fagan's side Basqued in the Bilbao pressure and shone in Benfica's Stadium of Light before a win in Romania meant it was Rome-mania for Kopites again and a fourth final in eight seasons

Round one

Round one, first leg
September 14 1983

BK Odense 0

Liverpool 1
(Dalglish 15)

Att: 30,000

Team: Grobbelaar, Neal, Kennedy, Lawrenson, Johnston, Hansen, Dalglish, Lee, Rush, Robinson, Souness.

IT was a winning start to Joe Fagan's first European Cup campaign as Liverpool manager but it should have been much more comprehensive than the scoreline suggests.

The Danish amateurs found themselves outclassed in every department and had it not been for a string of decent saves from their goalkeeper Lars Hogh, the tie would have been all but over ahead of the return.

An excellent early stop from Dalglish proved only light relief, however, Kenny making sure shortly after, firing home when Michael Robinson miscued a Craig Johnston cross.

Round one, second leg
September 28 1983

Liverpool 5
(Robinson 14,72, Dalglish 32, 40, Clausen (og) 64)

BK Odense 0

Att: 14,985

Team: Grobbelaar, Nicol, Kennedy, Lawrenson, Johnston, Hansen, Dalglish, Lee, Rush, Robinson, Souness (Hodgson).

WHERE Liverpool had been wasteful in the first leg there was no saving the Danish champions' bacon at Anfield.

A Kenny Dalglish brace saw him surpass Denis Law's British scoring record in the European Cup and Michael Robinson scored his first goals since joining the Reds.

An Odense player did manage to get on the scoresheet but unfortunately for them it came at the wrong end as Clausen hit a disastrous back pass into his own net.

Zubizarreta of Bilbao gathers as Rush comes close after mounting pressure from Liverpool

Round two

Round two, first leg
October 19 1983

Liverpool 0

Athletic Bilbao 0

Att: 33,063

Team: Grobbelaar, Neal, Kennedy, Lawrenson, Johnston, Hansen, Dalglish, Lee, Rush, Robinson, Souness.

NOT concerned with taking an away goal back to Spain, Athletic left Anfield with exactly what they came for - a goalless draw.

Hardly threatening Grobbelaar's goal throughout, they restricted Liverpool to just a couple of chances also, the best of which saw a 30-yard Phil Neal effort tipped over by Andoni Zubizarreta.

Any attacks the Reds could muster tended to come from the wings as Bilbao crowded out the midfield threat. Astute defensive work and a penchant to waste time shamelessly made way for a daunting trip to the Basque country.

Round two, second leg
November 2 1983

Athletic Bilbao 0

Liverpool 1
(Rush 66)

Att: 47,500

Team: Grobbelaar, Neal, Kennedy, Lawrenson, Nicol, Hansen, Dalglish, Lee, Rush, Robinson (Hodgson), Souness.

GIVEN that Bilbao went on to complete a league and cup double over Barcelona and Real Madrid this season, Liverpool's win at the San Mames was all the more remarkable.

As Athletic rediscovered their attacking endeavour on home soil, the Reds soaked up the early pressure before turning the screw as the game went on.

Noriega and Gallego had both shot wide to get the vocal Basque crowd on its feet, but as Souness began to dictate in midfield and Nicol forced a good save from Zubizarreta their cheers turned to cries of angst.

As Liverpool sucked the drive out of the home side, it was a sweet move that found Rush in the box after the break. Hansen found Kennedy on the left who crossed to the Welshman whose downward header bounced over the Spanish international to grant safe passage to round three.

Quarter-final

Quarter-final, first leg
March 7 1984

Liverpool 1
(Rush 67)

Benfica 0

Att: 39,090

Team: Grobbelaar, Neal, Kennedy, Lawrenson, Whelan, Hansen, Robinson (Dalglish), Lee, Rush, Johnston, Souness.

KENNY Dalglish provided the invention to spark this game into life.

Returning after a long injury lay-off, it was only after the Scot's half-time introduction that Liverpool really began to threaten the Portuguese champions. Almost immediately Benfica found themselves on the back foot as the Reds began to penetrate with more imagination.

Following Rush's decisive header from Kennedy's cross, Souness saw a 20-yard strike saved by Bento. The last 15 minutes brought constant pressure from Liverpool, but with three good chances spurned and a penalty appeal turned down Joe Fagan's men still had it all to do in Portugal.

Quarter-final, second leg
March 21 1984

Benfica 1
(Nene 74)

Liverpool 4
(Whelan 9, 87, Johnston 33, Rush 79)

Att: 70,000

Team: Grobbelaar, Neal, Kennedy, Lawrenson, Whelan, Hansen, Dalglish, Lee, Rush, Johnston, Souness.

THE Eagles were well and truly grounded as Liverpool took flight in the Stadium of Light.

The home side started brightly enough but the whole complexion of the game changed when Benfica keeper Bento allowed a Whelan header to slip between his legs and over the line. From here it was one-way traffic.

Again it was Dalglish who tormented the hosts as he played a part in the next three goals, setting up Johnston to score from 20 yards before crossing for Rush to head home and finally freeing Whelan for his second.

Nene's looping header past Grobbelaar in between proved scant consolation for Benfica.

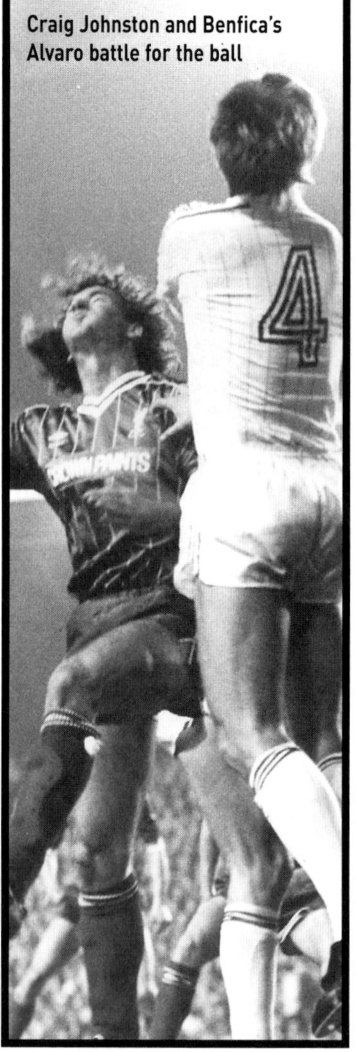

Craig Johnston and Benfica's Alvaro battle for the ball

Dalglish is brought down and Rush is about to lead appeals for a penalty

Sammy Lee thinks he has made it two goals for Liverpool but the referee disallows this effort for offside

Semi-final

Semi-final, first leg
April 11 1984

Liverpool 1
(Lee 25)

Dinamo Bucharest 0

Att: 36,941

Team: Grobbelaar, Neal, Kennedy, Lawrenson, Whelan, Hansen, Dalglish, Lee, Rush, Johnston, Souness.

THIS was never the most memorable of games but it did at least conjour a collector's item by way of a rare headed Sammy Lee goal.

What the visitors lacked in grace they made up for with aggression. A string of malicious fouls disrupted Liverpool's flowing style early on and so it was no surprise when the goal came as a result of a free kick.

Johnston was hacked down, Kennedy crossed and Lee escaped his marker to find the net.

The Reds applied heavy pressure as they looked for a second but the Romanians packed their penalty box. Despite Liverpool's authority though, Dinamo nearly stole a late equaliser as Augustin broke on the counter only to see his shot come back off the post after beating Grobbelaar.

Semi-final, second leg
April 25 1984

Dinamo Bucharest 1
(Orac 38)

Liverpool 2
(Rush 11, 84)

Att: 60,000

Team: Grobbelaar, Neal, Kennedy, Lawrenson, Whelan, Hansen, Dalglish (Nicol), Lee, Rush, Johnston, Souness.

IAN Rush's early goal was the perfect way to calm the nerves as Liverpool opened up a two-goal lead.

It was poetic justice that Graeme Souness was instrumental in the build-up after being singled out for close attention at Anfield in the first leg. It was the skipper's volley back into the box from a Sammy Lee corner that saw Rush sprint past a defender to chip delightfully over the Bucharest keeper.

Orac delivered a beauty of his own to give Dinamo hope just before half-time, his 20-yard free-kick curling over the wall and leaving Grobbelaar no chance.

Liverpool defended well to protect their lead before Rush broke six minutes from time to make sure of the Reds' place in the final.

★★★★★

ANFIELD GLADIATORS BACK IN ROME FOR SOME MORE CONQUERING

All roads lead to Rome again but this time the pilgrimage wasn't made by as many Kopites. Lying in wait were AS Roma and their fanatical fans who were fully expecting to see their heroes land the European Cup in their own back yard

TRANSFER GOSSIP

Reports in the Italian press linked Graeme Souness with Sampdoria ("I know nothing about it at all", said the Scot on the day of the final). Juventus were also linked with a £3.5million bid for Ian Rush 10 days before the final (while Barcelona were said to be preparing a £5m bid on the day of the final). "It is all so ridiculous that I don't even want to bother contradicting them," said Reds chief executive Peter Robinson.

ANY SPARES, TOM?

Tom Saunders, Liverpool's 'masterspy', recalled his journey to Rome to collect the 17,000 allocation for Reds fans. The incident occurred the night before scenes of violence in Rome as home fans clamoured for tickets. "It was obvious to us we could have done with a guard when we saw the crowd milling about. We were given a heavy parcel, and someone created a diversion as we got into the taxi and drove quickly away."

An estimated 10,000 fans (out of 60,000) were expected to be backing the side, with chief executive Peter Robinson revealing that 7,000 tickets had to be returned – and were subsequently burnt at the request of the Italian FA.

GIVE PEACE A CHANCE

To improve relations between British football and the rest of Europe, Liverpool sent 15 'ambassadors' to Rome (14 men and one woman) to hand out presents to Romans in a goodwill gesture before the final. The squad, who were to be guests of Mayor of Rome Ugo Vetere, were also planning to swap shirts with Roma fans on a stage in Capital Square 'as Paul McCartney's The Pipes of Peace blared from loudspeakers'.

The one woman in the party was Dorothy Lambert, an administration assistant in the city solicitor's department having been selected by trip organiser Barry Caldow. "I just can't believe it. It's like winning the pools", beamed Ms. Lambert.

TIPS AND ADVICE

By law you were only allowed to take 200,000 lire (around £87) in currency into the country.

Essential phrases given to fans included suggestions for

'Tah very much, la'; 'Eh la, d'yer speak de lingo like?'; and 'I've gorra 'ed like a bag of frogs, pal'.

Hotel prices were anything from £7 to £170 a night, £1 for a good cup of tea, £5 entrance to some clubs – while 'bar prices are extortionate'.

DIVINE INTERVENTION?

Tickets were fetching up to £100 the weekend before the final, which was a bit much for one Reds supporter. Robin Sutton was studying for the priesthood at the Vatican's Beda College in the lead-up to the game. "There are three other British students at the college as well as myself and we all want to go to the match. But we can't afford the black market prices – even if we could find the black market!"

However, a story was carried the following Tuesday telling how a supporter who had a ticket but could not afford the journey, got in touch with a local priest and offered his ticket to Mr Sutton – which was to be flown out with supporter Miss Sandra Harris.

WISH US LUCK

Retired ICI methods officer George Thornton was planning to invest in Liverpool's potential success after winning a competition to watch the final. The tradition of throwing three coins into Rome's Trevi fountain would then bring the Reds luck. He said: "I have never had the chance to see Rome before and we will be able to see the sights before the game."

GROUNDS FOR CHANGE IN EUROPE?

Chief executive Peter Robinson revealed some of the changes he had witnessed during Liverpool's 20 consecutive years in European football. These included the use of charter aircraft to speed up travel and prevent delays; the introduction of seeding in the wake of a European Cup Winners' Cup first-round tie with Juventus – which the Reds won; and the financial implications of continental football. "We virtually rebuilt Anfield from our success in the early years."

However, it seemed the chance to make big bucks had dwindled since. Robinson noted: "Nowadays you rarely make much from the first round or two and you have to rely on drawing a big name in the quarter or semi-finals.

PRICES

The football special (including match ticket) from Lime Street was £113.50 each (as advertised one week before the final). A flight from Liverpool and match ticket (£3.50 extra): was £169 while another deal offered flights to and from London, transfers, two nights' accommodation and ticket at £193.

LUCKY WELLIES

Roma had more than the threat of Ian Rush and Co. to cope with ahead of the final. Councillor Alec Doswell was planning to attend the match at the Olympic Stadium sporting his lucky boots – or 'desert wellies' as Alec preferred to know them. They had rarely let the Reds down, with Alec having started wearing them for big European games in 1977.

★★★★★

"At least you do get compensation from UEFA nowadays if your gate falls into a loss-making situation in the opening rounds, but European soccer certainly doesn't give you a licence to print money."

POLICE ESCORT

A bus strike stranded Reds fans at Rome's Ciampino Airport – although 100 fans were given a free ride on one of the police coaches. Five hundred Liverpool fans were travelling by train to the city while a fleet of coaches and planes were set to escort 10,000 fans to the Italian capital.

The American president was not on the side of Liverpool though. Ronald Reagan sent a message of good luck to Roma – with suggestions being that he had an eye on the Italian vote in election year.

NO HITCH OVER TICKET

One fan earned a ticket for the final having hitched his way to Rome. Stephen Bosoombe began his journey from Toxteth the Friday before the final – and arrived on the Monday night. A chance meeting with Euroline Travel representative Tommy Davies earned a ticket for the 24-year-old, and he said: "Now Liverpool can't lose!"

RADIO 'VATICAN' CITY

Wednesday included:
'Buongiorno – It's Norman Thomas' – Breakfast show live from Rome.
'Scousers in Rome' – Norman Thomas, Johnny Kennedy and Kieran Devaney bring all the pre-match atmosphere.
'The Road to Rome' – Clive Tyldesley recalls the highlights of the campaign, before providing commentary on the final (Gary Bloom brought the after-match interviews).

GRICE TO SEE YOU

The Grice family from Norris Green revealed their delight at the hospitality of the locals on the eve of the final. The contingent – father Davey Grice (66) and two sons David (37) and Billy (34) were regular European travellers. Mr Grice senior remarked: "Everybody has been so friendly. We heard before we came about possible trouble, but at the moment things couldn't be better. All the cafes we have been to, the locals have been very friendly."

LINK-UP PLANS

The genial atmosphere in the lead-up to the final impressed some Italian supporters so much that suggestions were made about possible ties being forged between the two clubs. President of the Roma Supporters' Club Adlo Sbaffo said: "We are thinking of going to Liverpool next Autumn, perhaps for a return match. Our supporters are very similar. They become enthusiastic and share their teams' joys and sorrows.

"We know the world is watching and we will prove we are the most polite supporters by our behaviour.

"We will give every Englishman a little flag with the symbols of both clubs. This will be the way to live 90 unforgettable minutes."

Indeed, Rome daily 'Il Messagero' gave their own special welcome to English fans:
"(We promise) Peace, love, song – and lots of mineral water!"

THE FINAL WORD

Joe Fagan: "Roma are a very, very good team. So are we, and I just hope that between us we can give Europe a game to remember with pride.

"Some people may be able to stay nice and relaxed, but not me. I can always see how the other side is going to break through and their players tend to look tremendous.

"This final in Rome has all the makings of a classic, because you have two fine teams who both like to attack and some of the best individuals in Europe.

"Make no mistake about it, we are going to Rome to try and win that cup and I am sure Roma feel exactly the same. We shall both be playing it fast and tight, and for us the result is almost everything.

"I think we have a reputation for sportsmanship and skilful play, and that we have earned respect wherever we go."

Captain Graeme Souness (on the potentially hostile atmosphere): "It puts you on your toes when practically every fan in the ground seems to be against you. It gives you something to react to.

EURO '84 SEND-OFF

"I think we showed in Bilbao and in Bucharest that we don't allow the crowd to get to us in the wrong way."

Bruce Grobbelaar: "I have a reputation for being a funny man, but believe me, I take my football very seriously when it matters. I feel that I have enough experience to handle the situation."

Peter Robinson: "The eyes of the world will be watching us, and it's the very best of occasions to prove to everyone that Liverpool fans are not hooligans. It is the perfect place to show the world that Liverpool is a city and a people to be proud of.

"We are going there not only to win the match, but to win the admiration of the world."

Mayor of Rome, Ugo Vetere: "We have the greatest respect for Liverpool, its club and its supporters. Like Roma, we believe they are the best in Europe. We hope that this will be a happy time for everyone – and of course, may the best team win."

On the Box

- Cagney and Lacey
- Chips
- The Price is Right
- Fame
- Winner Takes All
- Scully
- The Sweeney
- Metal Mickey
- Murphy's Mob
- Bullseye

The Top 10 Singles
May 30th, 1984

1. **WAKE ME UP BEFORE YOU GO GO** – Wham!
2. **LET'S HEAR IT FOR THE BOY** – Deniece Williams
3. **THE REFLEX** – Duran Duran
4. **AUTOMATIC** – The Pointer Sisters
5. **GROOVIN'** – The Style Council
6. **DANCING WITH TEARS IN MY EYES** – Ultravox
7. **I FEEL LIKE BUDDY HOLLY** – Alvin Stardust
8. **SEARCHIN'** – Hazell Dean
9. **I WANT TO BREAK FREE** – Queen
10. **AGAINST ALL ODDS** – Phil Collins

Anfield marathon men spot on for their finest hour

REDS LAND TREBLE

Liverpool 1
AS Roma 1 **(Liverpool win 4-2 on penalties aet)**

The big match verdict
by Ian Hargraves
Liverpool Echo, Thursday, May 31 1984

TWO months before the Olympic Games are due to start in Los Angeles, Liverpool last night completed the greatest marathon in modern times.

Their fourth European Cup victory, achieved after the most dramatic of penalty shoot-outs, proved a fitting climax to what has been a quite astonishing season.

They now hold the European Cup, the league championship, the Milk Cup and the Central League title, all achieved by the sterling British qualities of guts and sheer hard labour rather than by any individual genius.

No team has ever won so much in one season, or is ever likely to again. No team has ever earned its success in such a hard way.

And it is fitting that last night's victory, the greatest triumph of them all, was achieved not so much by individual brilliance as by unflagging teamwork and the refusal to give in when faced with adversity.

As in the previous rounds, when they won away four times in a row, Liverpool had to battle all the way. They had to beat Roma on their own ground, where the Italians had not lost all season, in front of a violently partisan crowd and a small army of police.

And what's more, they had to do it after surrendering an early lead and in the most unlikely manner conceivable.

Nobody who has watched Liverpool regularly over the last few years can have given much hope for their chances when extra time ended with the scores still level.

And when Steve Nicol, unexpectedly asked to shoot first, put his kick high over the crossbar the Liverpool cause

seemed hopeless.

Fortunately, those two European veterans, full-backs Phil Neal and Alan Kennedy, again rose to the occasion in the grand manner.

It was Neal, hero of three previous finals, who put Liverpool in front after 15 minutes - and it was the same player who got them back into the penalty race by netting confidently after Nicol's failure.

Then after Souness and Rush had netted their kicks and Roma's two Italian World Cup stars Conti and Graziani had both failed it was Barney Rubble who sent Tancredi the wrong way to put the issue beyond doubt.

The match itself never quite lived up to expectations in terms of sheer entertainment, though that was hardly surprising in view of all that was at stake.

However, it lacked nothing in incident or excitement, fluctuating first one way then the other, with neither team able to establish any clear advantage.

In the early stages it was Liverpool who looked the more impressive, and when they took the lead after 15 minutes it seemed the Italians were doomed to defeat. It was a very

good goal, created by Johnston's accurate cross which was never cleared, the ball rebounding off the hapless goalkeeper to Neal who banged it into the net in the manner born.

Liverpool could have increased their lead when a Johnston header was helped into the net by Souness only for the apparent 'score' to be disallowed for offside and Rush might well have scored on two other occasions but for Tancredi's agility, as might Nicol in the closing minutes.

However, towards the end of the first half and again early in the second Roma more than held their own. Though neither of their Brazilians were able to shake off the shackles imposed by Liverpool's tight midfield marking, their captain, Di Bartolomei exploited Conti's speed and skill with some lovely diagonal passes.

Roma had twice created havoc down Liverpool's right flank, and Graziani had forced Grobbelaar to a fine near-post save, when Roma got their equaliser almost immediately before the interval.

Neal and Lee seemed to have blocked Conti's way to goal out on the left but Conti collected a rebound and hit a perfect centre which found Pruzzo unmarked and perfectly placed to head past Grobbelaar.

In the second half, and again in extra time, there were

plenty of half chances at both ends but somehow one rarely felt there would be further goals. Liverpool seemed over-dependent on Rush to do their scoring while Roma seemed to lack confidence in their own ability to finish off the game.

Both sides were clearly exhausted going into extra-time and it was no surprise when the match became the first European Cup final to be settled by penalties.

Even Liverpudlians must have felt sympathy for Roma on being beaten in such an unsatisfactory manner but for all that it was a marvellous performance by Liverpool.

LIVERPOOL'S victory was essentially a team performance with every one of the 13 players used giving everything they had to the cause.

Grobbelaar had an outstanding game in goal, his best save coming from the dangerous Conti in the closing minutes and Lawrenson was a tower of strength in the centre of defence.

Rush also played well but perhaps the best player on the field was Liverpool's captain, Graeme Souness, who set an outstanding example both in attack and in defence and wins my nomination as man of the match.

MATCH FACTS

Liverpool (4-3-3): Grobbelaar, Neal, Kennedy, Lawrenson, Whelan, Hansen, Dalglish (Robinson, 94), Lee, Rush, Johnston (Nicol, 72), Souness. Unused subs: Bolder, Hodgson, Gillespie.

Roma (5-2-3): Tancredi, Nappi, Bonetti, Righetti, Nela, Di Bartolomei, Falcao, Cerezo (Strkelj, 115), Conti, Pruzzo (Chierico, 64), Graziani. Unused subs: Malgieglio, Oddi, Vincenzi.

Goals: Neal (15), Pruzzo (43).
Penalties: Nicol (0-0), Di Bartolomei (0-1), Neal (1-1), Conti (1-1), Souness (2-1), Righetti (2-2), Rush (3-2), Graziani (3-2), Kennedy (4-2)

Bookings: None
Conditions: Warm, dry
Referee: Erik Frederiksson (Sweden)
Attendance: 69,693

Graeme Souness

"WHEN you talk about character you are talking about what we have done tonight.

I feel sorry for Roma because they lost on penalties but I felt that overall we deserved our win. It may have been unfair for them to go down on spot kicks but it was unfair for Liverpool to have to play on Roma's home ground.

I think this could well be the greatest result ever achieved in any club's history. It has been a magnificent night and who is going to stop us next season?"

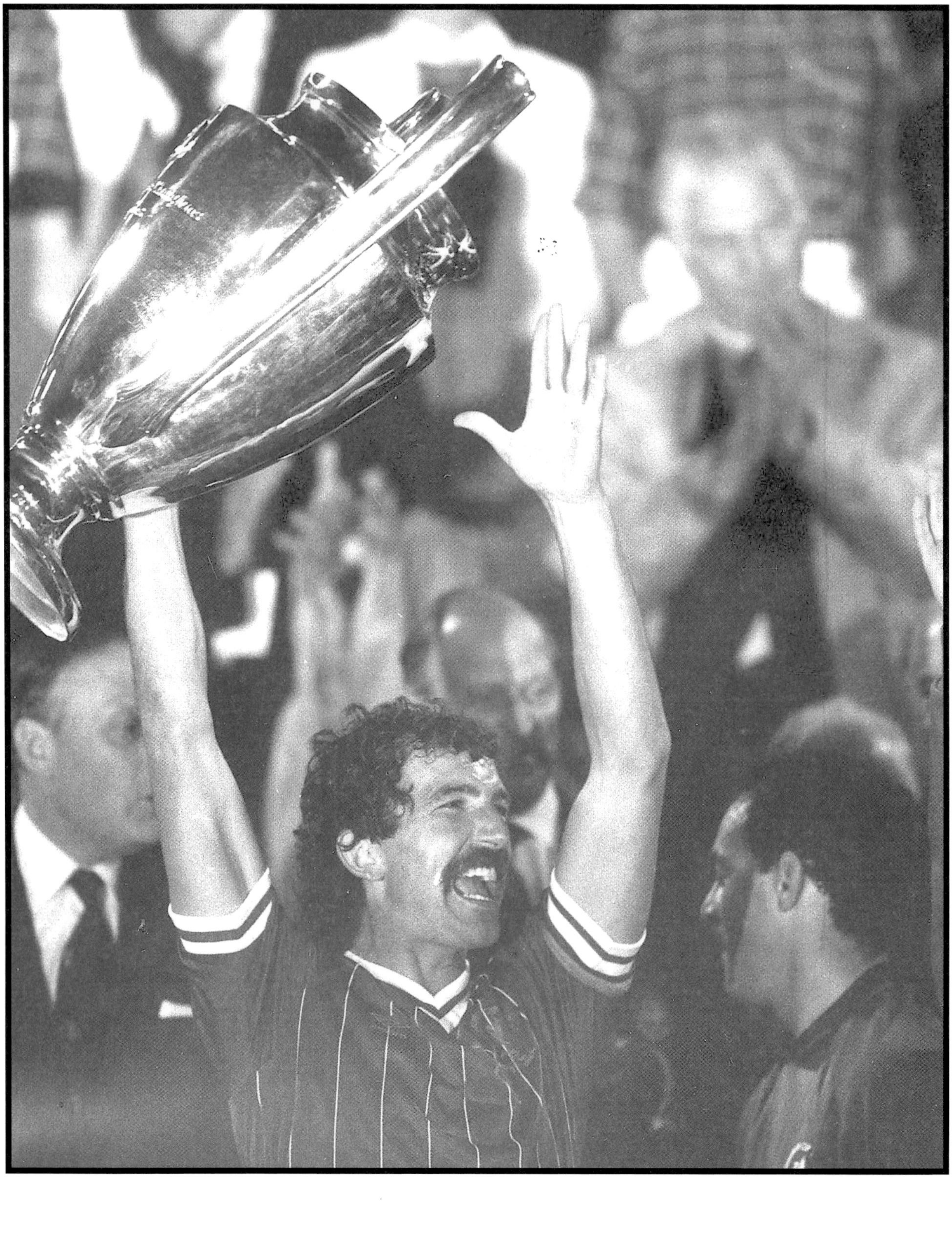

Bruce Grobbelaar

THE difference between success and failure is very much in the hands of the goalkeeper when it comes down to penalties and Bruce Grobbelaar certainly played his part in Liverpool's European Cup final fate that night.

But while he was in joyous mood in Rome he spared a thought for the losers: "It is a cruel way to lose a game but we are delighted to have won tonight.

"It is very special for me and, of course, great for the boss."

Following his 'wobbly legs' routine, Grobbelaar joked he had another trick up his sleeve: "I was due to take the last penalty but Alan Kennedy jumped in front of me to take it. I'm very disappointed!"

Brucie's goalline antics are one of the most striking images of the final, but while this appeared as nothing out of the ordinary for the eccentric keeper, the real reason lies elsewhere.

He said: "I will give all the credit for that decision to Joe Fagan. Joe came and put his arm round me and he said to me 'Son, if they cannot score from 12 yards, that's not our problem. We're not expecting you to save any of these penalties because they should be able to score from 12 yards.' As I was walking away, he said 'But try and put them off'. That stuck in my head. Bruno Conti came up. I put my hands on my knees and crossed them over like a '60s-style dance. He was an Italian international and he missed.

"The last penalty was [Francesco] Graziani. He was an Italian international and if he can't stand the pressure, it's not my problem. I bit the net and thought 'I'm in Italy - spaghetti' so I did the spaghetti legs and he missed."

Alan Kennedy

"ROMA had some great players: Cerezo, Graziani, Conte and we felt we were in the minority in terms of fans.

We didn't get the better of them, they didn't get the better of us. I suppose Joe Fagan was pleasantly surprised after 90 minutes. What he said was 'Don't let yourselves down'.

After extra-time, I thought the clock said something like 12 o'clock at night. It just seemed to go on and on and on; it was ridiculously late by the time it got to penalties.

Joe was looking for volunteers. I don't think anybody stood out. A couple had been substituted, including Kenny Dalglish. I'd missed them in a pre-season tournament. I'd practised them in training and I was pathetic, absolutely pathetic, but Joe didn't just look at the week before when we were practising; he looked at the game on the night, who felt confident, who felt decent. The big surprise was me.

Steve Nicol missed his, Phil Neal scored, then Graeme Souness and Ian Rush. I wasn't even thinking about scoring in two European Cup finals. I honestly don't recall what was going through my mind. I wanted it to end there and then. It was frightening, absolutely frightening. Millions of people were watching, 80,000 there on the night. If I could have 'beamed' myself up anywhere, I would have done it. I wouldn't have taken that penalty for all the money in the world, but Joe had given me strength. He'd given me the belief that I would be alright. Joe was great at looking at the character of people. He was proved right, the way it went.

I don't know how you describe the feeling; it was wonderful, great. People think it was coolly and calmly placed; it wasn't anything of the sort. It was a quick movement, run up, open the body up and place it to the goalkeeper's right-hand side. Nothing made my mind up until that final second.

The lads came running over and I famously did what looked like a parachute jump landing. It wasn't a great way to celebrate winning a European Cup final but it didn't particularly matter.

We had a great night afterwards. We were invited to a villa on the outskirts of Rome and all had a meal together - loads and loads of wine. I remember someone said at five in the morning that we had to get back to the hotel and when we did it was absolutely buzzing. Loads of supporters. A wonderful night shared by a lot of people, a lot of our friends and family were there. It was a great laugh, we had a sing-song. I was looking at a picture the other day and the colour of the clothes we were wearing . . . my God – it was definitely the eighties, absolutely terrible."

Steve Nicol

"IT was an awful feeling seeing my shot go over and I just wanted the ground to open up and swallow me. That penalty miss was something I'll never forget."

Sammy Lee

"I ALWAYS remember Graeme Souness taking us out onto the pitch in what was a fantastic atmosphere. As a team in unison we all just walked around in front of the Roma fans. This was the type of bonding and togetherness we had in the camp."

Phil Neal

"WELL that day, I joined the attack and I can hear Joe and Bob saying, if you're going to join the attack, stay with it until it breaks down. In other words you push yourself getting back very quickly. Well I joined the attack and all of a sudden it continued, a ricochet falls in the six-yard box, and who's in there? Me!"

Ian Rush

"PLAYING on Roma's own ground didn't really bother us. Looking back now you think it must have been intimidating but at the time it didn't worry any of the players. Mainly because we were so confident and had such a good team.

We weren't the best at penalties and we struggled to get five to take them! We'd had a shoot-out in training before we went to Rome and I think only Phil Neal scored, so I think that's why everyone was reluctant to step up. I didn't volunteer. Only Graeme (Souness) and Phil (Neal) did. Souness then asked myself and Steve Nicol to take one but we were still one short so Alan Kennedy offered."

Graeme had told us not to worry and we went into the shoot-out thinking 'let's just do our best'. But I was still nervous and that walk up to the spot, with 70,000 Italians whistling and booing, was very nerve-wracking.

As soon as the ball hit the back of the net though I was engulfed by a great sense of relief."

Nils Liedholm

ROMA'S Swedish manager Nils Liedholm felt aggrieved to have lost the European Cup final on penalties and would have preferred a trip to Anfield for a replay.

"I'm not complaining because we knew the rules, but I think it would have been much fairer to have played another match rather than go to a penalty shoot-out," he said afterwards.

"I would not even have minded the second game being in Liverpool. At least it would have meant the match being decided by football."

Liverpool boss Joe Fagan sympathised with Liedholm over the outcome of the match but didn't agree with the idea of another match.

"I am always sorry for any team beaten in a cup final, particularly a European Cup final.

"Personally I would not like the final to be played over two legs. A final is of such importance that it needs to be a one-off occasion, played on a neutral ground.

"It may sound a bit funny but this was a neutral ground tonight, because when it was selected nobody knew that Liverpool and Roma would be in the final."

Joe Fagan was asked if he thought some of Roma's star players such as Brazilian ace Falcao were a little under par. His response was that this was more to do with the orders handed out to his own players. He said:"Instructions were given to our players that whoever was close to Falcao at any one time was to try and close him down.

"The lads did this well and they never allowed Roma to settle on the ball and play as well as they can."

His final message to the team came before the penalty shoot-out and was short and simple: "When the penalties were about to begin, I gathered the whole team together and said 'I am proud of every one of you this evening. No matter what happens now that will not change.'"

Djimi Traore - 2005

DJIMI Traore revealed that the AC Milan players had helped inspire Liverpool to stage the amazing second-half comeback in Istanbul.

The Reds defender explained that from being so low as they trailed 3-0 at half-time, the sound of Milan's premature celebrations coming through the dressing room walls fired him and his teammates back up again.

Combined with Rafa Benitez's words of wisdom and a few tactical changes, the dishevelled Liverpool lads started to believe they could overturn the deficit.

The rest, as they say, is history...

"Honestly, when I sat listening to the manager at half-time I did not really believe we could do it," said Traore.

"Against AC Milan even less, as they have some great players.

"But when we were back in the dressing room the Milan players were outside already celebrating that they were champions, celebrating the victory. That really got to us and gave us the hunger to come back at them.

"Once we scored the first one they were scared, and they fell back. When we brought Didi [Hamann] on it gave us a lot of experience in midfield and it really disrupted them.

"It is just unbelievable for me, to think we were 3-0 down at half-time.

"But when we got back into the dressing room the manager told us we could still do it if we scored in the first five minutes. He said if we did that we could keep scoring and they would wilt."

Steven Gerrard - 2005

AT half-time the player who dragged his team back into the Champions League final had all but given up hope of lifting the trophy.

Steven Gerrard was down and thought his beloved Liverpool were out, but his manager had other ideas.

Such had been AC Milan's dominance in the opening 45 minutes that the Reds appeared to be shell-shocked into submission.

"It was just weird because I thought the dream was over...over," admitted Gerrard afterwards.

Rafael Benitez didn't.

It was his job to pick his players up and instil some belief in what little chance remained to try and salvage the club's fifth European Cup.

Whatever he said worked.

"The manager came in at half-time and he calmed us down basically," reveals the captain.

"He first had to silence us down because we were all talking 19-to-the-dozen.

"We could hear Milan celebrating and there was nothing we could do about it.

"The manager calmed us down and drew some things on his board, he made a few changes and there were new instructions and plans.

"He said if we scored early, it would change the game. I couldn't concentrate. I don't know what was going through my head. It was weird.

"I was sitting there and my head was in my hands.

"But I heard him say we need a goal and that is what stuck. I knew we had to chase the three Milan goals and get some respectability back."

DRESSING ROOM SECRETS

Alan Hansen - 1984

"JOE Fagan pulled off a masterstroke even before we flew out to Rome. While Roma were locked away in some Italian mountain training retreat we holidayed in Israel. Joe told us to just relax and let our hair down. We had a couple of Italian journalists with us and they couldn't believe what they were seeing. We were actually drinking beer two weeks before a European Cup Final."

Craig Johnston - 1984

"I HAD given Chris Rea's album a hiding to such an extent that all the players knew the songs off by heart, especially 'I Don't Know What It Is (But I Love It)'. When one of us would sing a verse, the rest would come in on the chorus, clapping and chanting, evoking those images of unity and victory.

"After the pitch inspection in Rome we made the long trek down the tunnel back to our dressing room, deep within the bowels of the Olympic Stadium. The tension among the squad was palpable as we walked in silence down that dark corridor. Inexplicably, Davey Hodgson then broke into a solo rendition of the opening verse of that song. One or two joined in and by the time we drew abreast of the Roma dressing room the whole Liverpool squad had joined in. The Roma players just looked on bemused, thinking this must be the super relaxed Liverpool squad they'd heard about!"

Ian Rush - 1984

"THE Liverpool crowd that night were brilliant, even though they were vastly outnumbered. As regards to the intimidating atmosphere, I remember Graeme Souness and Kenny Dalglish making sure it didn't affect any of the players. They were laughing and joking before the game and this increased our confidence. I think the Roma players were more scared than us, because they knew we were a good team."

Alan Kennedy - 1984

"THERE was very little atmosphere in the Liverpool dressing room: actually, it seemed quite nervous. Ronnie Moran was scurrying around, busying himself and trying to calm people, but was mislaying things and getting in the way, making things worse. People just wanted to get out, get it over with.

At the time, most of the Liverpool lads liked the singer Chris Rea and a few of us had even gone to see him before. We had a Chris Rea tape in the dressing room and Dave Hodgson, one of the subs, said, as we were about to come out, that he thought the Italians looked a bit nervous. So why don't we sing them a Chris Rea song, 'I Don't Know What It Is (But I Love It)', just to wind them up? Everyone said not to be so stupid - that this was the European Cup final. But when we got in the tunnel, Hodgy and Craig Johnston both started singing it and the rest of us just joined in. It was a way of breaking our nerves, and putting the wind up them. The Roma players were gobsmacked: they must have thought we were lunatics. As we got on the pitch we were still singing and we were even getting louder. All these cool, international footballers, now they all just looked scared s***less. First blood to Liverpool." **Taken from his autobiography**

10 GREAT ANFIELD EURO NIGHTS

Over the years there have been some magical European nights at Anfield. From Inter Milan '65 to Chelsea '05, the noise, colour and emotion has made Anfield one of Europe's top footballing cathedrals. You'll all have your own favourites - here are 10 of the best as we see it...

v INTER MILAN

European Cup
Semi-final, first leg
May 4 1965

Liverpool 3
Inter Milan 1

THE injured Gordon Milne and Gerry Byrne paraded the FA Cup, won for the first time just three days earlier, before kick-off at a packed Anfield and the amazing atmosphere shook the Italian champions.

Roger Hunt gave Liverpool the lead but Mazzola equalised following a mistake by Ron Yeats.

With the Kop in full voice behind them, Shankly's side scored two more through Ian Callaghan and Ian St John to put Liverpoool in a commanding position but a highly controversial 3-0 defeat in the San Siro ended hopes of an appearance in the final.

v BAYERN MUNICH

MUNICH arrived at Anfield with a team packed full of stars but were taken apart by a brilliant hat-trick from Alun Evans.

He cleverly converted a Steve Heighway cross for the first on the half-hour, hooked home Lawler's header just after the break and completed his treble from close range in the 73rd minute.

The Reds went through with a 1-1 second leg draw in Germany but went out to Don Revie's Leeds in the semi-final. Bayern got revenge in the following season's Cup Winners Cup when they beat Liverpool 3-1 on aggregate before going on to win three Bundesliga titles and three European Cups in a five-year spell.

European Fairs Cup
4th round, 1st leg
March 10 1971

Liverpool 3
Bayern Munich 0

v BORUSSIA MOENCHENGLADBACH

UEFA Cup
Final, first leg
May 10 1973

Liverpool 3
Borussia Moenchengladbach 0

A HUGE downpour forced Austrian referee Erich Linemayr to abandon the game after 27 minutes so it was replayed the following night and Bill Shankly made a key tactical change.

Shanks had spotted that Moenchengladbach were weak in the air and brought in John Toshack for Brian Hall, a plan that worked wonders as Toshack created two first half goals for Kevin Keegan.

Larry Lloyd headed home a third to give the Reds a three-goal advantage - which was preserved by a crucial Ray Clemence penalty save - and although they were beaten 2-0 in Germany in the second leg, the club's first piece of European silverware was secured.

v BRUGES

IT wasn't quite a comeback of Istanbul proportions but it wasn't far off as the Belgians raced into a 2-0 lead after just 12 minutes.

Bob Paisley's decision to bring Jimmy Case on for John Toshack changed the game and goals in the 59th and 61st minute from Ray Kennedy and Case levelled matters.

With the Kop now in full-voice Liverpool continued to push and in the 64th minute Steve Heighway was fouled in the box and Kevin Keegan converted the penalty to complete an amazing six-minute turnaround.

Bruges took an early lead again in the second leg but Keegan fired home a free-kick and Liverpool won the UEFA Cup for the second time in four seasons.

UEFA Cup
Final, first leg
April 28 1976

Liverpool 3
Bruges 2

★★★★★

v ST ETIENNE

European Cup
Quarter-final, second leg
March 16 1977

Liverpool 3
St Etienne 1

AFTER losing 1-0 in France to a side widely regarded as the best in Europe at the time, Bob Paisley's men needed to win by two clear goals at Anfield.

Kevin Keegan opened the scoring after just two minutes but Bethenay equalised early in the second half.

Ray Kennedy made it 2-1 and with just six minutes remaining, supersub David Fairclough charged through to put the ball into the net in front of an ecstatic Kop on a night that rocked Anfield to the rafters and ultimately led to the glory of Rome and that first European Cup triumph.

v BORUSSIA MOENCHENGLADBACH

AFTER beating them in the 1973 UEFA Cup final and the European Cup final less than a year earlier, Liverpool broke Moenchengladbach hearts for a third time.

The Germans had won the first leg 2-1 but Paisley's men turned in their best performance of the season and - given their opponents - arguably their most convincing ever European display at Anfield.

Ray Kennedy headed home Kenny Dalglish's cross after six minutes, Dalglish volleyed Kennedy's header home in the 35th minute and Jimmy Case completed an emphatic victory after the break to send the European champions down to Wembley were they retained their trophy by beating Bruges 1-0.

European Cup
Semi-final, second leg
April 12 1978

Liverpool 3
Borussia Moenchengladbach 0

v AUXERRE

UEFA Cup
second round, second leg
November 6 1991

Liverpool 3
Auxerre 0

AFTER losing 2-0 in France, Liverpool overturned a two-goal first leg deficit for the first and only time in their European history.

Jan Molby opened the scoring with an early penalty and after half-an-hour Mike Marsh levelled the tie with a diving header.

The visitors were reduced to 10 men after the break and with just seven minutes left Mark Walters burst through to slide the ball home at the Kop end and send the 23,094 fans inside Anfield wild.

v AS ROMA

LIVERPOOL knew they needed to win by two goals to progress from the second group stage to the last eight of the competition.

The atmosphere was cranked up before kick-off when boss Gerard Houllier returned to Anfield for the first time since recovering from a life-saving heart operation five months earlier.

Jari Litmanen opened the scoring with a first half penalty and after the break, Emile Heskey rose like a salmon to send the Reds through on a night that was dubbed 'the St Etienne of a new generation' by Liverpool legend Phil Thompson.

Champions League
Second group stage
March 19 2002

Liverpool 2
AS Roma 0

★★★★★

v OLYMPIAKOS

Champions League
Group stage
December 9 2004

Liverpool 3
Olympiakos 1

NEEDING to win 1-0 or by two clear goals to progress, Rivaldo stunned Anfield with a first-half opener.

But a couple of inspired substitutions by Rafa Benitez turned the game on its head with Florent Sinama-Pongolle equalising in the 47th minute and Neil Mellor making it 2-1 with just nine minutes left.

Liverpool still needed a goal and it was inspirational captain Steven Gerrard who provided it when he smashed a stunning half-volley into the Kop net from 20 yards out to begin some of the wildest celebrations Anfield had seen in years.

v CHELSEA

ON an atmospheric night to rival anything ever produced in the 1960s and 1970s, Rafa Benitez's Liverpool booked their place in the Champions League final with a single goal victory over recently crowned Premiership champions Chelsea.

Chelsea pushed for an equaliser late on but a stubborn rearguard display, led by the outstanding Jamie Carragher, kept them at bay and when the full-time whistle went Anfield erupted to celebrate Liverpool reaching their first European Cup final for 20 years.

Three weeks later and over 40,000 travelling Kopites were celebrating a fifth European Cup after a penalty shoot-out victory over AC Milan following a comeback of epic proportions.

Champions League
Semi-final, second leg
May 3 2005

Liverpool 1
Chelsea 0

EUROPEAN CUP

★★★★★ Liverpool Roll

The men who played in Liverpool's

Xabi Alonso 05

Milan Baros 05

Jimmy Case 77, 78, 81

Ian Callaghan 77

Jamie Carragher 05

Djibril Cisse 05

Ray Clemence 77, 78, 81

Kenny Dalglish 78, 81, 84

Jerzy Dudek 05

David Fairclough 78

Steve Finnan 05

Luis Garcia 05

Steven Gerrard 05

Bruce Grobbelaar 84

Alan Hansen 78, 81, 84

Dietmar Hamann 05

Steve Heighway 77, 78

Emlyn Hughes 77, 78

Sami Hyypia 05

Joey Jones 77

Goalscorers (not including penalty shoot-outs)

Xabi Alonso 1, Kenny Dalglish 1, Steven Gerrard 1, Alan Kennedy 1,

FINAL HEROES

of Honour ★★★★★

FIVE European Cup final winning teams

David Johnson 81

Craig Johnston 84

Kevin Keegan 77

Alan Kennedy 81, 84

Ray Kennedy 77, 78, 81

Harry Kewell 05

Mark Lawrenson 84

Sammy Lee 81, 84

Terry McDermott 77, 78, 81

Phil Neal 77, 78, 81, 84

Steve Nicol 84

John Arne Riise 05

Michael Robinson 84

Ian Rush 84

Vladimir Smicer 05

Tommy Smith 77

Graeme Souness 78, 81, 84

Phil Thompson 78, 81

Djimi Traore 05

Ronnie Whelan 84

Terry McDermott 1, Phil Neal 2, Tommy Smith 1, Vladimir Smicer 1

1981

★★★★★

The road to
Paris

AFTER scoring 10 of the best against Palloseura, Bob Paisley taught Alex Ferguson a harsh lesson about the realities of the European Cup when the Reds thrashed his Aberdeen side 4-0. Sofia were so far away from causing an upset before an injury-hit Liverpool went to Munich and enjoyed one of their finest away days

Round one

Round one, first leg
September 17 1980

Oulu Palloseura 1
(Puotiniemi 82)

Liverpool 1
(McDermott 15)

Att: 14,000

Team: Clemence, Neal, Cohen, Thompson, Ray Kennedy, Hansen, Dalglish, Lee, Fairclough, McDermott, Souness.

THE European Cup campaign got off to a stuttering start as Liverpool were held by the Finnish amateurs, on a pitch that Graeme Souness compared to a "farmer's field".

Terry McDermott nodded the Reds in front but Oulu grew in confidence, as further chances weren't converted. Eventually, Puotiniemi drove in an equaliser eight minutes from time.

Round one, second leg
October 1 1980

Liverpool 10
(Souness 5, 24, (pen) 52, McDermott 29, 41, 83, Lee 53, Ray Kennedy 66, Fairclough 68, 81)

Oulu Palloseura 1
(Armstrong 47)

(Liverpool win 11-2 on aggregate)

Att: 21,013

Team: Clemence, Neal, Cohen, Thompson, Ray Kennedy, Hansen, Dalglish, Lee, Fairclough, McDermott, Souness.

LIVERPOOL'S second biggest win in their European history redressed the balance after a bitty first leg performance, with Graeme Souness and Terry McDermott both hitting hat-tricks.

Also finding the target were Sammy Lee, Ray Kennedy and David Fairclough, who managed a double.

David Fairclough makes it eight as Liverpool cruise to victory in the second leg against Oulu Palloseura

See you Jimmy. Phil Neal fires past Jim Leighton to put the Reds 2-0 up against Fergie's Aberdeen

Round two

Round two, first leg
October 22 1980

Aberdeen 0

Liverpool 1
(McDermott 5)

Att: 24,000

Team: Clemence, Neal, Alan Kennedy, Thompson, Ray Kennedy, Hansen, Dalglish, Lee (Case), Johnson, McDermott, Souness.

THE 'Battle of Britain' pitted the Reds against Alex Ferguson's Aberdeen and Bob Paisley's men gained an important edge at Pittodrie.

McDermott was to the fore again, beating Jim Leighton with an angled chip from 12 yards.

Aberdeen pressed but Ray Clemence was able to deny Mark McGhee. Liverpool left Scotland confident the job was largely done.

Round two, second leg
November 5 1980

Liverpool 4
(Miller og 38, Neal 43, Dalglish 57, Hansen 71)

Aberdeen 0

(Liverpool win 5-0 on aggregate)

Att: 36,182

Team: Clemence, Neal, Alan Kennedy (Cohen), Thompson, Ray Kennedy, Hansen, Dalglish, Lee, Johnson, McDermott, Souness.

THE job was done but it was finished in style at Anfield. Aberdeen did create some early pressure but two goals late in the first half killed them off.

First, Willie Miller diverted a Hansen header into his own net before Phil Neal took advantage of a Dalglish backheel. Dalglish and Hansen completed the scoring.

Quarter-final

Quarter-final, first leg
March 4 1981

Liverpool 5
(Souness 16, 51, 80, Lee 45, McDermott 62)

CSKA Sofia 1
(Yonchev 58)

Att: 37,255

Team: Clemence, Neal, Alan Kennedy, Thompson (Irwin), Ray Kennedy, Hansen, Dalglish, Lee, Heighway, McDermott, Souness.

GRAEME Souness hit another European hat-trick as Liverpool showed a greater cutting edge in front of goal than their Bulgarian opponents.

Sammy Lee and, almost inevitably, Terry McDermott also scored. Yonchev gave CSKA the faintest of hopes for the second leg, but the Reds could be well satisfied with such a performance against the team who had knocked out the holders, Nottingham Forest, in round one.

Quarter-final, second leg
March 18 1981

CSKA Sofia 0

Liverpool 1
(Johnson 10)

(Liverpool win 6-1 on aggregate)

Att: 65,000

Team: Clemence, Neal, Alan Kennedy, Irwin, Ray Kennedy, Hansen, Dalglish, Lee, Johnson (Heighway), Case, Souness.

THIS match was something of a non-event as an early David Johnson goal silenced 65,000 fans at the Levski Stadium.

CSKA did win a late penalty but Clemence saved from Markov.

Graeme Souness scoring one of the greatest hat-tricks at Anfield in the first leg

McDermott celebrates adding to the goal tally in the 62nd minute

Ray Kennedy seals victory for Liverpool with an away goal late in the game

Semi-final

Semi-final, first leg
April 8 1981

Liverpool 0

Bayern Munich 0

Att: 44,543

Team: Clemence, Neal, Alan Kennedy, Thompson, Ray Kennedy, Hansen, Dalglish, Lee, Rush, McDermott, Heighway (Case).

THIS was Liverpool's first major test in the competition and Bayern gave a disciplined performance, which left Paisley's men with a lot to do in Germany.

Bayern appeared the more likely to score for much of the Anfield encounter, with Niedermayer hitting the bar and Paul Breitner and Karl-Heinz Rummenigge also going close.

Semi-final, second leg
April 22 1981

Bayern Munich 1
(Rummenigge 87)

Liverpool 1
(Ray Kennedy 83)

(Liverpool go through on the away goals rule)

Att: 77,600

Team: Clemence, Neal, Money, Irwin, Ray Kennedy, Hansen, Dalglish (Gayle, Case), Lee, Johnson, McDermott, Souness.

THE Olympic Stadium was the scene of one of Liverpool's more unlikely European triumphs.

With Phil Thompson and Alan Kennedy absent injured, reserves Richard Money and Colin Irwin came in. So confident were Bayern of reaching the final, they famously handed out leaflets to their supporters, which showed the best route to Paris.

The Reds' prospects looked even bleaker when Kenny Dalglish was forced off seven minutes in.

However, Liverpool absorbed the home pressure and were able to exert some of their own through Howard Gayle, Dalglish's replacement, who unsettled the opposition defence.

The match was still at stalemate with seven minutes left when Ray Kennedy all but put the Reds into the final with a 16-yard shot. Rummenigge caused some late anxiety with an 87th minute strike but the away goal was enough to ensure it was Liverpool's fans that had to check the route to the French capital.

★★★★★

TO GAY PAREE WITH BOB PAISLEY

Allez Les Rouges was the cry from Kopites as they travelled across the Channel to see number three in Gay Paree. Tickets were harder to find than Evertonians in France but that didn't stop Liverpool's fans from following their heroes again

PARIS MATCH

The Liverpool Echo was offering a luxury trip for two to Paris. Questions were as follows:

1 What two countries were represented in the very first European Cup final? (Spain – Real Madrid, France – Stade Reims)

2 Who scored Liverpool's first goal against Borussia Moenchengladbach in the 1977 final? (Terry McDermott)

3 What Everton player made his club debut against Inter Milan? (Colin Harvey)

4 Who won the home game at Anfield when Liverpool played Ajax in 1966? (Neither side – it was a 2-2 draw)

5 Name four English-born managers to have led their side out in a European Cup final. (Bob Paisley – Liverpool, Brian Clough – Nottingham Forest, Jimmy Armfield – Leeds, Bobby Houghton – Malmo).

TICKET COMPLAINTS

Only 12,000 tickets were given to Reds fans (the capacity was 48,000), although the French Football Federation defended their decision, despite the fact that £2 tickets were being sold on the black market for £10. Prices for more expensive face-value tickets had risen to £120 less than a week before the final.

Liverpool were apparently receiving complaints on a daily basis regarding the allocation, and the limited degree of priority afforded to season ticket holders. A certain Mr F Evans from Rainhill was unhappy that tickets for the special trains to Paris (£50 each) were only being sold in the daytime: "Whoever made that decision must be under the impression that all Liverpool supporters are unemployed". Mr K Clayton and Mr G Jones were also set to give up their season tickets in protest.

General secretary Peter Robinson appealed to UEFA to change their system of nominating the stadiums to be used for the major European finals six months in advance. "When clubs like ourselves, Real Madrid, Inter Milan and Bayern Munich are involved, they should consider switching the final."

PARIS SHERATON (NOT HILTON)

Gullivers Travel of Gloucester were offering deals for £165 that included a coach to and from Heathrow Airport from Liverpool, flights to and from Paris, a match ticket and one night in the Sheraton Hotel.

BIGGEST WELCOME

Plans were revealed for Liverpool's biggest-ever welcome home party, with 500,000 expected – around the same mumber that cheered them back from Wembley three years earlier. The open-top bus was set to leave on the squad's arrival back at Speke Airport on the Thursday afternoon, and airport director Rod Rufus hailed the influence of the club for the city. "In Yugoslavia, for example, they have almost as big a following as they have on Merseyside. They are more popular than the Yugoslav national side."

WORTH A PUNT

A Norris Green punter stood to scoop £33,225 should Liverpool be successful in Paris. The figure, which would have been a record pay-out by Ladbrokes on Merseyside, came about after he placed three £50 doubles and one £50 treble linking West Ham to win the Second Division title at 5-1 and Tottenham to win the FA Cup at 16-1 – Liverpool were a 7-2 shot. He had already won £5,100 before the final.

LIKE YOUR STYLE, LA

The club shop was selling a new range of memorabilia ahead of the final, including t-shirts, scarves, ties, hats, caps, pennants, banners, stickers and flags. Liaison chief Jim Kennefick said: "It's like Woolworth's in here at the moment." Sales of programmes too were providing big business, with the original stock of 1,000 selling out a week before the showpiece, and an extra 9,000 being ordered. "I think we have contributed something to the French printing industry there. Originally they were only going to produce 5,000 copies until we said that we would take 10,000 – now we understand they will print in the region of 50,000," added Kennefick.

TIPS AND ADVICE

Phrases such as 'Where's the ground? 'Which underground train do we take?' and 'Any spares mate?' were provided in the native tongue – so too was You'll Never Walk Alone:

En marchant sous l'orage,
Pourquoi baisser la tete?
N'aie pas peur quand le ciel s'assombrit.
A la fin de l'orage,
Au chant de l'alouette,
Le soleil viendra chasser la nuit.
Qu'importe le vent?
Qu'importe la pluie?
Quand tes reves sont en danger,
Courage, courage
Jamais tu n'es seul,
Car tes reves sont partages,
Tes reves sont partages!

Reporters were also marvelling at the prices of scrambled eggs on offer at certain 'upper-scale' establishments in the city (Maxims) – a mere £8. Prices to enter the Moulin Rouge...£40. It was almost £2 a pint in the increasing number of 'pubs' which were becoming more common in the city, with Worthington and Guinness on draught.

Duty free – 'It is cheaper to buy cigarettes and alcohol in France than on the ferry crossing'. 200 cigarettes cost around £3.90 in France, with a litre of whiskey a similar price.

A three-course meal was said to cost £2.50; and a large french loaf with a hunk of cheese and a bottle of wine: £1.50.

On tipping taxi drivers: '...drivers prefer their tip in cash and not a typical Scouse gentleman's gesture of supplying 'straight from the horse's mouth' what might win the next day's 3.30 race at Sandown.'

★★★★★

OLD BIG 'EAD HAS HIS SAY

Nottingham Forest boss Brian Clough: "Although we are still bitterly disappointed at missing out on the chance of winning the European Cup for a third time, our hopes and thoughts are with Liverpool. I hope they clinch the title again. Between us we've shown there isn't much wrong with the best clubs in England."

TEAM OF TERRY MACS

Most of Kirkby-born Terry McDermott's family were travelling to the Parc de Princes from the Quarry Green Tenants' Club. The 47-strong contingent **(pictured below)** boarded the coach from his home town.

BARNIE RUMBLE

Hundreds of cheering fans turned up at Speke Airport. One banner read: 'Three times Kings of Europe'. The squad were aparently hoping for the luck of the Irish. For every European trip they had made since 1964, Captain Barnie Croghan had been on board – he was a passenger for the trip to Paris.

PAINTING THE TOWN ROUGE

Up to 30,000 fans flooded Paris the day before the final, to the alarm of Paris police officials who had advised fans not to travel without a ticket. Stories included one fan who had paid £7 to get to France – by hitching lifts and bribing foreign bus drivers, while an ex-Walton prisoner, who hitched after being released a week early, failed to inform his wife of said release.

Gary Newall, a 21-year-old out-of-work labourer originally from Walton, saved two weeks' dole money in a bid to buy a ticket. He hitched lifts to Dover before giving a Spanish coach driver £5 to drop him off near Paris. "I'm living on bread, margarine and tubs of paste all week because the money is so tight. Coming across on the ferry I bought a bottle of Pernod for £4.50 and 200 ciggies. I got the French ones 'cos they were cheaper, but they're awful, and I'll end up selling them."

His friend – the recently-released Walton inmate on his first trip abroad, added: "I expected to come to paradise. But it's just like England innit – same weather like. And the cops won't stand any mucking around either."

Kevin Frangleton and Denise Platt from near Warrington

were determined to net a bargain from the touts: "One guy with a wad of tickets wanted £50 each. We told him: 'On you're bike pal'."

Bill Smith of Huyton was among the 900 fans who arrived on the first football special into Paris's North Station. "We have had a ball and are just looking forward to celebrating a Liverpool victory on the way home."

RADIO GAGA

There were doubts over radio broadcasts of the match on the day of the final. A bulldozer had carved through a mass of cables outside the stadium, with French engineers working flat out to repair the damage. Deputy station manager at Radio Merseyside Ian Judson said: "The TV pictures are safe, but the commentators might have to give their commentaries over the telephone."

PERFECT SETTING

Ahead of the final, Liverpool stayed at the same hotel where the terms of the Treaty of Versailles were presented to the German government to signal the end of the First World War.

In the Second World War, it was used as RAF headquarters until 1940 when it was taken over as the German HQ in France – where Hitler visited several times.

THE FINAL WORD

Bob Paisley: "I hope we can reach the same standard as we did in Rome, and I hope the spectators give us the same type of support they gave us then. This is the big thing. We need their support, but we need it to be clean and well-behaved. I'm looking for a repeat of Rome both on and off the field."

"I am not worrying about who is in the Madrid team. All that concerns me is getting our own people fit. We can

TWO POTS AND A PIANO

Wirral grandmother Dorothy Williams, 65, and her friend Dorothy Jenkins, 62, **(pictured below)** added their own contribution to the Liverpool songbook. Enititled 'Kings of the Kop', the ditty was given a rousing reception having been premiered at the Black Horse Hotel in West Kirby. Mrs Williams, of the singing and piano-playing duo, known as 'the two Pots', said: "Although we don't go to the games, we both support Liverpool and obviously want to see them win. We hope that the song could spur the lads on." The lyrics are as follows:

Bring out the glasses.
Stack up the champagne.
The Kings of the Kop are playing again.
They're going to put the lid on Real Madrid.
They're going to work the miracles
They always did.
And they're going to paint Paris red.
They're going to paint Paris red.
And they'll never give up.
Till they come home with the cup.

have no beef about anything providing we have a full side out.

"They are all in the right frame of mind. It's going to be a hard game and different from the usual European games because it is a one-off affair."

"The excitement and anticipation are starting to build up and I hope it's an entertaining match with good behaviour from the supporters whatever the outcome."

Skipper Phil Thompson: "Real are more individual than we are; we work as a team. We have heard about the skills of Juanito and Santillana and we know about (Laurie) Cunningham, but if they think that they can win the game on their own they will find it a very hard, daunting task."

"We could have the edge on them as a team. Possibly their only player who has the same approach as ourselves is (Uli) Stielike, and he could be the main threat."

Phil Neal: "It's a very impressive stadium. It's just a crying shame that there will be so many of our supporters locked outside."

Ray Kennedy: "Madrid are unpredictable. You know what to expect from sides like Ajax and Bayern Munich, but Real can be brilliant or they can be rubbish – nothing in between."

"If Madrid are rubbish tonight then we are in the right mood to give them a hammering."

"Without all our injuries I think we would have won the League. Ray Clemence and Phil Neal are the only two of the team who haven't seen specialists this year and having the full-strength squad has given us a boost."

"Everyone associates Liverpool with the European Cup and that's the one we want to be in next season, as defending champions."

ON THE BOX

- Terry and June
- Sportsnight – which included a feature 'Whatever happened to the next Fred Perry? Why can't we produce a Wimbledon winner?'
- Crossroads
- The Benny Hill Show
- Family Fortunes
- The Cannon and Ball Show
- Only When I Laugh
- Magnum
- Hart to Hart
- Tales of the Unexpected

THE TOP 10 SINGLES

May 27th, 1981

1. **STAND AND DELIVER**
Adam and the Ants

2. **YOU DRIVE ME CRAZY**
Shakin Stevens

3. **STARS ON 45**
Star Sound

4. **CHEQUERED LOVE**
Kim Wilde

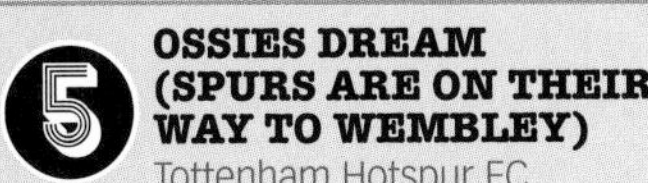

5. **OSSIES DREAM (SPURS ARE ON THEIR WAY TO WEMBLEY)**
Tottenham Hotspur FC

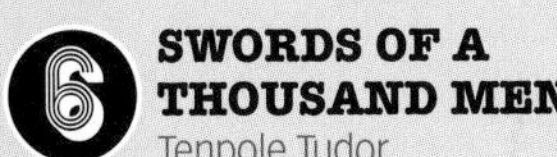

6. **SWORDS OF A THOUSAND MEN**
Tenpole Tudor

7. **BEING WITH YOU**
Smokey Robinson

8. **KEEP ON LOVING YOU**
REO Speedwagon

9. **I WANT TO BE FREE**
Toyah Safari

10. **BETTE DAVIS EYES**
Kim Cames

Goal of a lifetime sinks Real

IT'S A CRACKER

Liverpool 1
Real Madrid 0

The big match verdict
by Charles Lambert
Liverpool Echo, Thursday, May 28 1981

IT WAS just past 9.50 in the stylish bowl of the Parc des Princes last night when Alan Kennedy earned himself instant immortality. What the assembled masses from all corners of Europe made of the "Barney, Barney" chant, which rose from the Red sections of the arena as Kennedy's clubbing left-footer hit the Real Madrid net, no-one knows.

But this was the moment that Kennedy, the man the Kop call Barney Rubble, wrote his name on to an international stage and shattered that most aristocratic of football clubs, Real Madrid.

It was an unexpected end to a game, which failed to provide the spectacle that had been predicted, but more than compensated by producing the result of our dreams.

Liverpool's 1-0 win not only secured the European Cup for the third time after two years in which the trophy was on loan to Nottingham Forest, it also gave them a European trophy for the fifth time and that is a record only Real themselves can beat.

The winning goal came with only nine minutes to go.

Although Liverpool had looked consistently the more threatening side, their momentum seemed to have gone and the match was slowing to a virtual standstill. That was when Kennedy took a hand.

Receiving the ball from Ray Kennedy's throw, he bustled past a surprised Garcia Cortez and, as goalkeeper Agustin advanced in desperation, the Liverpool left-back drove the ball fiercely past him.

At the Madrid end, where 12,000 white bowler hats were still for the first time, the drums, which had pounded a

5

Latin beat from the first minute, were silent.

At the other end and in the pockets of scarlet throughout the stadium and most noticeably in the heart of the Real accommodation, they were dancing an unashamed Can-Can of pure exaltation.

There was no way Liverpool would lose. And in fact, they nearly doubled the scoreline, with Graeme Souness having a powerful shot brilliantly stopped by Agustin, and Terry McDermott tormenting the Spanish defence with crosses from the right, which almost gave David Johnson a goal.

So it was another memorable night for this exceptional club which has earned its place at the top of football's roll of honour. They adjusted intelligently to the formidable threat posed by a frigid Madrid formation early on and gradually drew the sting from the Spanish.

Real gambled heavily on grabbing an early goal. With Stielike a forceful presence and players switching positions with bewildering speed, they gave Liverpool a number of early problems. But it was a condemnation of them for all that, and for all the skilful ploys of Juanito and the devilish head work of Santillana, that Real hardly gave Ray Clemence anything serious to worry about.

Laurie Cunningham's most dangerous contribution came in the first minute when he beat McDermott and Phil Neal and played a cross to the near post where Clemence held on as Stielike moved in. But by the 11th minute Liverpool were sorting out a situation in which Kenny Dalglish, Johnson and Souness were all the targets of close man-to-man marking.

MATCH FACTS

Liverpool (4-4-2): Clemence, Neal, A Kennedy, Thompson, R Kennedy, Hansen, Dalglish (Case), Lee, Johnson, McDermott, Souness. Unused subs: Ogrizovic, Irwin, Money, Gayle

Real Madrid (3-4-3): Agustin, Sabido, Navajas, Cortes (Pineda), del Bosque, Angel, Camacho, Steilike, Juanito, Santillana, Cunningham. Unused subs: San Jose, Gonzalez, Angel, Garcia, Fernandez, Iaidro

Goal: Alan Kennedy (81)

Bookings: R Kennedy, Steilike

Conditions: Weather fine, pitch greasy

Referee: K Palotai (Hungary)

Attendance: 48,360

Alan Kennedy joined the attack and sent Agustin sprawling to save a low drive, McDermott in the 12th minute put a first-time effort just over and two minutes later Dalglish turned superbly and hit a shot, which Agustin saved.

This was encouraging, but then Real began to come into the picture. After a couple of threats from Santillana they went close in the 26th minute as Camacho, moving forward from shadowing Souness, hooked the ball just wide, after Juanito had craftily threaded it through.

Although manager Bob Paisley was to call for better use of the ball in his half-time talk, Liverpool almost took the lead eight minutes from the interval when Hansen, Neal and Dalglish cut through the defence and Souness drove a first-time effort which Agustin only held at the second attempt.

The second half started with a moment of pure horror, as Camacho, beating the offside trap, found only Clemence between him and the first goal. But his chip went over the bar.

The night will be remembered for the pageant of Red loyalty that illuminated the stadium and for the glamour of Europe's top two clubs fighting it out for the 1981 crown.

But most of all, this trip to Paris in the springtime will be remembered for the goal of a lifetime by one of Anfield's less celebrated sons, Alan Kennedy.

Alan Kennedy

"BECAUSE of my broken wrist I'd been sweating on whether I would play in the final. When Bob told me I would I just remember thinking 'I can't let him down.' The other lads like Richard Money and Colin Irwin had done extremely well without me to reach the final and he could have played one of them, or Avi Cohen in my place. But Bob took a chance on me, probably because he knew I was a natural left-footed player who could defend and get forward to support the attack.

I don't think it was a dreadful match; it wasn't an exciting match. People don't remember the pitch, which was in a terrible state. There had been rugby on it the week before and it wasn't well looked after. Finals should have the best pitches and stadiums.

I remember Graeme Souness got injured very early on. It was a case of not conceding, that's what we decided on. No goalkeeper was tested.

The manager always encouraged you to get forward. When Sammy Lee picked up the ball, he shouldn't have been in that position in the first place. He left the ball to Ray Kennedy. You don't think about what you're doing, you just do it. You make a run, you may not even get the ball. Bob liked players, such as Terry McDermott, who made runs for the sake of the team, to create space and confusion.

Ray Kennedy took the throw-in, I have to say I didn't particularly want the ball, I wasn't looking for it, I was just trying to help other players out to create a little bit of space. He threw the ball in, it hit me on the chest, and it bounced down. It was one of those occasions that the player came in - Cortez - to take me out of the game and nothing happened. Then you're thinking, 'What are you going to do? What are you going to do? Is it a shot? Is it a cross?' and basically I just blasted the ball towards the goal with the best shot I could muster and the goalkeeper made the fatal move to the left. The ball went over his shoulder and into the back of the net. I just set off behind the goal to celebrate in front of all the jubilant Liverpool fans. It was what dreams are made of. I was just pleased for myself, my family and for the whole of Merseyside. I just ran and ran and ran; it seemed like it took ages to get to the Liverpool fans. I was fortunate it was at that particular end. It was reminiscent of Kenny Dalglish against Bruges in '78.

Some lads went out that night. I stayed in, being the good, clean little lad that I was. My girlfriend at the time said we were not going out."

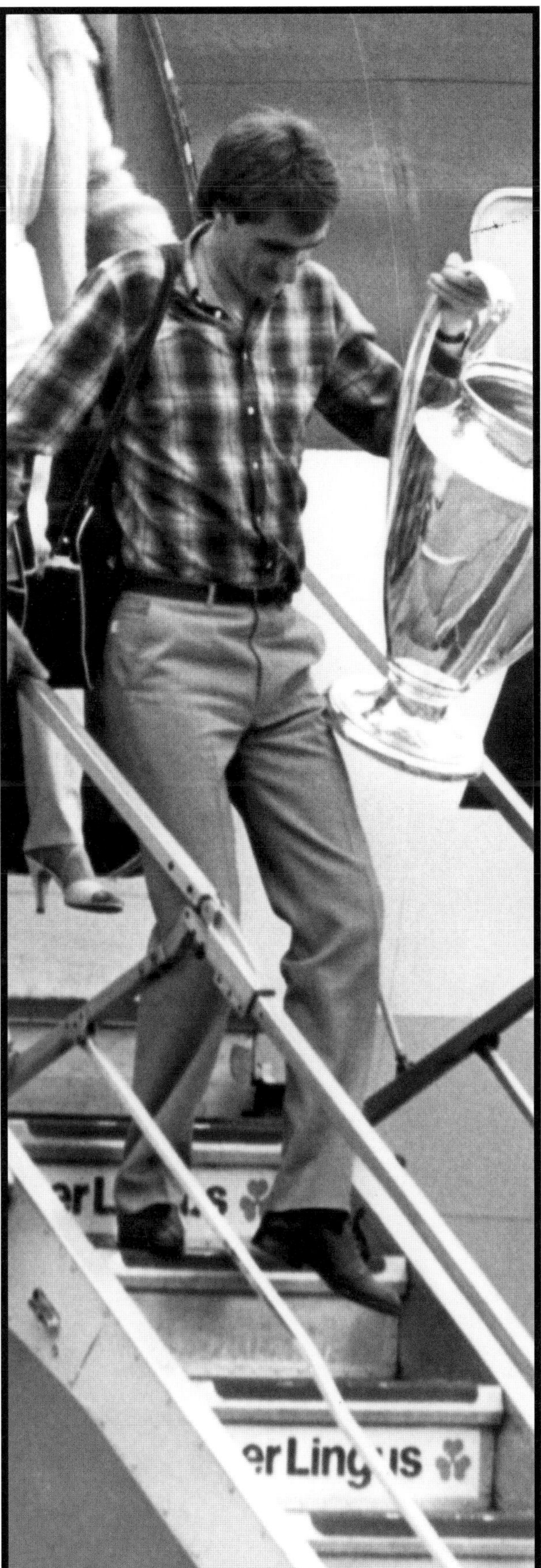

Phil Thompson

"IT was a terrific occasion. The all whites versus the all reds: Real Madrid versus Liverpool FC, in a packed stadium, it was a wonderful occasion.

The game wasn't the best in the world, but when you win, it doesn't matter how you play, it's the winning that counts when you get that far. To win in Paris was something I'll always remember.

That was the finest moment of my life, without question. To have gone from watching my heroes from the Kop to captaining the team I loved and leading them to victory in the European Cup final was just unbelievable. There is no way I can express that feeling in words. Proud doesn't begin to describe how I felt. I remember lifting it towards my mates from my Sunday League team in Kirkby who were in the crowd that night - I could see them on the front row of the top balcony. It was for them, for me, for everyone in Liverpool.

The weirdest thing was when we got back to Liverpool and the European Cup ended up in The Falcon, my Sunday team's local in Kirkby. [Club secretary] Peter Robinson told me that, as captain, I was in charge of it and should take care of it, even if it meant taking it home. Did I need telling twice when it's the European Cup? I'd got it in this big red velvet bag and put it in the back of my Capri and off I went to the Falcon. It's a bloody massive thing and it ended up taking pride of place behind the bar. Word soon spread that the European Cup was in The Falcon and hundreds of people started rolling up to have their photo taken with it. It was quite an incredible sight to see.

People were on the phone telling friends that Phil Thompson was in the Falcon with the European Cup. Some people thought they had had one drink too many and didn't believe them. Other people did head down there. It was a great story.

Peter Robinson had to ring me the next morning because the world's press were waiting to take pictures of it. I'd promised all the guys in the Falcon I would bring it in so their children could have their pictures taken. I stuck to my word and was there at 11am to have these pictures taken with the kids. I got down to Anfield about 12 o'clock. All the press were there with Peter Robinson. He was fantastic, there was no rollocking, and Phil Thompson, bleary-eyed, returned the European Cup."

Souness celebrates

GRAEME Souness had a double celebration in the final week of May 1981, as he became a father for the first time.

Only 48 hours after the Paris final, his then wife, Danielle, gave birth to a baby which they named Fraser Scott, who weighed in at 8lb 2oz.

Souness said: "It was a marvellous experience, one I will treasure all my life. I would recommend it to all fathers. The last few days have been the best in my life."

Bob Paisley

"IT was a very physical first half and some of the Real Madrid tackling was outrageous, to say the least. But at the same time they had players of real quality. We started quite well but we were upset, probably, by some of the tackles.

It was a triumph for our character once again. We started with three players - Dalglish, Thompson and Alan Kennedy - short of match practice, and Souness was hurt shortly after the kick-off. I'm sure Real didn't begrudge us our victory. I am so proud to be the manager of the first British club to win the European Cup three times."

Graeme Souness

"SOME of their tackles were X-certificate and in the first few minutes we were knocked out of our stride by the violence of their challenges. I decided that they needed a little of their own medicine to slow them down and to show that we could not be intimidated. It was then that I picked out the nasty Camacho, but as I closed in to give him a little nip, the German Stielike came in on my blindside and left me a limping passenger for the remainder of the game."

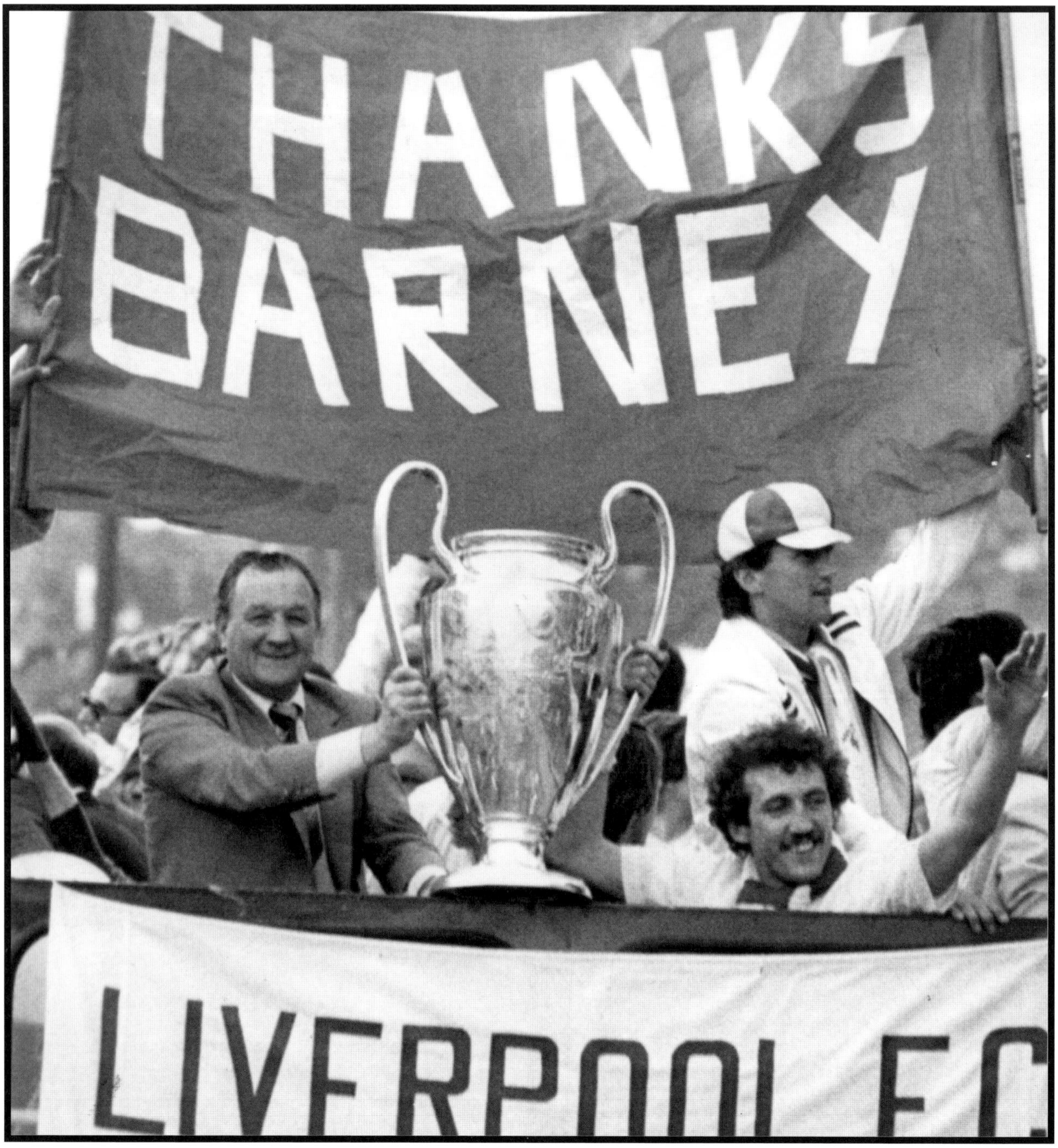

David Johnson

"IT was the most satisfying night of my European career. It meant so much to me after being on the bench in '77 and on crutches in '78. This time I actually played, and for the whole 90 minutes too."

England international and Real Madrid star, Laurie Cunningham is pictured above, bottom left, with his Madrid team mates

Laurie Cunningham (Real Madrid)

"I COULD have been used a bit more. There were times when I was playing for a one-two, but the return ball never came when it should have done. This is something that has got to be talked about a bit more in our dressing room.

Liverpool were lucky. We should have won it, but football is never like that, and luck came for Liverpool eight minutes from the end."

Phil Neal

"I KNEW Laurie Cunningham from the England set-up and it was my job to make sure he had no impact on the game. Bob Paisley warned me beforehand that I would have a big defensive job on my hands in order to contain him. But looking back I'd say I put in as good a defensive job as I could that night and Laurie rarely troubled us.

We've had such a terrible year in many ways, and fancy capping it with this. This is really an even more victorious feeling than on the two previous occasions. Before, we had always played well throughout the season, but this time we have stuttered a bit and that makes it more fulfilling to finish like this."

Jacqui and Stephen Small with their teddy, Barney Rubble, who was later passed to Alan Kennedy whilst he was on the open-top bus parading the city

Ooh la lah – we've won it in Paris la!

THERE was a Scouse party in Paris after Liverpool's magnificent victory against Real Madrid.

The win was toasted with beer and champagne as droves of delirious supporters sang their hearts out in the bars and cafes in the Champs Elysees.

Liverpudlians hugged and kissed each other - and waiters - in true French style.

As fans strolled along the boulevards, groups shook hands with solemn Real Madrid followers.

Scarves, flags and banners adorned famous buildings, including the Arc de Triomphe where thousands of motorists beeped their horns and waved to the fans.

Kenny Dalglish - 1978

"IT helped that Wembley staged the final. Those Twin Towers felt like a second home to Liverpool. We had been there twice already that season, although we'd failed to score on either occasion. So near to achieving my ambition, I became very nervous. My normal matchday afternoon routine was disrupted because I was unable to sleep. All I could do was lie on my bed at the hotel and think of what lay ahead - the atmosphere, the opponents, whether chances would fall my way, whether I would get the chance to touch that famous old trophy."

Phil Thompson - 1977

"THERE was a real togetherness about the squad and for my part it was still great to be a part of an historic occasion, even though I was hurting inside because I could not play.

Tosh and I travelled with the team and Bob Paisley ensured we were involved in every way. The atmosphere amongst the lads was tremendous.

Nothing ever fazed this Liverpool team because of the self-belief we had. There was always a lot of humour in the dressing room and the players revelled in the challenge. We would always be focused, but relaxed and this was the mood as Bob led everyone out to inspect the Olympic Stadium pitch.

I will never forget what happened next. As soon as we entered the tunnel area, a wall of noise swept over us. Then we caught our first glimpse of the terraces and it seemed as if the whole arena was a sea of red and white. Red and white chequered flags were everywhere. Someone must have made a fortune outside the ground. Liverpool's travelling army exploded when they glimpsed the players. It was the kind of deafening roar that made the hairs stand up on the back of your neck. As a Scouser and a Liverpudlian, I was so proud.

The lads returned to the comparative quiet of the dressing room, but I can tell you that the mood in there was electric. We couldn't wait to get out there to see the fans again. Everyone was saying: 'That was only the rehearsal. What's it going to be like when the curtain goes up for real?'

We couldn't wait to get down that tunnel. We couldn't wait to hear the singing and the chanting and see those red and white chequered flags held high. It got to 7.30 and we were really hyped up. If Jim Carrey had been in our dressing room, the team talk would have been just three words.

'It's show time'!"

Joey Jones - 1977

"THE day before the game we did some light training and had our regular team talk from Bob Paisley, who said: 'Don't do any sight-seeing because there's nothing to see. I was here in the war with a tank and I knocked it all down'.

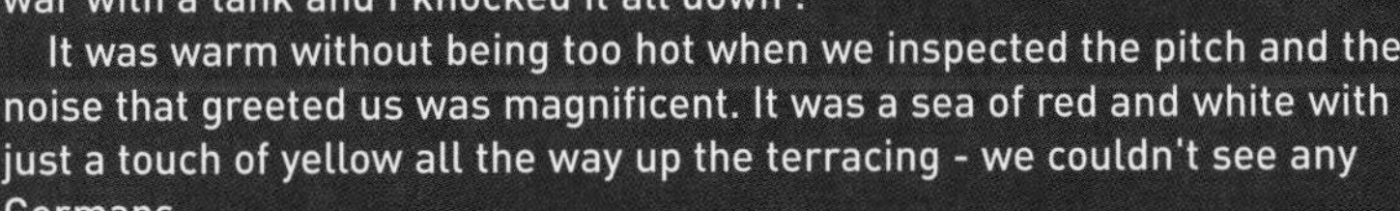

It was warm without being too hot when we inspected the pitch and the noise that greeted us was magnificent. It was a sea of red and white with just a touch of yellow all the way up the terracing - we couldn't see any Germans.

It was an incredible sight and right in the middle was a massive banner stretching across the Liverpool end.

'Joey ate the Frogs legs, made the Swiss roll, now he's munching Gladbach.'

As well as making us laugh it gave me one helluva boost. I don't think I've ever felt so proud in all my life. What an honour!"

Afterwards in the dressing room the singing went on and on with all the cameras there. I never let my medal out of my hand once. I wanted to hide it in my pocket under my hanky, but I couldn't trust it to be safe."

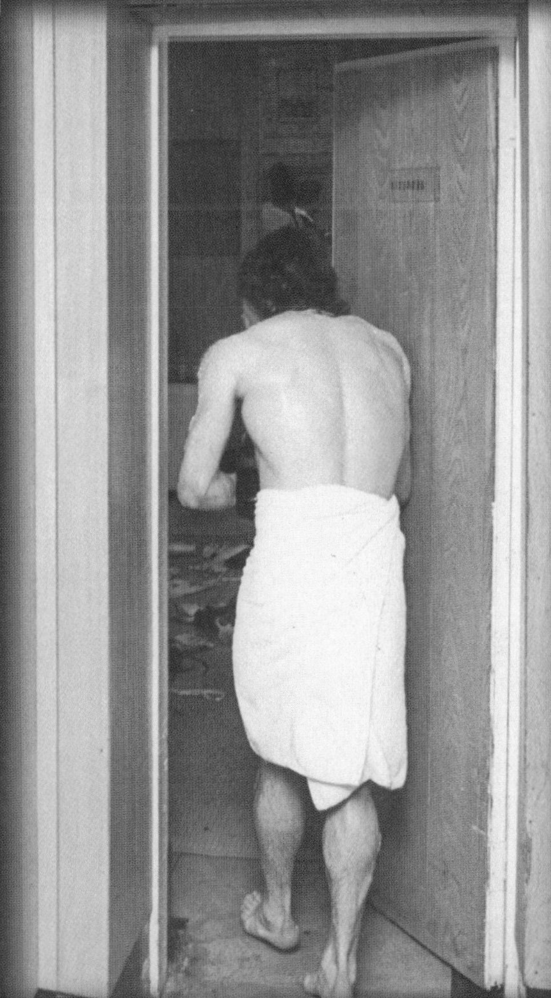

Alan Hansen - 1981

"I WAS even more nervous in Paris then I'd been in the 1978 final against Bruges at Wembley.

"Usually when I got out on to the pitch I felt better. But not that night.

"As we ran towards the fans we were stunned by seeing the biggest banner I've ever clapped eyes on.

"It covered one entire end of the stadium and in letters as big as houses said starkly, "Real Madrid." Bloody hell, I thought. I tried to ignore it but I couldn't. Intimidating? It was terrifying."

1978

The road to London

As Champions of Europe Liverpool received a bye into the second round - a far cry from the modern rules - and found themselves playing on both sides of the Berlin wall to defend their trophy. A visit to Lisbon was sandwiched in between our two trips to Germany but no-one could stop Bob's boys from reaching the final again

Kenny Dalglish strikes and Liverpool take a 2-0 lead at Anfield against Benfica

Round two

Round two, first leg
October 19 1977

Liverpool 5
(Hansen 14, Case 21, 57, Neal (pen) 44, Kennedy 66)

Dynamo Dresden 1
(Hafner 76)

Att: 39,835

Team: Clemence; Neal, Jones, Hansen, Kennedy, Hughes, Dalglish, Case, Heighway, Toshack, Callaghan.

THE Reds began their defence of the trophy in emphatic style against a Dresden team who were unable to make their mark on the game.

John Toshack was the main thorn in their side and although the Welshman did not find the target himself, he claimed three assists as the Reds romped into a healthy first-leg lead.

Round two, second leg
November 2 1977

Dynamo Dresden 2
(Kotte 46, Sachse 52)

Liverpool 1
(Heighway 67)

(Liverpool win 6-3 on aggregate)

Att: 33,000

Team: Clemence; Neal, Jones, Hansen, Kennedy, Hughes, Dalglish, Case, Heighway, McDermott (Fairclough), Callaghan.

DRESDEN were unrecognisable from the side which lost at Anfield and when Sachse headed home the East Germans' second goal seven minutes after the break, Liverpool were wobbling. Fortunately, the home side squandered a couple more chances and 'Supersub' David Fairclough broke clear on a counter-attack and crossed for Steve Heighway to stab home and settle the jangling nerves in the away end.

Terry McDermott puts Liverpool 3-1 up against Benfica at Anfield

Quarter-final

Quarter-final, first leg
March 1 1978

Benfica 1
(Nene 18)

Liverpool 2
(Case 37, Hughes 72)

Att: 70,000

Team: Clemence; Neal, Smith, Thompson (Hansen), Kennedy, Hughes, Dalglish, Case, Heighway, McDermott, Callaghan.

ON a filthy night in which the teams were forced to contend with torrential downpours, Liverpool's evening became even more murky when Nene gave Benfica an early lead.

But Bob Paisley's men showed their appetite for the fight and gave a gritty display which was rewarded by goals from Jimmy Case and Emlyn Hughes as the Reds silenced the partisan crowd in the Stadium of Light.

Quarter-final, second leg
March 15 1978

Liverpool 4
(Callaghan 6, Dalglish 17, McDermott 78, Neal 88)

Benfica 1
(Nene 25)

(Liverpool win 6-2 on aggregate)

Att: 48,364

Team: Clemence; Neal, Smith, Thompson, Kennedy, Hughes, Dalglish, Case, Heighway, McDermott, Callaghan.

IT was scrappy and disjointed but Liverpool fans weren't complaining. Ian Callaghan's cross was deflected in after just six minutes and when Kenny Dalglish seized upon a poor backpass from Toni, the tie was effectively over.

Late goals from Terry McDermott and Phil Neal gave the Reds an emphatic 6-2 aggregate victory.

Semi-final

Semi-final, first leg
March 29 1978

Borussia Moenchengladbach 2
(Hannes 28, Bonhof 89)

Liverpool 1
(Johnson 88)

Att: 66,000

Team: Clemence; Neal, Smith, Thompson, Kennedy, Hughes, Dalglish, Case, Heighway (Souness), McDermott (Johnson), Callaghan.

A CAUTIOUS tie saw Liverpool licking their wounds when Hannes opened the scoring from a corner but the Reds hit back after the break and thought they'd snatched a draw when David Johnson headed home the equaliser two minutes from time.

But before the travelling Kop could begin their celebrations, Bonhof hit a free-kick through the Reds' defensive wall and past a startled Ray Clemence to give the Germans a handy lead.

Semi-final, second leg
April 12 1978

Liverpool 3
(Kennedy 6, Dalglish 35, Case 56)

Borussia Moenchengladbach 0

(Liverpool win 4-2 on aggregate)

Att: 51,500

Team: Clemence; Neal, Smith, Thompson, Kennedy, Hughes, Dalglish, Case, Heighway, McDermott, Souness.

CHANTS of "Wembley, Wembley" rang out around Anfield as Liverpool produced one of their best performances in European competition to sweep aside Moenchengladbach.

The Kop choir reached a crescendo as goals from Ray Kennedy, Kenny Dalglish and Jimmy Case set up a title defence in the capital.

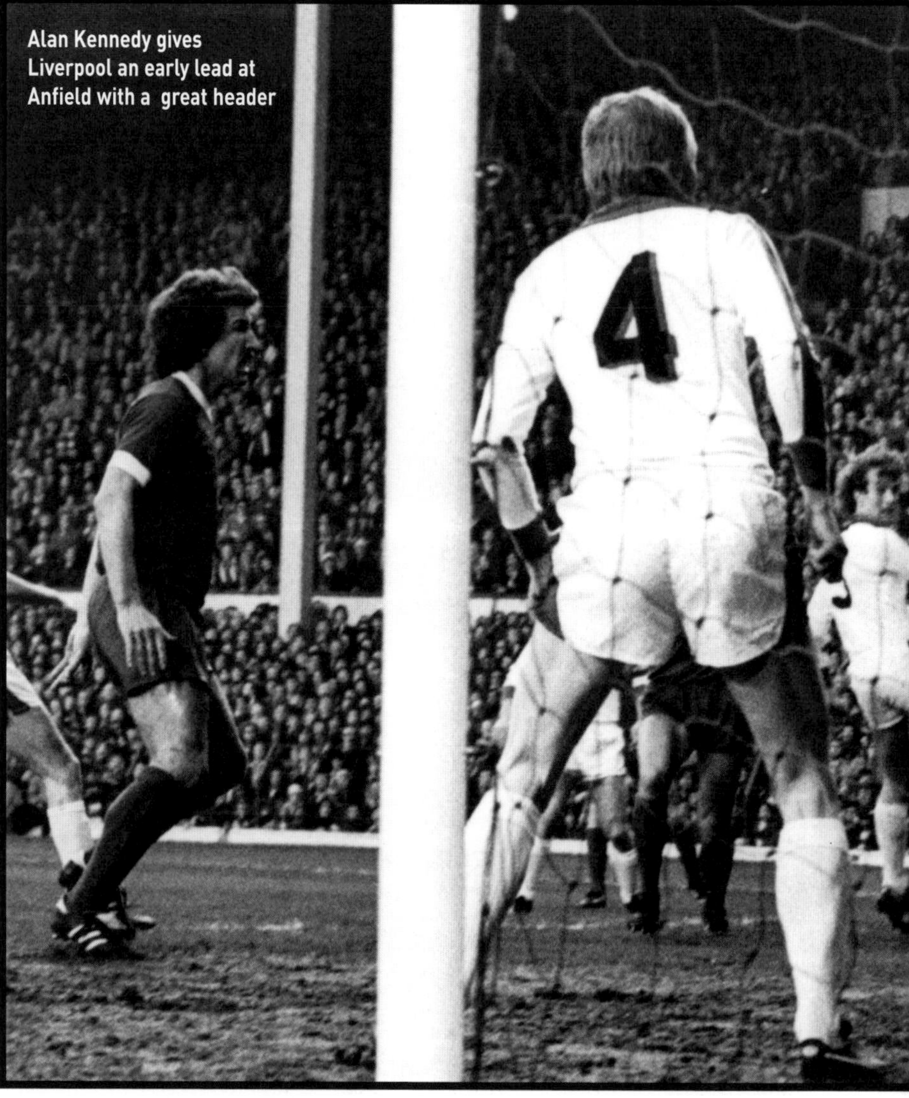

Alan Kennedy gives Liverpool an early lead at Anfield with a great header

David Johnson scores a late away goal in the first leg

Donhof scores a last ditch free-kick which gives the Germans the advantage heading to Anfield

WE'RE THE GREATEST TEAM IN EUROPE AND WE'RE GOING TO WEM-BER-LEE

The travelling Kop had been all over Europe following the Redmen but in 1978 the final was held at a very familiar location. Over 80,000 Liverpool fans were estimated to have ventured across the Watford Gap to turn Wembley into Anfield South

MINI BONUS

Bootle-based firm Sturdy Finance offered various incentives to Liverpool's potential matchwinner for the final. The Reds' first goalscorer was offered a red Mini, while the man who laid on the pass for the first goal (Graeme Souness) was also set to benefit - to the tune of Hi-Fi equipment. Regardless, each player was due to receive a watch on the Friday after the final.

BEATING THE BARRICADE

Wembley officials prepared for the Reds' support by stepping up security in a bid to ward off ticketless fans on the day of the final. A 'Colditz-style' operation was launched, though a police spokesman in Liverpool claimed: "I wouldn't be surprised if some of them are not already in there."

TV TIMES

An audience of more than 100 million people was anticipated for the final, with the game being broadcast live or recorded to most of Europe. ITV were hoping for near to 26 million viewers.

STAR GAZING

John Peel: "I come up to Liverpool for most of the home matches on my own, and I'll be on my own when I go to Wembley. The beautiful thing is that I know I won't be on my own for very long there."

Tom O'Connor: "If we're lenient they'll be let off 3-0, but if we're merciless it wouldn't surprise me if it was five or six. To Liverpool of course."

Adrian Henri (poet and painter): "I've managed to get a lift with some friends in a XJ6 and we're going down in style."

Ken Dodd: "I'm not prejudiced you know. I'll support anyone...I don't care who beats Manchester United."

WELCOME HOME

No grand finale was planned like 1977's Picton Library celebration due to safety concerns, though city officials promised a bigger, better route for the salute (14 miles), with 250,000 fans expected to come out - nearer 500,000 was the more accurate figure.

SCHOOLS OUT

There was outrage as a kids' army of fans (some as young as nine) descended on London - many without tickets - in a bid to break through the security barriers at Wembley. One 12-year-old from Dovecot said: "I've missed school to get here. I'm not bothered about not having a ticket - because I've sneaked into Wembley before. Me and my mates will probably go to the Soho markets to scrounge some food for the day."
Another young 'scal' said:
"My mum thinks I'm staying at a friend's home tonight. After the match I'll try and sneak on to one of the special trains - or I'll just have to hitch back to Liverpool."

Other tales in preparation for the big night included:
Leyland bosses ordered that both car plants at Speke should delay the late shift by two hours so that fans could watch the final.

FINAL WORD

Kenny Dalglish:
"Bruges had defeated Atletico Madrid and Juventus to reach the final, but we felt it would help that Wembley was staging the final."

Bob Paisley: "We have seen enough of the Belgian champions to know that they will attack us. And we'll certainly attack them."

It should provide entertainment, excitement and thrilling football."

Although their goalkeeper Jensen is agile, he still prefers to punch the ball rather than catch, like all Continental goalkeepers."

★★★★★

Vauxhall's Ellesmere Port plant were not due to start until 9.30pm. "We just hope everyone will be coming to work with a smile on their face," said a plant spokesman.
One in four buses in the north end of the city were set to be off the road as drivers turned down voluntary overtime.

PARTING THE RED SEA

The message was defiant from Wembley bosses ahead of the final. Security chief Michael Sykes stated: "There is just no point in trying to get inside without a ticket or the proper credentials. Even Bob Paisley won't get past the first gate if he hasn't got a ticket. We reckon it's harder to get into Wembley without one than it is to get out of a high-security prison."

Reds chairman John W. Smith wanted fans to heed the warnings on the eve of the showpiece. He said: "Our fans made themselves a marvellous reputation with their good-humoured behaviour in Rome last year for our first European Cup final. I want them to repeat that now."

TICKET TO RIDE

Controversy reigned regarding the success of touts in the days leading up to the May 10 clash. Around 50,000 fans (from an original allocation of 23,000) were expected to back the Reds after an extra 20,000 purchased tickets - most on the black market. For a £2.50 ground ticket £15 was paid, and a dealer said: "We have made a killing. The supporters have been going frantic and there are thousands more who are still looking for a ticket."

PRICES

- T-shirts worded: 'Liverpool, European Champions' were available for £1.75 - plus 20p postage - from The Sign Shop on Victoria Street.
- Train to the final (one of the 16 football specials) - £8
- Train plus meal - £20

KEN'S BALL'S UP

Ken Bowman came up with a novel plan to glean a ticket for Wembley. Despite already having a ticket, his wife

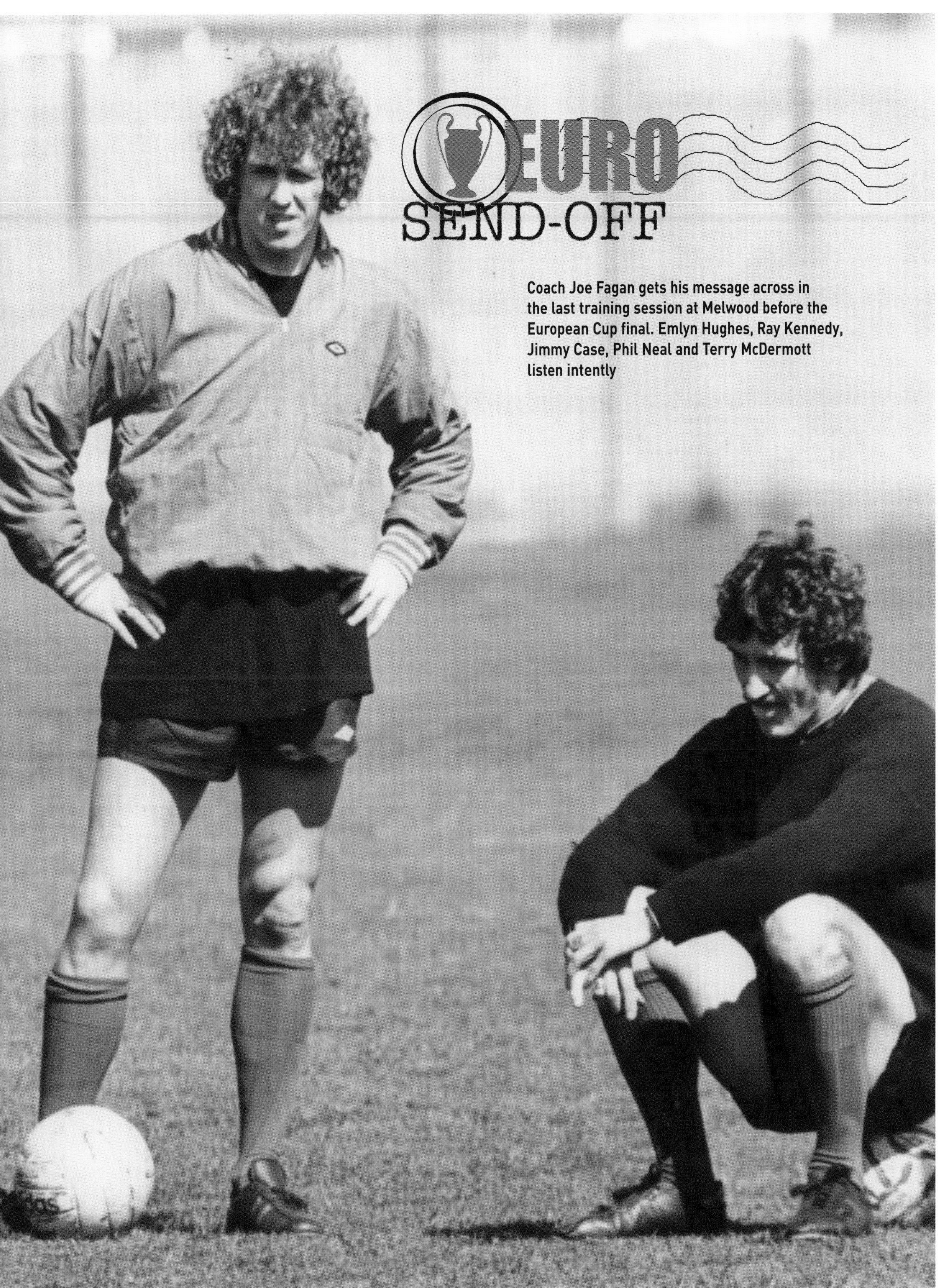

EURO SEND-OFF

Coach Joe Fagan gets his message across in the last training session at Melwood before the European Cup final. Emlyn Hughes, Ray Kennedy, Jimmy Case, Phil Neal and Terry McDermott listen intently

★★★★★

EURO SEND-OFF '78

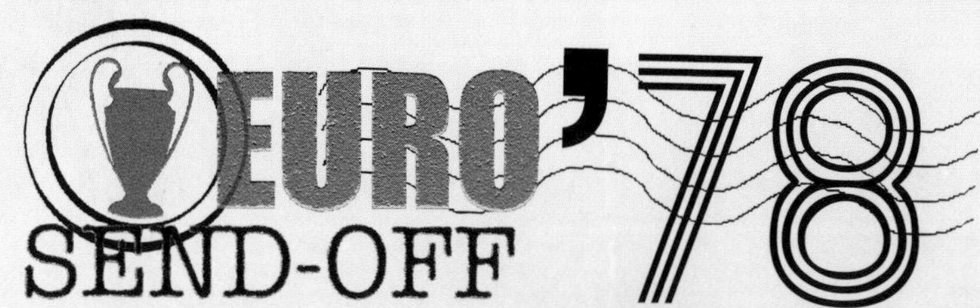

Francis was unable to claim her place so Ken, of Stoneycroft, sacrificed his most treasured possession - a football signed by the European Cup winners of 1977 - in a bid to secure a ticket. "I think it's worth it, even though I'm proud of that football."
A woman from Wrexham duly obliged and the happy couple were granted their wish.

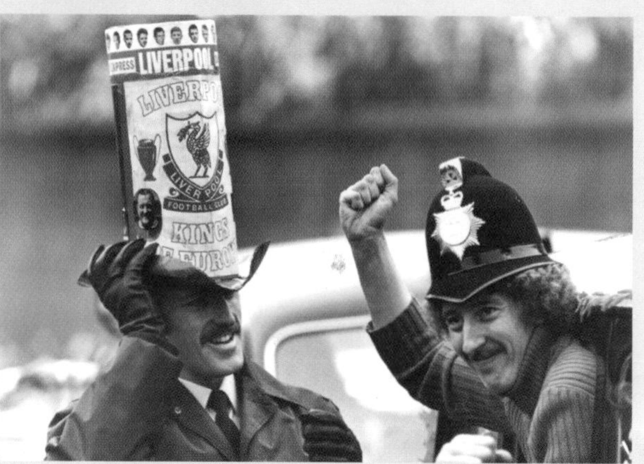

RAY OF LIGHT

Having forgotten to post his entry for a competition to win an all-expenses paid trip for two to the final, Ray McCarthy was as shocked as anyone on being informed he had won. The thoughtfulness of his mother saved the day, having put a stamp on the completed entry and posted it off.

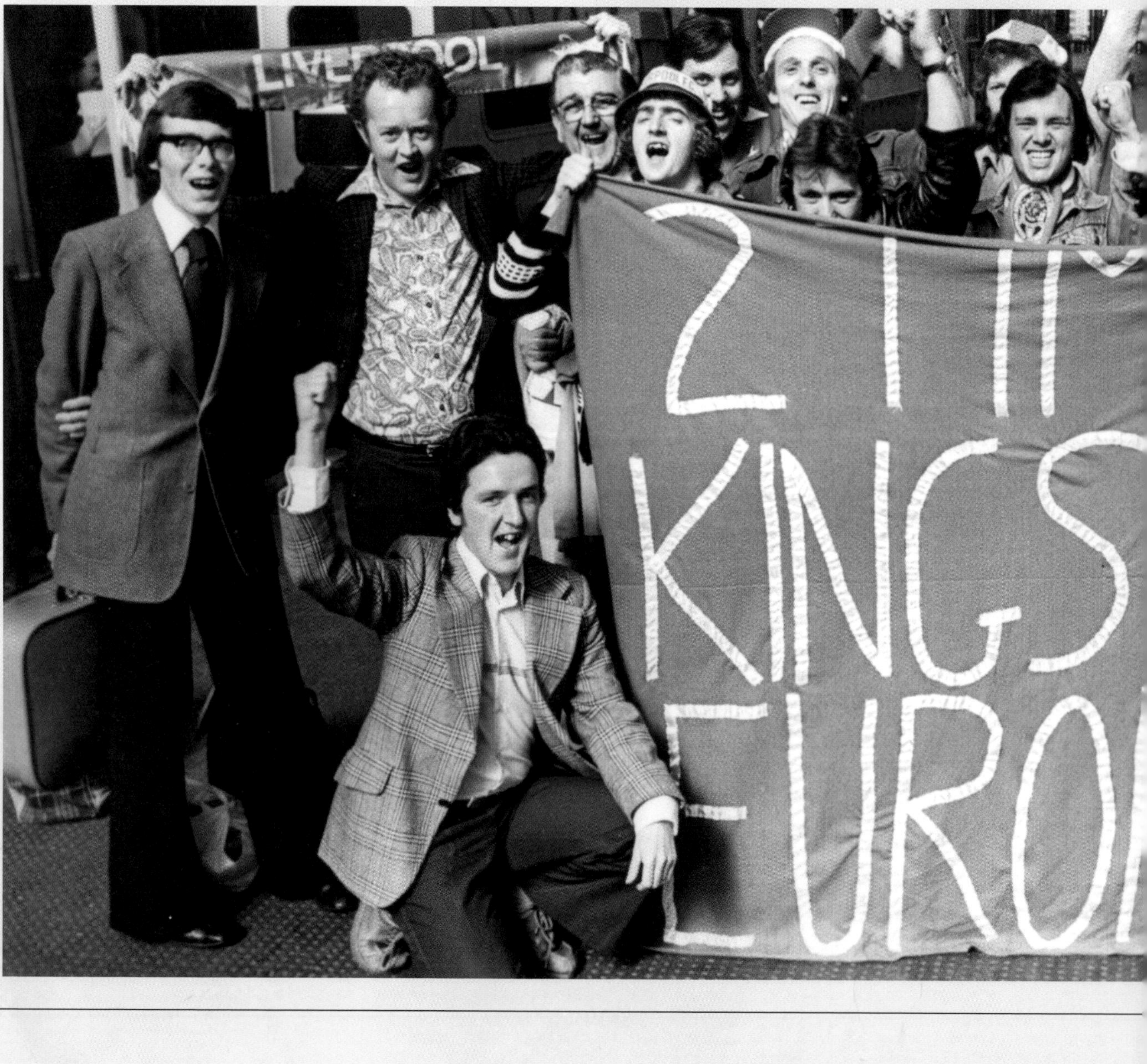

ON THE BOX

- The Val Doonican Music Show
- The Life and Times of Grizzly Adams
- Celebrity Squares
- Sale of the Century
- Rising Damp
- It Ain't Half Hot Mum
- The Standard: Win a Few, Lose a Few
- The Old Grey Whistle Test

THE TOP 10 SINGLES
May 10th, 1978

1. **RIVERS OF BABYLON** Boney M
2. **NIGHT FEVER** The Bee Gees
3. **TOO MUCH TOO LITTLE TOO LATE** Johnny Mathis and Deniece Williams
4. **AUTOMATIC LOVER** Dee D. Jackson
5. **NEVER LET HER SLIP AWAY** Andrew Gold
6. **MATCHSTALK MEN AND MATCHSTALK CATS AND DOGS** Brian and Michael
7. **BECAUSE THE NIGHT** The Patti Smith Group
8. **LET'S ALL CHANT** The Michael Zager Band
9. **EVERYBODY DANCE** Chic
10. **BOY FROM NEW YORK CITY** Darts

The golden goal that broke the Belgians . . . and

RED HOT! KINGS IN CONTROL

Liverpool 1
FC Bruges 0

The big match action
by Michael Charters
Liverpool Echo, Thursday, May 11th, 1978

LIVERPOOL took over Wembley last night. Players and fans combined to provide a night of magic on the field and the terraces which will live on as long as this famous stadium exists.

It was more than the magnificent fact that the champions had retained the European Cup by beating FC Bruges 1-0, it was as if Anfield (giant-sized) had been moved lock, stock and barrel into the national stadium.

On the field the players produced that cultured mixture of sophisticated, European-style football combined with British strength to overwhelm the outplayed Belgian champions.

There must have been more than 80,000 Liverpool fans in the capacity 92,000 crowd. They created a great heaving mass of red and white, all round the stadium to greet their heroes after another great triumph with a reception which hurt the eardrums.

It was moving, magnificent and totally fitting that they had seen their team win the cup twice...and it had been done in immense style.

The only possible criticism of their smooth and elegant exhibition was that they won by only one goal, scored midway through the second half by ace finisher Kenny Dalglish. It was his 30th of the season and it clinched what Bob Paisley called the most important game in the club's history.

They won more easily than they had done in Rome a year ago. The Scrooge-like scoreline cannot pretend to tell the story of their total command. Bruges were never in the game, always struggling to compete, and Liverpool confirmed, without the shadow of an argument, their reputation as the top team in Europe.

In a brilliant, all-round team display, Graeme Souness stood out on his first Wembley appearance to play with such assured poise and class that he must surely develop into one of the great midfield players in the world with the help of the Liverpool players around him.

And if he and Dalglish can play for Scotland as they did for Liverpool last night, then the World Cup hopes north of the border must soar.

Bob Paisley's choice of David Fairclough was a winner - the lad played brilliantly - and the well-timed substitution of Steve Heighway in the second half was another masterstroke. It all fitted in so neatly, with tremendous performances from Phil Thompson and Alan Hansen - this boy came of age in the Liverpool red last night.

The champions took a bit of time to move smoothly into their stride, but long before half-time, it was a stride of such power and persistence that the Belgians were pinned in their own half for minutes on end.

Bruges were rarely seen in attack, and apart from a header by Ku which cleared the bar just before half-time, it was all Liverpool - a steadily increasing weight of red pressure.

An early feature which continued to irritate was the Bruges use of an offside trap which seemed to be the only tactic they knew capable of stopping the Liverpool threat when in full flow.

In fact the first major incident took 23 minutes to arrive as Fairclough, moving smoothly and with ever-increasing confidence, raced down the left and passed inside to Case, who looked a certain scorer until Bastijns made a fine interception.

sent Kenny away with a smile as wide as the Kop

But this was the signal for more positive action by Liverpool, who launched assault after assault. Kennedy missed a fine chance with a shot across the goalface, a header by Neal was well saved, before Case, trying to reach the ball at full stretch, brought down Maes with a tackle which earned him a booking.

Vandereyoken soon made it clear that Case was the target for retaliation, and was also booked. He nearly paid dearly for his loss of temper, because from the free-kick Case hit one of his specials which Jensen turned away with the save of the game.

The longer the game went, the more Liverpool looked like champions.

They could have scored twice in the first few minutes of the second half. Fairclough beat Bastijns, crossed the ball low and hard, and Dalglish was a tantalising inch away from turning it into the net.

Then a super inter-passing link between Souness and Dalglish sent McDermott streaking through the middle. Jensen, who became the Belgian's hero in holding out Liverpool, moved quickly out of goal to block the shot.

Liverpool had had so little to do defensively that it was a major shock to see Sorensen, who had hardly touched the ball before this, beat Hansen, only to waste an opening he had created brilliantly.

Liverpool's problem was a familiar one - total domination without a goal to show for it at that stage. Manager Bob Paisley decided then to inject more attacking strength with a forward replacing a midfield man after 64 minutes - Heighway in place of Case.

Heighway had been on the pitch only for seconds when the warm night air over Wembley was split by the biggest Liverpool roar I've heard for years. It was the clincher goal that won this great game.

McDermott and Souness switched the ball down the right in search of an opening in the compact Bruges defence. Souness found it with yet another of his inch-perfect floaters, landing the ball at Dalglish's feet.

Dalglish, looking up with that calm authority that makes him outstanding, saw Jensen slightly off his line and out of position, drove the ball, not quickly but so accurately, just inside the far upright.

He raced off the pitch in joy to stand and greet the Liverpool fans at that end of the ground. His team-mates enveloped him and their congratulations and You'll Never Walk Alone soared into the night.

Liverpool's domination was even more pronounced now, as Heighway brought additional attacking skills to a team which had paralysed Bruges but had only one goal to show for it.

Ten minutes from the end Hansen, who had played so well, made a careless back pass which put Clemence in trouble against Sorensen. The ball flew wide to Simoen whose shot, with Clemence yards out of position, was turned off the line by Thompson.

And in the closing minutes Liverpool kept their heads and their skills, fashioned through years of European experience and non-stop tensions of football at the highest level.

MATCH FACTS

Liverpool (4-4-2): Clemence; Neal, Thompson, Hansen, Hughes; Case (Heighway), McDermott, Souness, Kennedy; Dalglish, Fairclough. Unused subs: Callaghan, Jones, Irwin, Ogrizovic

Bruges (4-4-2): Jensen; Bastijns, Krieger, Leekens, Maes (Volders); De Cubber, Cools, Vandereycken, Sorensen; Simoen, Ku (Sanders)

Goal: Dalglish (65)

Bookings: Case, Vandereycken

Conditions: Perfect

Referee: C Corver (Holland)

Attendance: 92,000

Bob Paisley

MANAGER Bob Paisley wrote himself into the history books after presiding over back-to-back triumphs and immediately announced his aim to make it a hat-trick in 1979.

"We'll be going for three times next season and I believe we have the squad capable of winning the European Cup again next year," he said. "If there was another Dalglish available, we'd go for him. But I don't see anyone better than what we've got now. This squad can do it again.

"We needed a spark of individualism to give us victory and it was provided by Graeme and Kenny, two players comparatively new to our set-up. Graeme's sense of awareness allowed him to spot the opening and put Kenny in a one-on-one situation with the keeper, which he thrives on. When Kenny scored I sensed that would be enough because of the Belgians' attitude."

Paisley admitted he was always determined to make sure matchwinner Dalglish, a £440,000 recruit from Celtic the previous summer, joined the Reds ahead of the cut-off for playing in the competition.

He explained: "When we first heard from Jock Stein at Celtic that Kenny was talking about leaving, we made our move to keep him in Britain. But there was a lot of dithering going on and I insisted we wanted him to sign by the qualifying day for the European Cup.

"We put a bit of pressure on Celtic for that reason and we got him. It has all paid off now."

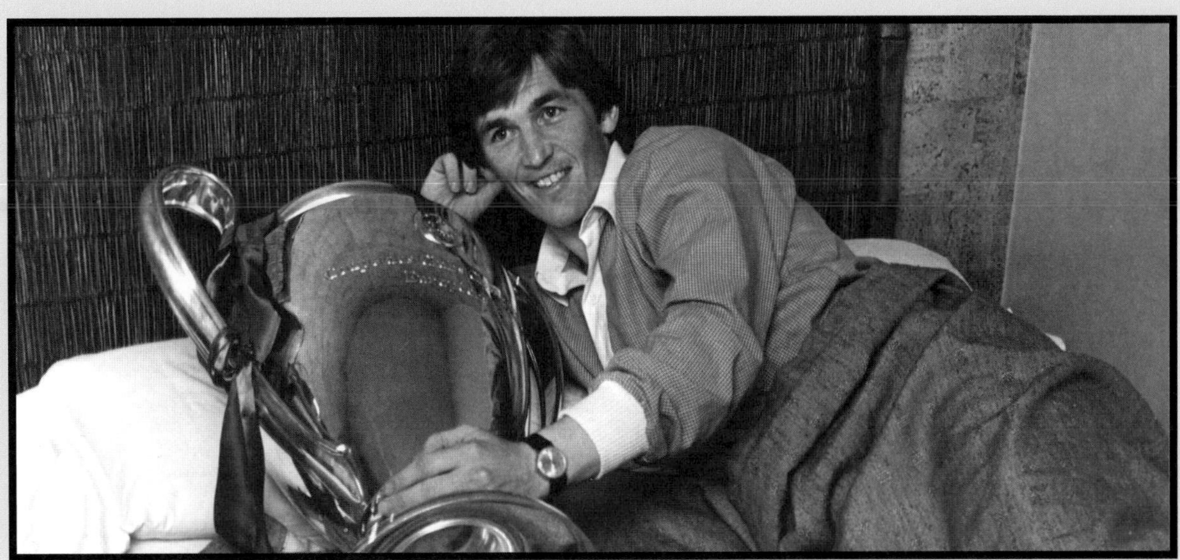

Kenny Dalglish

MATCHWINNER Kenny Dalglish grabbed most of the headlines for his fine finish that proved enough to keep the trophy at Anfield.

"Graeme Souness played the ball through to me on the edge of the box and I just clipped it over the keeper into the goal," he said.

"Everyone seems to be saying how badly Bruges played, but performances don't matter. We have won the European Cup and that's what is important.

"I wanted to run over to our fans and give them a salute. I don't remember jumping over the boards but I do know I couldn't leap over them on the way back because the emotion made my legs weak. Seeing that goal go in was the greatest moment of my football life. Getting a European Cup winner's medal is every player's dream."

Emlyn Hughes

EMLYN Hughes was thrilled after lifting the European Cup for the second successive year and showing off the famous piece of silverware to the massed Red ranks beneath the twin towers.

He said: "I can't really believe it. After all the excitement of Rome last year to win it again is just incredible.

"It's a funny feeling really. You can't take it in that we have done it again, winning a cup like that twice in a row. I don't really think it will sink in until later.

"Liverpool are the greatest club in the world and that's what motivates everyone connected with it. The cup felt as if it had never been out of my hands.

"Our fans expected us to go out and take Bruges apart, but we couldn't do that because they gave us a harder game than Borussia Moenchengladbach. In the first 20 minutes, we didn't really get a grip, but ten minutes from half-time we began to think we were going to win.

"Bruges seemed beaten before they started. It seemed to me that they were playing for a goalless draw, hoping in their wild despair the match might eventually be decided on penalties. What an attitude to take into a European Cup final. We were not at our best. I suppose we had the experience to do just what we needed.

"It has been a long hard season but to win the European Cup in front of so many of our fans is fantastic. It couldn't have been written better if it was a fairy story."

Terry McDermott

TERRY McDermott missed out on scoring in successive finals but as he clutched his second winners' medal that fact paled into insignificance.

"It would have been nice to have scored in two European Cup finals but the main thing is that the result is right.

"The boss told us that Bruges would play an offside game and we worked hard in training to counteract it. It was difficult to break them down, but we got through two or three times, David Fairclough had a couple of chances and I had one which I should have put away.

"The support couldn't have been better anywhere in the world. Eighty per cent of the crowd must have been Liverpool supporters."

Alan Hansen

ALAN Hansen had to pinch himself as he received his first winners' medal. A year earlier he had been playing with Partick Thistle.

"If anyone had told me I would play more than 20 first team games for Liverpool this season, I would have been made up. To finish with a European Cup winners' medal is fantastic," he said after the game.

Looking back at the game more recently, the Scottish defender recalled: "It was a very special night. For five to six years beforehand I'd been watching the European Cup final and dreaming about playing in that match. The year before I was still at Partick and we watched Liverpool and Moenchengladbach with a six-pack. No way did I think that the next year I'd be playing in the final. When I ran out to the pitch at Wembley five minutes before kick off I was just thinking to myself 'this is what it's all about.'

"It wasn't the best game in the world, but Kenny scored a great goal and we won 1-0 and joined the ranks of the great players who had won the European Cup. I remember going through Wembley about half an hour after the match with Terry McDermott and just saying: 'This is the greatest feeling I've ever had.'

'Liverpool coppers celebrated on train with us'

DECADES before she became known as television's toughest quiz show host, ANNE ROBINSON was reporting for the Liverpool Echo. She was given the task of being the paper's watchdog on the celebrations as she boarded the last train back from London with revelling Reds. Here, we reproduce her account of a night when there were no weak links to be found as far as Liverpool were concerned:

IF Kenny Dalglish could have a pound note for every time his name was mentioned between Wembley and Lime Street last night, he could retire immediately.

We were like a band of jubilant but exhausted refugees by the time we staggered onto the last train at 11.07.

We were hoarse from yelling and winded from running to catch it. Nobody, we moaned, had remembered the station was a good two-mile hike from the ground.

By Watford Junction, the Presbyterian minister in our carriage was accepting a Newcastle Brown. By Rugby, Fred 'The Vicar' had passed round his dog collar and was joining in the canonisation of Kenny.

There were action replays of the famous goal in the corridors, on the tables and from the luggage racks.

When we got on we agreed it wasn't as good a match as the one in Rome. By the time we got off there was nothing to compare with it.

At Wembley Central Station, the cockney British Rail officials tolerated us but on the train the Liverpool coppers took off their hats and celebrated with us.

Typically the heating in the train failed, but we had Union Jack flags and an amazing collection of black and blue scarves which someone said had come from a coach load of Bruges fans.

The train was only three-quarters full and at least 1,000 of the original 11,000 passengers on the soccer specials had stayed behind.

I don't know how much their absenteeism will be noticed. As the whistle went for kick-off one fellow on my row announced: "Great, my mate's just clocking on for us."

On the way down, the packed train was more like a Sunday school outing than a Wembley special.

It was as if the fans were determined to restore their reputation after the debacle at Dusseldorf.

And even the veteran B.R. man remarked: "We had more trouble with the women going to the ladies' hockey international than this lot."

And if my return journey was anything to go by, we should be quite certain we are still the best-humoured, best-mannered soccer fans in the country.

Ray Kennedy

RAY Kennedy admitted few of the Liverpool side felt any pressure going into the game.

The midfield maestro said: "We never felt under any pressure. The only way we were going to lose was if we made mistakes ourselves. We managed to get the one goal and that made life much easier for us."

Graeme Souness

GRAEME Souness supplied the pass for Kenny Dalglish's winner - but admitted the through-ball was not what he intended.

"I was credited with the pass for Kenny's goal but the reality was that it was a complete fluke. The ball came out of the air on the edge of their box, as it was coming down I saw two players converge on the ball, I thought I was going to get clattered, so I leaned back, closed my eyes and the ball just dinked off my foot perfectly. It was perfectly weighted and it ran into the space that Kenny was running into. He did the hard work.

"They never came to make it a game. We were a very good team then, they were frightened of us and didn't step out. We had most of the ball and I'm sure it was quite a dull game to watch for the neutral."

Tommy Smith

TOMMY Smith delighted Reds fans despite having to take his place in the stands after being ruled out with a broken toe.

Smith waved his walking sticks in jubilation at the travelling Kop as he was hoisted aloft by Joey Jones and Colin Irwin on the lap of honour.

After munching his way through chicken legs he said: "I'm really chuffed. Obviously, I was sick at not playing but now everything has turned out great. We've won the Cup again and I am going to America later this week as planned. I know it took us some time to score, but there was no doubt in my mind that we would do it. There was only one team in it."

Phil Neal

RIGHT-BACK Phil Neal agreed the game wasn't much of a spectacle, but didn't care a jot.

"Football-wise it was boring. The Bruges manager came to stifle us and it needed some divine intervention from Kenny to earn the spoils."

David Fairclough

DAVID Fairclough, for so long known as Liverpool's Super-sub, cherished being given a place in Bob Paisley's starting line-up.

"I remember walking out at Wembley before the game and seeing that almost the entire stadium was decked out in red and white," he said. "At that point I knew there was no way were ever going to lose.

"Beating Bruges and retaining the trophy confirmed Liverpool's position as the outstanding team in Europe."

Souness denies romantic link with Swedish beauty

IN the days following the Reds' second European Cup triumph, Graeme Souness spent some time denying newspaper speculation of a relationship with Swedish Miss World Mary Stavin.

The Swedish beauty had been a guest of the Scot at the final and the pair were pictured celebrating with the trophy on the train back to Liverpool.

But the Scot was quick to play down rumours of a romantic link.

"We are just good friends. There's nothing more to it than that," he said.

Stavin added: "I have only come to see the football match. It was a good game. I see Graeme sometimes and I might see him again if I am in Liverpool."

The pair met when Stavin made a promotional visit to the city.

Phil Thompson

PHIL Thompson had missed out on an appearance in the 1977 final and was delighted to sample victory first hand.

He said: "It was very hard for me and John Toshack at the end of last year's final. We were involved to an extent, but the big thing is to play.

"Not many people get a second chance to win a European Cup final. It is unbelievable. "

Thompson made a vital goalline clearance from Simoen 10 minutes from time to preserve the Reds' advantage.

"The thought flashed through my mind that I couldn't afford to miss it. Our kid would have killed me. I just managed to make contact with my left foot. I was lucky to get there.

"Although we'd dominated the game for 89 minutes, it didn't matter how we won, just as long as we won in front of what seemed like about 95,000 Liverpool fans inside Wembley. The last 15 minutes though were the longest of my life!"

Reflecting on the triumph more recently, Thommo said: "Only Istanbul could compare to beating Moenchengladbach in Rome. That was very special in everybody's hearts and minds. But having missed that one through injury this was even more important to me personally. I was determined for us to get through to the final so I could experience what the lads had enjoyed the year before. Although I'd got a medal because I'd played in most of the games in '77 it wasn't the same. That's why '78 is a very special memory for me."

"People always remember Kenny Dalglish's dink over the goalkeeper. But after that, although we'd dominated the game completely, I remember big Al trying a backpass that never reached Ray Clemence. The fella jinked around him and I just got back and my long skinny legs just happened to get there. I remember the ball coming at the goal and by stretching my left leg out I was able to just steer it around the other side. That as much won us the game, because they didn't deserve anything out of it, we had dominated it completely, but it was a vital moment in the game."

Semi-final scorer David Johnson had to settle for putting his feet up for the 1978 European Cup final at Wembley after being a substitute in 1977

Final reminders

We all remember Liverpool's European Cup final winning heroes but what about the men who didn't play quite as prominent a part in the final?

For every Tommy Smith there's a Richard Money and for every Jerzy Dudek there's a Peter McDonnell. Some players missed out on the final through injury after helping Liverpool get there. Others got their chance because of team-mates being injured or ineligible. There's also one or two who found themselves with winners' medals despite never making a senior appearance for the club.

We turn the spotlight on the men who should never be forgotten after playing their own part in the glorious history of Liverpool Football Club . . .

IF Phil Thompson and John Toshack had been fit for the 1977 European Cup final then the chances are that both would have started. Both men were first team regulars under Bob Paisley.

Thommo got injured in March and missed the rest of the season but Toshack, who had picked up an Achilles tendon injury, was named in the 17-man party for the final in Rome.

Paisley was well aware of how Toshack's towering aerial presence had turned the 1973 UEFA Cup final against Moenchengladbach in Liverpool's favour and wanted to give the Welsh international striker every chance of being fit to partner Kevin Keegan.

But Toshack failed to recover and his place went to the fit-again Ian Callaghan. That meant disappointment for David Johnson, who had started in the FA Cup final defeat to Manchester United four days earlier, and David Fairclough who joined him on the bench.

Tommy Smith took Thompson's place for what was initially supposed to be his 600th and final appearance for the Reds but after scoring a Roy-of-the-Rovers goal he ended up staying.

The injuries to Thommo and Toshack meant that Alec Lindsay and Alan Waddle got a place on the bench.

Left-back Lindsay was right at the end of his eight-year Anfield career and made just one appearance all season. He moved on to Stoke for £20,000 four months later.

Waddle, a centre-forward, hadn't started a game for the Reds since April 1974 and his only goal in 22 games for Liverpool had been a Merseyside derby winner in December '73. Like Lindsay he also left four months later, joining Leicester City for £450,000.

Liverpool's unused goalkeeper on that famous night was Peter McDonnell who had joined the Reds from Bury in 1974.

McDonnell, who was born in Kendal, never made a single appearance for Liverpool before moving to Oldham in 1978 but had the distinction of being part of that first European Cup winning squad.

Sadly he doesn't have a medal to show for the experience as it was 'lost' in the aftermath of the game although a rumour that it was handed to one of Liverpool's injured first team players has never gone away.

McDonnell went on to play in Dallas and Hong Kong before eventually becoming player-manager of non-league Barrow AFC.

He later worked at Cropper's Papermill in Burneside and in 2005 was a committee member of the Westmorland FA council.

John Toshack trains in Rome on the day of the final but fails to make it for the game

1977

Unused subs	Injured
David Fairclough	John Toshack
David Johnson	Phil Thompson
Alec Lindsay	
Alan Waddle	
Peter McDonnell	

Ray Kennedy shares a moment with David Johnson as the Reds do a lap of honour at Wembley

Smithy helps the builders and ends up with his foot in plaster before the final

AFTER being left on the bench for the final a year earlier, there was more heartbreak in store for David Johnson.

The 'Doc', who had scored in the semi-final first leg against Borussia Moenchengladbach, suffered a serious knee injury playing against Leicester City just a month before the final and was still on crutches when Liverpool went down to Wembley.

After famously scoring in Rome, Tommy Smith had extended his Anfield stay by signing a new two-year contract and was in line to play in the final.

That was until the Anfield Iron dropped a pick-axe on his foot while doing some building work at home just a fortnight before the game against Bruges and broke his toe, which thus ruled him out.

That opened the door for a young Alan Hansen, who had only been at Anfield for just over a year, to start at the back.

The injuries saw Paisley include youngsters Sammy Lee and Trevor Birch in his 18-man squad but neither made the final 16.

Three of the 1977 winning team were on the bench.

Steve Heighway came on as a second half substitute but Ian Callaghan and Joey Jones - who had lost their first-team places that season - never made it on to the pitch. Both moved to pastures new that summer.

Liverpool's other two subs at Wembley were Colin Irwin and Steve Ogrizovic.

Irwin, a young centre-half, was still over a year away from making his Liverpool debut and was only on the bench because of Smithy's injury.

Big Oggy, Ray Clemence's understudy for five years, had been signed from Chesterfield in November '77 for £70,000.

He played twice in March '78 when Clem was out injured - Liverpool lost 4-2 at Derby on his debut but beat Leeds 1-0 at Anfield three days later - and finished the season with a European Cup winners' medal.

1978

Unused subs	Injured
Ian Callaghan	David Johnson
Joey Jones	Tommy Smith
Colin Irwin	
Steve Ogrizovic	

A young Ian Rush (second left) and Avi Cohen (right) inspect the pitch before the final, but it was the closest they got to playing on it

PAISLEY went into his third European Cup final with five players all considered as injury doubts.

He was already without David Fairclough, who had only made six league appearances all season because of injury, and Kenny Dalglish, Phil Thompson, Alan Kennedy, David Johnson and Sammy Lee were all being treated for various injuries in the run-up to the game against Real Madrid.

That meant that squad players Richard Money, Colin Irwin, Howard Gayle, Ian Rush and Avi Cohen were all on standby to make unlikely appearances in Paris.

As it turned out all the injured players - with the exception of Fairclough - had recovered in time and as a result Rush and Cohen missed out on a place on the bench.

A place in the starting XI was particularly poignant for Johnston as he had finally got on to the pitch in a European Cup final at the third time of trying.

Jimmy Case was on the bench and replaced the not fully-fit Dalglish in the second half.

Gayle, Irwin and Money were named among the substitutes and that was just reward for their efforts in the semi-final second leg against Bayern Munich.

With the injuries taking their toll, Money and Irwin had both started at the back in Germany and were part of a heroic rearguard display that helped Liverpool to a 1-1 draw and a victory on away goals thanks to Ray Kennedy's strike.

Lowestoft-born Money, who had been signed from Fulham for £50,000 in May 1980, only made 17 appearances for the Reds and that night in Munich was undoubtedly his best as a Liverpool player. He joined Luton in 1982.

Scouser Irwin, who according to the injured Phil Thompson was man-of-the-match in Germany, did slightly better making 44 appearances and scoring three goals.

Trying to displace Thommo and Jocky permanently was too big a task for him though and he moved to Swansea after the final. Sadly, injury ended his career at the Vetch Field prematurely.

At the other end of the pitch young Gayle was thrust into the limelight as a substitute for the injured Dalglish.

Despite it only being his second appearance, he ran the established Munich defenders ragged with his blistering pace and they could only respond by committing a barrage of fouls that eventually forced Paisley to withdraw the Toxteth-born striker as he was in danger of reacting.

Gayle made just five appearances for the Reds before joining Birmingham in 1983 but played a huge part in ensuring Liverpool reached Paris.

Just like in 1978, Ogrizovic was the substitute keeper again.

He'd only made two appearances since that '78 final and when Paisley brought in Bruce Grobbelaar to replace Clemence after the final in Paris he moved on to Coventry City where he won the FA Cup in 1987 and was still playing into his early 40s.

1981

Unused subs	**Injured**
Steve Ogrizovic	David Fairclough
Colin Irwin	
Richard Money	
Howard Gayle	

Unused substitutes Bob Bolder (centre, back row) and David Hodgson (right, behind Rushie) leave Liverpool airport

ALAN Hansen was Joe Fagan's only injury worry going into the 1984 final in Rome.

Jocky was receiving round-the-clock treatment on a hamstring injury and as a result Gary Gillespie, who had made just one senior appearance (against Walsall in the League Cup) since his £325,000 arrival from Coventry the previous summer, was on stand-by to play at the back.

Hansen was declared fit 48 hours before the game and Gillespie took his place on the bench alongside Steve Nicol, Michael Robinson, David Hodgson and Bob Bolder.

John Wark was the only player Fagan was without as he was ineligible following his £450,000 move from Ipswich just two months earlier.

Robinson and Nicol were both brought on by Fagan - with the young Scot missing Liverpool's first penalty in the shoot-out - so Gillespie had to wait until the following season to make his European debut.

Amazingly, that came in the 1985 European Cup final when he was brought on as an early substitute for Mark Lawrenson against Juventus but events off the pitch at Heysel overshadowed the match.

For the record, Gillespie conceded the penalty (although video evidence clearly shows the offence took place outside the box) that Michel Platini converted to win the trophy and that was to be the only time the Stirling-born centre-half played in Europe for Liverpool.

Fellow bench-warmer David Hodgson had made a couple of substitute appearances, against Odense and Athletic Bilbao, on the way to the final but was behind Dalglish, Rush and Robinson in the striker's pecking order.

Bob Paisley had paid Middlesbrough a hefty £450,000 for him in August 1982 but he never lived up to the price tag and after scoring 10 goals in 47 appearances he was sold to Sunderland a couple of months after the final for a cut-price £125,000.

Bolder was the reserve keeper and, like 1977 counterpart Peter McDonnell, never made an appearance for Liverpool.

He was signed from Sheffield Wednesday for £125,000 in 1983 as back up for Bruce Grobbelaar but the Zimbabwean's incredible fitness levels - he made 310 consecutive appearances for the Reds between his debut in 1981 and August 1986 - meant that Bolder never got a sniff of a game.

The Dover-born keeper moved on to Sunderland in 1985 although is probably best remembered for his stint as Charlton's number one.

He has regularly featured as the Liverpool Master's first choice keeper when they play in their indoor six-a-side competitions.

1984

Unused subs
Bob Bolder
David Hodgson
Gary Gillespie

Injured
No-one

Ineligible
John Wark

Igor Biscan turns in a great performance against Bayer Leverkusen at Anfield

AFTER an injury-dogged first season at Anfield, Rafa Benitez finally had an almost full-strength squad to select from for the final against AC Milan in Istanbul.

He was without strikers Neil Mellor (tendonitis) and Florent Sinama-Pongolle (cruciate knee ligaments) who had both scored in the crucial 3-1 group stage win over Olympiakos to ensure Liverpool reached he last 16.

Chris Kirkland, who had kept goal in four of the six group games, was also out with a back injury.

The only other players Benitez couldn't select were Fernando Morientes and Mauricio Pellegrino who were both cup-tied after playing for Real Madrid and Valencia respectively in Europe earlier that season.

Dietmar Hamann and Djibril Cisse had both been in contention for a starting place in Turkey but began the game on the bench.

Both were introduced in the second half. Fellow substitute Vladimir Smicer, who came on in the first half to replace the injured Harry Kewell, scored one of Liverpool's goals as they staged a remarkable second-half comeback to force a 3-3 draw and penalties.

In a quirky twist of fate it was the three substitutes who scored Liverpool's three cup-winning penalties in the shoot-out.

Igor Biscan was somewhat unlucky to find himself on the bench in Istanbul.

The Croatian midfielder had played a key part in Liverpool reaching the final, appearing nine times and turning in excellent displays against Deportivo La Coruna, Bayer Leverkusen and Juventus in particular.

Spanish summer signings Antonio Nunez and Jose Miguel Gonzalez Rey (Josemi) spent the 120 minutes on the bench.

Josemi had figured in seven of Liverpool's first eight Champions League games until injury ruled him out for five months.

He returned just in time for the final and with Steve Finnan carrying a knock he was preferred on the bench to the unlucky Stephen Warnock who had been in the squad for 13 of Liverpool's previous 14 Champions League games and was expected to be named among the substitutes.

Nunez had started at home to Olympiakos and away to Juventus but had spent most of the campaign injured or on the bench.

For substitute goalkeeper Scott Carson, receiving a Champions League winners' medal completed a fairytale five months for him.

The 19-year-old from Whitehaven had been playing for Leeds reserves until Benitez signed him for £1million in January.

At the start of April he was handed his Champions League debut when Liverpool faced Juventus at Anfield and produced a brilliant save from Alessandro Del Piero, although was later at fault for Fabio Cannavaro's goal that gave Juve a glimmer of hope for the second leg.

Jerzy Dudek regained his place for the second leg in Turin and Carson spent the rest of the campaign, including the final, on the bench.

His remarkable season finished with a trip to the USA to link-up with England on their two-game tour after receiving his first call-up to the full squad by Sven-Goran Eriksson.

2005

Unused subs
Josemi
Scott Carson
Igor Biscan
Antonio Nunez

Injured
Neil Mellor
F. S-Pongolle
Chris Kirkland

Ineligible
F. Morientes
M. Pellegrino

1977

The road to Rome

Liverpool's crusade to win their first European Cup started in Northern Ireland and ended up in the eternal city of Rome. On the way there was a tricky trip to Turkey, a Swiss mis-match in the semi-final and arguably Anfield's greatest night of them all when Les Verts of St Etienne came to town

Round one

Round one, first leg
September 14 1976

Liverpool 2
(pen) Neal 18, Toshack 64)

Crusaders 0

Att: 22,442

Team: Clemence, Neal, Jonses, Smith, Kennedy, Hughes, Keegan, Johnson, Heighway, Toshack, Callaghan.

THIS should have been straightforward against the Irish part-timers but the resilience and determination of the Ulstermen caught Liverpool by surprise. It looked like easy street after Phil Neal's early penalty but the Reds didn't add to their lead until midway through the second period.

Crusaders felt harshly treated with the award of what was undoubtedly a dubious penalty but they could have few complaints about Liverpool's second. Heighway's cross was nodded powerfully into the net by John Toshack to make life more comfortable for Liverpool.

Round one, second leg
September 28 1976

Crusaders 0

Liverpool 5
(Keegan 34, Johnson 81, 90, McDermott 84, Heighway 87)

(Liverpool win 7-0 on aggregate)

Att:10,000

Team: Clemence, Neal, Jones, Smith, Kennedy, Hughes, Keegan, Johnson, Heighway, Case (McDermott), Callaghan.

CRUSADERS would have kept the score respectable had the referee ended the game on 80 minutes. At that stage the Reds led just 1-0, 3-0 on aggregate, after Keegan's early goal.

But as the part-time minnows tired, David Johnson - twice - Terry McDermott and Steve Heighway all found the net to seal a 5-0 win.

David Johnson puts Liverpool 2-0 up after just ten minutes at Anfield against Trabzonspor

Round two

Round two, first leg
October 20 1976

Trabzonspor 1
(pen) Cemil 63)

Liverpool 0

Att: 25,000

Team: Clemence, Smith, Jones, Thompson, Kennedy, Hughes, Keegan, McDermott, Heighway (Fairclough), Toshack (Johnson), Callaghan.

LIVERPOOL had travelled to Trabzon in Eastern Turkey determined to keep things tight. They succeeded until the Romanian referee was fooled by an obvious and cynical dive and awarded a penalty - which Trabzonspor duly converted.

That stung Liverpool who decided to flex their muscles and take the game to their opponents. They still didn't get a shot on target but were hardly helped by a misshapen ball. But all was far from lost with Anfield playing host to the second leg.

Round two, second leg
November 3 1976

Liverpool 3
(Heighway 8, Johnson 10, Keegan 18)

Trabzonspor 0

(Liverpool win 3-1 on aggregate)

Att: 42,275

Team: Clemence, Neal, Jones, Thompson, Kennedy, Hughes, Keegan, McDermott, Heighway, Johnson, Callaghan.

IT took just eight minutes for Steve Heighway to level the aggregate scores from very close range. Two minutes later Liverpool were ahead when David Johnson nipped in ahead of Cemil to force the ball over the line.

Keegan wrapped up the points on 18 minutes with a fine header before Trabzon began kicking everything that moved.

Quarter-final

Quarter-final, first leg
March 2 1977

St Etienne 1
(Bathenay 80)

Liverpool 0

Att: 28,000

Team: Clemence, Neal, Jones, Thompson, Kennedy, Hughes, McDermott, Case, Heighway, Toshack (Smith), Callaghan.

ST ETIENNE'S reputation as one of Europe's most exciting sides saw Liverpool approach this away tie cautiously. A rearguard action denied the Frenchmen space to play and they were allowed just one unanswered goal to take to Anfield.

The strike owed much to the gods of fortune after right back Janvion sliced a shot well off target - perfectly for Bathenay who volleyed beyond Clemence.

Quarter-final, second leg
March 16 1977

Liverpool 3
(Keegan 2, Kennedy 58, Fairclough 84)

St Etienne 1
(Bathenay 51)

(Liverpool win 3-2 on aggregate)

Att: 55,043

Team: Clemence, Neal, Jones, Smith, Kennedy, Hughes, Keegan, Case, Heighway, Toshack (Fairclough), Callaghan.

OUR start to this match was perfect - Kevin Keegan curling a cross-come-shot beyond the goalie's desperate dive to send a packed Anfield into raptures. But Bathenay repeated his trick from the first leg and levelled on the night.

That meant Liverpool had to score twice in little more than 35 minutes or we were out. Ray Kennedy pulled one back with a low shot from the edge of the box then lofted a pass into Fairclough's path with six minutes left. The rest is history.

Liverpool take the lead at Anfield as Kevin Keegan's chip drops over the helpless Curkovic

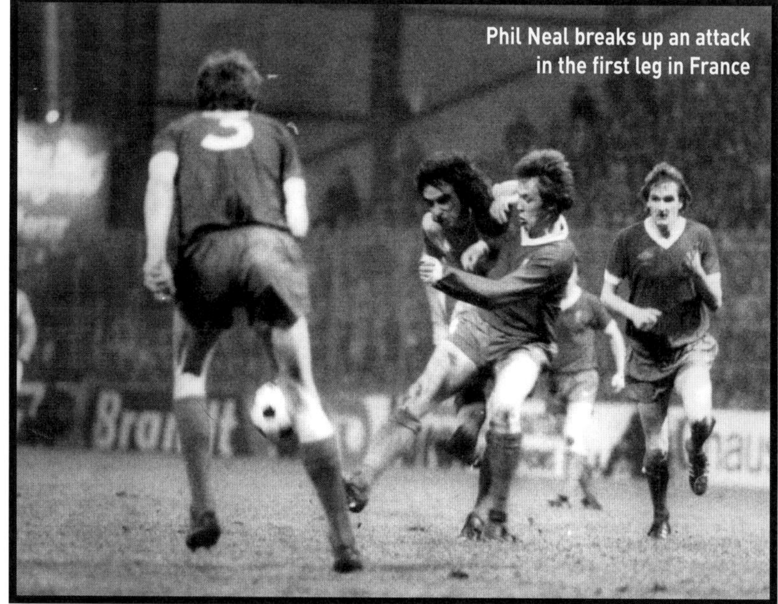

Phil Neal breaks up an attack in the first leg in France

David Fairclough seals victory for Liverpool with his famous late strike at Anfield

Semi-final

Semi-final, first leg
April 6 1977

FC Zurich 1
(pen) Risi 5)

Liverpool 3
(Neal 14, (pen) 67, Heighway 47)

Att: 30,500

Team: Clemence, Neal, Jones, Smith, Kennedy, Hughes, Keegan, Case, Heighway, Fairclough, McDermott.

RISI'S early penalty for Zurich should have had Liverpool sweating but they knew they had the measure of the Swiss. Phil Neal scored from an acute angle to level and after that the result was never in doubt.

Steve Heighway scored a cracker, evading three challenges on his way to a clever finish, before Phil Neal converted a penalty comfortably to complete the scoring and leave Zurich with an Alp to climb at Anfield.

Semi-final, second leg
April 20 1977

Liverpool 3
(Case 33, 79, Keegan 83)

FC Zurich 0

Att: 50,611

(Liverpool win 6-1 on aggregate)

Team: Clemence, Neal, Jones, Smith, Kennedy, Hughes, Keegan, Case, Heighway (Waddle), McDermott, Johnson.

THE clinical nature of Liverpool's first-leg performance in Switzerland meant this game was devoid of the tension normally associated with semi-finals. It was a cruise for the Reds who completed a 3-0 win through a Jimmy Case double and Kevin Keegan's late strike.

Steve Heighway puts Liverpool 3-1 ahead in the first leg

The Zurich keeper dives in vain as Case puts Liverpool 2-0 up at Anfield

Jimmy Case and Kevin Keegan celebrate reaching the European Cup final

★★★★★

ALL ROADS LEAD TO ROME...

There had never been a Scouse exodus quite like it. When the Reds reached their first European Cup final in 1977, it seemed like half the city followed Bob Paisley and his men to the Eternal City for what was an eternal night for Liverpool Football Club

THE 2-1 FA Cup final defeat to Manchester United served only to increase the travelling Kop's appetite for success.

So much so that many decided to extend their pilgrimage to the continent and the Olympic Stadium in Rome where the Reds where set to face Borussia Moenchengladbach four days later in the club's first European Cup final.

After picking themselves up from the woes of Wembley, the buoyant mood within the Liverpool camp was summed up by Bob Paisley who set the tone by telling the press:

"The last time I was in Rome was 33 years ago. I helped capture it."

Natives of the Italian capital must have thought they were under siege again as Reds' fans flocked to the Eternal City creating scenes that will be passed from one generation to the next and live in the memory forever.

With the league title already in the bag, all roads led to Rome for this momentous occasion - and half the population of Liverpool by all accounts!

Official figures had less than 10,000 Liverpudlians arriving in Italy, but as former striker David Johnson recalls, it was much, much more.

"The lads knew that a lot of our fans - between 5000 and 8000 according to the media - had made the trip and we were anxious to give them something to cheer after the disappointment of losing to United.

"On arrival, we disappeared into the bowels of the Olympic Stadium and it was some time before we strolled out to look at the pitch. When we did, we were absolutely staggered by the atmosphere that greeted us. The place had been taken over by Liverpool fans.

"We later learned that there were 26,000 of them.

"All we could take in was this heaving mass of red and white. We all looked at each other and grew about four feet taller. With such support, there was absolutely no way we could possibly lose.

"The Germans are traditionally loud supporters, but they were absolutely overwhelmed. Our section of the crowd swayed like the Kop, having one hell of a party, while Borussia's contingent stood still. It was no contest."

While many fans booked holidays or parted with their

life savings to make the trip, some simply failed to mention it at work and went on a whim straight from Wembley.

By car, boat, coach, plane and train, they came, they saw and indeed, they conquered.

COSTLY EXERCISE

The build-up to Rome was marred by fans being asked to cough up inflated prices in their bid to follow the Reds in the final. As early as May 2, Eddie Loyden, Labour MP for Garston, wrote to then Prices Secretary Roy Hattersley and Sports Minister Denis Howell regarding a complaint from a constituent over the cost of a round-trip to Rome. Prices had risen 40% to £100 since Liverpool's progress to the final had been confirmed on April 20 - the price now not including the cost of a ticket. "It just indicates what many people are coming to feel, that there is no control whatever over prices," remarked Loyden.

Four days later, and Jet Set Travel were advertising an extra flight - their 10th - costing £115, which included two nights at the Holiday Inn Hotel (B&B) - with match tickets guaranteed, at extra cost...

MONEY TALKS

May 3rd: A report confirms that UEFA have decided to cut capacity of the Olympic Stadium by 15,000 to 65,000 - so that advertisements can be placed around the pitch. An allocation of 16,000 - all seated - was confirmed for each side, with expectations from the authorities that the showpiece would not be a sell-out, due to the final being televised throughout Europe. Prices were approximately £9, £8 and £3, thought to be reasonable for the occasion.

A LETTER FROM MOENCHENGLADBACH

May 7th: Exiled Scouser Don Troake observed the quality of Borussia Moenchengladbach and their dangerman "Bonhof, the Borussia No 5." Regarding final preparations, he observes: "Significance must be attached to this low number of fixtures, as in comparison to Liverpool's hectic programme, they can prepare for the European Cup final with time on their side."

WARNING FOR FANS

May 9th: British Embassy officials issued concerns over the imminent invasion of Liverpool fans in the Italian capital

SONG FOR EUROPE

Inspired by Eurovision, the Liverpool Echo launched a contest for readers to cheer the Reds to glory in Rome. Inspired by Tommy Smith's 'hearty' renditions of readers' entries, Mrs Margaret Martin of Formby prevailed, having been motivated while musing among the dirty plates and cutlery on the family tea table. "I pictured it being sung as the fans sway from side to side holding up their scarves and rosettes."

To the tune of 'Sailing' by Rod Stewart, the ditty went:
We are with you,
We are with you,
We are with you,
here in Rome.
Red flags flying,
You'll be trying
To bring that cup
back home.

Can you hear us,
Can you hear us,
Can you hear us,
Liverpool.
You'll be scoring,
We'll be roaring,
All of Europe,
you will rule.

WHEN IN ROME...

The novelty of Mediterranean conditions was too much for John Fredericks of Anfield, who was forced to receive treatment from first aiders in Rome. "They were smashing, but my back is giving me jip. I thought I'd enjoy the sun, but I overdid it."

★★★★★

(9/5/77). Warnings included Italian policing ('A fan risks six months imprisonment if he is found drunk'; '...insulting a police officer carries a maximum prison sentence of six months and a fine'). Indeed, Mr Ronald Jochau, a former Consul in Barcelona and Italy, claimed the Carabinieri (the 'crack' section of the Italian police force) "are far less tolerant than the British police, and will not hesitate to use force."

PRETTY-BOY TOMMY

One male fan felt inclined to issue his backing to Smithy, declaring that 'Tommy Smith is prettier than Sophia Loren' on a badge pinned to his 'red and white uniform' - although German fans were apparently backing Danish winger Allan Simonsen.

SOMETHIN' BORROWED

Steve Spencer and Mark Cunliffe were able to travel for the historic occasion despite financial difficulties. Unemployed Steve travelled to Wembley days earlier for the FA Cup final, having only been able to afford to attend one final - but benefited from his sister's wedding money to the tune of £100. "But when they lost my sister said you are not missing out this time and handed me the cash. She's great."

Mark meanwhile had the more pressing concerns of a City and Guild Engineering exam on the Friday - and thus would not have made it back in time by train due to strikes in France. "I would have got back just too late...so it had to be by air."

However, two fans were less fortunate, having been thwarted in their bid to stow away on the 10.15 flight to Rome from Speke. A Brittania Airways spokesman said: "Two had climbed over the railings and boarded the plane, but airport police spotted them and pulled them out."

ALL TRAINS LEAD TO...

Schoolboy Stephen Dodgson, 10, and his dad, John, were number one and two on the first train to leave Lime Street for Italy. "It will be an exhausting trip for the lad, but wild horses wouldn't have kept him away." An estimated 5,000 supporters were due to leave the city on the 36-hour train and boat journey, extended due to a rail strike in France meaning trains would have to travel via Germany and Switzerland. With 12 hours added to the trip and an extra £10 per ticket, the cost was £70. The main advice from rail chiefs for fans was: "Make sure you take plenty of food with you".

RUG PULLED

Having spent two weeks in Rome fitting new carpets at the Holiday Inn, Reds fan Peter Wetherall was hoping for a night off to take in the final. But having finished the contract the weekend before the final, he was forced to fly

back from Italy and spent the day of the final hard at work at a hotel in Bristol. "I was hoping the job would last longer but with another contract to go there's no way I could stay," remarked the Anfield regular from Formby.

OUR MAN SALVADORE

Anyone needing a ticket for the final need never fear when our business-minded Italian friends are in control. Salvadore was met by reporters on a preliminary look around the stadium and realising they were from England, our Italian counterpart produced '100 or so tickets', offering up his name and phone number in full view of security inside the stadium. With a price of nearly £7 each, the touts looked to be on to a loser.

MAKE A NOTE

May 24th: Liverpool's record 'We Can Do It' climbed to No 15 in the charts, having moved up from No 50 a week earlier.

ROME TURNS RED

Alan Fazakerley of Norris Green summed up the mood: "Everyone has been smashing to us. All the Italians tell us they want Liverpool to win the European Cup - I'm only sorry we haven't found any German fans to tell them how much we'll beat them by."

Alan Thomas from Vale Road, Walton, was dressed in a red and white top hat, a white boiler suit covered in badges and the signatures of Liverpool players and a long cloak made from the Union Jack. "I don't know what they'll say at work if they see my picture in the Echo dressed like this - I'll never live it down."

GEE BERT

A new job for Bert Ashcroft looked set to scupper his plans for Rome. Having worked on the construction of the Wirral section of the Loop Line, opened on May 9 1977, Bert and his wife Winnie took the first train on the line at 5am. A certificate, given to all the first passengers, had the lucky number 773 winning Bert the ticket. But the job at Ince Power Station, starting the Monday before the final, meant handing Bert the dilemma of asking his new bosses for time off. No fear though - Bert is an Evertonian and his son, who was set to benefit, was a Reds fanatic.

'TIPS AND ADVICE'

- Travellers were advised that they were only allowed to take the equivalent of £24 in Italian money - but could have up to £300 in traveller's cheques. They were also warned about a permanent shortage of change and coins - 'shopkeepers sometimes give packets of sweets in exchange'.
- Bottled water was recommended.
- 'Only the rich should consider visiting a Roman nightclub, they are very expensive'
- 'Italian motorists think of themselves as Grand Prix drivers'
- 'Rome has an international reputation as a pick-

★★★★★

EURO '77 SEND-OFF

pocketing centre'
• Three-course meal with wine in a good restaurant - £4
• Half-pint of Italian lager - 30p
• Cigarettes (Italian - for pack of 20) - 20-30p

THE FINAL WORD

Before flying out from Speke Airport on the afternoon of May 24, hundreds of fans gave the squad a memorable send off. Among the banners were the legends: 'Paisley's Infra-Red Army is Red Hot'; and 'Joey eats Munchen for Lunchen'.

Bob Paisley (on the fans): "They have been great all season and I hope win, lose or draw, they will be the same in Rome. I am very pleased with the way they behaved after Saturday's disappointment."

Ahead of the game, Paisley said: "The heat will play a big part on how we approach this game. There's nothing we can do about it; UEFA lay down where the final is to be played a year in advance and we have to accept it.

"We know the importance of this game. It must be the ambition of every club and every player in England to reach the European Cup final and we realise that we are representing the country as well as ourselves.

"We won't let anyone down. I don't think you could get a better team than Liverpool to tackle this job. Of course it will be difficult. The Germans are a good side but so are we.

"We'll be patient at the start, treating it as a typical European tie. Wembley is way behind us now and the players' spirits have lifted amazingly since then. They are ready to go.

"This is the final we've all been looking forward to. We've won the title at home and that is always the greatest thing to achieve. But you only get to this final perhaps once in a lifetime so everything depends on what we do tonight."

Skipper Emlyn Hughes: "We are feeling confident but it's going to be a tough match. Obviously just losing one Cup final and going into another is going to affect us, but we will be giving everything.
"We've got over Wembley now. We're in the mood to play well for Liverpool and England."

David Fairclough: "I'm looking forward to it. I was very disappointed to be left out at Wembley. Now I'll be happy to get just one goal to make up for it - the winner."

Temperature in Rome 87F day before the final - compared with 65F in Liverpool

ON THE BOX

- Mash
- Crossroads
- University Challenge
- Bless This House
- Dawson and Friends
- This is Your Right
- Mr and Mrs
- Don't Forget to Write!

THE TOP 10 SINGLES

May 25th, 1977

1. **I DON'T WANT TO TALK ABOUT IT**
   Rod Stewart

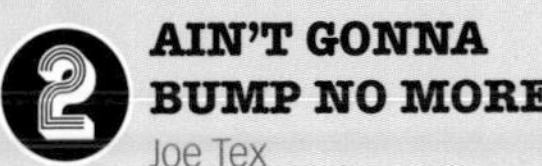

2. **AIN'T GONNA BUMP NO MORE**
   Joe Tex

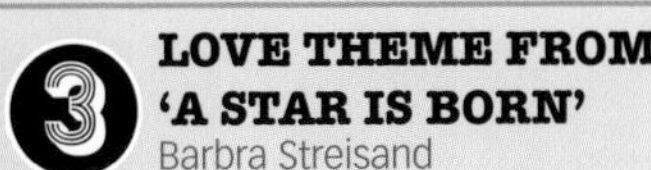

3. **LOVE THEME FROM 'A STAR IS BORN'**
   Barbra Streisand

4. **LUCILE**
   Kenny Rogers
5. **GOOD MORNING JUDGE**
   10 C.C.

6. **THE SHUFFLE**
   Van McCoy
7. **FREE**
   Deniece Williams
8. **MAH NA MAH NA**
   Piero Umiliani
9. **GOT TO GIVE IT UP**
   Marvin Gaye
10. **HOTEL CALIFORNIA**
    The Eagles

Biggest boost to English football since World Cup

TONIGHT LIVERPOOL DID US PROUD

Liverpool 3
Borussia Moenchengladbach 1

The big match report
by Michael Charters
Liverpool Echo, Thursday, May 26 1977

LIVERPOOL are the masters of Europe - and the masters of how to play European football with style and efficiency, class combined with effort, individual brilliance with superb teamwork.

On an unforgettable night in Rome, on a night that will live for ever as the highlight of a thousand sporting memories, this magnificent team completed the greatest season in the history of any English club by adding the European Cup to their league championship - the third British club to win the highest prize in world inter-club football.

They did more than beat the German champions Borussia Moenchengladbach - they obliterated them - and don't forget they were playing against a world class team. They won 3-1 with a display of the highest quality which must be the biggest single boost to English football since the World Cup triumph of 11 years ago.

Liverpool did more than win a football match in the heat of Rome last night. They lifted our hearts and strengthened our patriotism. They won a victory on a foreign field which makes them, in my view, the finest club side England has ever seen.

And, as skipper Emlyn Hughes led his team on a rapturous lap of honour with the giant cup at the end I felt honoured to be there to see it. It was the crowning and

ultimate glory of a season of the highest possible achievement. Merseyside and all Britain should salute them.

There were two outstanding moments in this unbelievable and unforgettable final. Did the Liver Birds take wing when Tommy Smith, in his last game for the club before retiring tomorrow after a distinguished 16 years at Anfield, score a goal which, in effect, won the cup for Liverpool? If they didn't, they should have done.

And did those same Liver Birds almost fall from their perch when Ray Clemence produced one of the greatest saves of his life - with his legs - to prevent the Germans going in front and possibly taking the cup to that West German town with an unpronounceable name? If they didn't, I'm sure they wobbled.

But before all this happened, in a second half of such drama and tension that was almost unbearable to watch, there had been the glorious spectacle of watching Liverpool dominate and control one of the finest teams in the world.

The essence of their control was that they did not allow the Germans to build up attacks from their own half of the field. They challenged for every ball and usually won it.

Give a team like Moenchengladbach the slightest chance to exploit their quick striking strengths, and you'll be taken to the cleaners. Liverpool, operating perfectly to a tactical plan which proved to be a triumph for the genius of manager Bob Paisley, dominated the game leaving the Germans so well beaten that they trailed off at the end unsung, unheralded and unwanted by their own supporters.

Through all this, the magnificent Liverpool fans, a sea of red and white at one end of the ground with others bunched in a patch-work quilt fashion all over the ground, roared their team to victory.

It was truly a night when Liverpool clinched their reputation as the soccer capital of England.

From the start Liverpool pushed the ball around with patient skill and tactical superiority which made the German team look almost second rate at times. This alone indicates how well they played. Hughes and Smith, operating in smooth harmony at the back, inter-passed until the time was right to move forward with a move of penetrating efficiency.

In midfield, Callaghan, Kennedy, Case and McDermott were the backbone of it all. Callaghan was superb. Recalled to the team after his injury problems he showed all his skill and smooth operating efficiency to dominate such World Cup stars as Bonhof and Wimmer.

Keegan and Heighway were the two target men up front and whatever criticism has been levelled at Keegan in recent weeks he more than compensated in this critical match with one of his greatest performances in what was, like Smith, his last competitive game for the club.

In the Germans' system of man-for-man marking Keegan was tightly shadowed by the famous full-back Vogts of World Cup fame and the current West German team captain. They had a tough and unrelenting physical duel with Keegan coming out on top, always there for colleagues to find, coping with physical challenges and coming back for more. He has never worked harder, never been more effective. He gave his all to bring the European Cup to Liverpool.

Heighway was also closely marked by a man born with a defender's name - Klinkhammer. He got the hammer from this character more than once but he and Keegan gave their defence not a moment's peace - a tremendous performance in harmony and individuality.

It wasn't long before Liverpool took a massive grip on the game. They kept it to the end, except for a 15-minute spell early in the second half when the Germans were in with a chance of victory. Yet Moenchengladbach did not win a single corner - a statistical testimony to Liverpool's greatest display in Europe.

The writing was on the German wall as early as the 13th minute when Kennedy ended a crisp Keegan-McDermott move with a shot which the giant goalkeeper Kneib turned over the bar. Apart from brief sorties, the Germans were pushed back on defence as Liverpool built up decisive attacks which only needed a more punishing finish to have settled the game there and then.

Their first goal, at 28 minutes, was a gem. It began with Callaghan, busy, effective and supreme in the middle, winning a tackle in a tight challenge. He pushed the ball through quickly to Heighway who took it forward on one of those typically jinking runs of his before delivering the perfect pass to McDermott.

McDermott's role in this superb goal was the crux of it all, he must have run 50 yards to be in the right spot to take Heighway's pass and drive the ball just inside the upright. He vanished from sight beneath his team-mates - the European Cup was on its way to Anfield.

In the first half, the Liverpool defence was calm and efficient. Clemence was a lonely spectator and the Germans looked short of ideas. The first half ended with the Reds in total control.

But, early in the second half, the situation changed dramatically. It was moving along smoothly until Case, trying to turn the ball into the path of Neal to complete a clearance, sent it straight to Simonsen, the Danish World Cup winger.

Simonsen, a small man with devastating pace and a powerful shot, accepted the Liverpool gift and ran forward with the ball. He hit a superb angled shot past Clemence. So it was 1-1 against the run of play but now Liverpool had to do it all again after dominating the play.

The fans roared their support as, for the only time in the game, the team struggled. There were defensive slips, a bit of chaos at the back and suddenly Steileke was clean through from a typical German breakaway and only Clemence stood between the Germans and a firm grip of the cup.

But Clemence rose to the emergency. He came swiftly and boldly from his goal, blocking the shot with his legs and as it turned out that was the Germans' last chance.

Simonsen's goal came after 51 minutes but there were thoughts that extra-time would be necessary until Smith, in a storybook effort that a fiction writer would not dream up, headed Liverpool back into the lead from Heighway's corner-kick after 65 minutes.

Smith had moved up frequently for set-pieces but this, surely, must be the greatest goal, certainly the most decisive, of his career.

The 14 minutes of German pressure collapsed. Liverpool strode smoothly forward to a magnificent and famous victory with Neal scoring an 83rd minute penalty after Vogts had brought down Keegan.

The decision, by a top-class French referee, was right. Vogts had flirted with danger several times in his challenges on Keegan who, this time, took the ball past him in a brave and critical run but had his legs ruthlessly hacked from under him.

Kneil moved to his left, Neal drove the ball to his right and there it was in the back of the net, safely landed and that was that. The European Cup belonged to Liverpool.

The fans went wild and rightly so. With their hero Joey Jones leading the run of triumph after the game the greatest moment in the history of this greatest of English clubs ended amidst scenes of unbelievable excitement, emotion, tears and joy.

There was only one tiny regret through all the celebrations which followed this triumph. How on earth did Manchester United beat them at Wembley to mar the bid for a unique treble?

But nothing must hide the glory of this European Cup victory. You can get no higher than this in football. Liverpool have scaled the heights like true Champions of Europe.

MATCH FACTS

Liverpool (4-4-2): Clemence, Neal, Smith, Hughes, Jones, Callaghan, Case, McDermott, Kennedy, Heighway, Keegan. Unused subs: Fairclough, Lindsay, Johnston, Waddle, McDonnell

Borussia Moenchengladbach (4-4-2): Kneibl, Schaeffer, Wittkamp, Klinkhammer, Vogts, Simonsen, Wohlers (Hannes), Bonhof, Wimmer (Kulik), Stielike, Henyckes. Unused Subs: Kieff, Del Haye, Heidenrich

Goals: McDermott (28), Simonsen (52), Smith (64) Neal (82pen)

Booking: Stielike

Conditions: Hot, dry, pitch good

Referee: Robert Wurtz (France)

Attendance: 60,000

Emlyn Hughes

CRAZY Horse Emlyn Hughes thought his team had taken a wrong turning somewhere between Rome's airport and the Olympic Stadium and had somehow ended up back at Anfield!

That was the only way the skipper could describe the scene inside the ground that night, a swaying mass of red and white scarves, flags and banners.

"I remember walking out onto the pitch before the game and I thought to myself 'Jesus Christ we're back in Liverpool!' There was that many punters from Liverpool there, we were greeted by a sea of red and white.

"The support of the fans gave us all a terrific lift and all the lads were saying to each other how there was no way we could lose the match now.

"It was like playing at home. I can imagine what the Borussia players must have thought when they walked out. They must have looked around and thought they had no chance against such support. It must have seemed like they were playing at Anfield."

Liverpool's passing, poise and preparation made this one of the most one-sided European Cup finals on record, but despite their dominance of proceedings, Emlyn knew Moenchengladbach would have at least one chance.

"Every team, no matter who you are playing, get at least a couple of chances in a match. Borussia were no different.

"They had a five-minute spell were they were on top and they took full advantage by grabbing an equaliser. We had a game-plan though and we stuck to it and that spell was all they had in the game. Smithy scored that header and we didn't look back.

"It wouldn't have mattered who we'd played that night. Moenchengladbach were a great team, but we were better on the night."

This should have been Emlyn's crowning glory, but his thoughts, as he strode forward to collect the trophy, were of others.

"I remember walking up those steps to lift the cup and I felt privileged to do so. I was not thinking about myself, Kevin Keegan or the rest of the lads who'd just won the match.

"The names that were flashing through my mind were the likes of Roger Hunt, Ian St John and Ron Yeats, Shanks and Rueben Bennett.

"These were the men who had given us the chance to win the European Cup and who had put us in the position that we were in. As I reached out to collect the cup I knew that it was as much for them as for us."

Phil Neal

PHIL Neal admits his walk to the penalty spot in Rome's Olympic Stadium was the longest of his career, but he wasn't nervous as he placed the ball and stepped back on his run-up.

Neal had caught sight of the German's giant goalkeeper in the pre-game warm-up and decided there and then what he would do with a spot-kick should one arise.

"It was up to me to finish the game off and it was a long agonising walk up to that penalty spot. It was Kevin's swansong game. He took Berti Vogts everywhere and in the end Berti got frustrated, brought him down, penalty!

"I've got a 50-yard walk to that penalty spot and what I remember most before taking the kick is Cally, who has played a million games for this club, on the edge of the box and his hands are in a prayer position saying: 'Come on Nealy, please!'.

"I knew that if I scored it would finish the game off but I wasn't nervous when I stepped up.

"When I walked out of the tunnel before the game it struck me that Wolfgang Kneib was about two or three inches taller than Clem and I decided then that if I got a penalty I would keep it low because he would struggle to get down for it. That's what I did and it rolled in off the post and we were European champions."

Tommy Smith

TOMMY Smith played in some massive games during a long and distinguished Liverpool career, but even the Anfield Iron was taken aback by the sight he witnessed in Rome's Olympic Stadium.

"The '77 European Cup final one was the one when I did notice the crowd. We went out to have a look what was going on in the Rome stadium and three-quarters of it was Red.

"I couldn't believe it and it did hit you, 'we've got more supporters than the Germans' and bearing in mind it's not that far away you thought that they (the Germans) would be there."

Even after Bob Paisley's side had been hauled level at a time when they were dominating the game, Smithy insists they never thought for even one minute they wouldn't be lifting the cup at the end of 90 minutes.

"We got out there and it was untrue and I think on that night, we not so much became a European side, but we played like a European side. Terry McDermott's first goal was outstanding. The little one-two, bang, bang, bang and he lifts it over the goalkeeper. Absolutely brilliant.

"They scored a goal, a bad pass by Jimmy Case, but we took the game to them, were patient and we didn't go gung-ho.

"It was 1-1 and then I scored, which was very unusual. They failed to do their homework. We had arranged beforehand that I should go up for corners but they hadn't prepared for it and I was left unmarked.

"Stevie (Heighway) was expected to chip the corner in and the idea was for me to flick it on to Keegan and generally cause confusion in their penalty area. Instead he drove the ball into the centre, I ran to meet it and connected with a perfect header.

"The goalkeeper never moved. I'd compare it to serving an ace in tennis or hitting a hole in one in golf. Everything about it was perfect."

Ian Callaghan

IAN Callaghan was the only player who took part in the European Cup final in Rome who was also in the starting line-up for the Reds' first European encounter with Reykjavik some 13 years previously.

Despite playing at World Cup finals, and winning just about every major honour the game can bestow, he remembers Rome 1977 as a magical time.

"Rome was special. The first time you win something it always was. It was like winning the FA Cup for the first time in 1965.

"It was a great performance especially after the disappointment of losing to United on the Saturday. It was special for me too because it was Kevin's last game for Liverpool.

"He'd done so much here, was a great player, and was off after the game. It was a combination of everything. It was just a fantastic achievement."

Joey Jones staggered by his tribute banner . . .

AMONG the mass of flags that greeted the Liverpool players the most eye-catching was without doubt the one in tribute to the European heroics of popular full-back Joey Jones. With reference to the games against St Etienne, Zurich, and now the final against Moenchengladbach it read 'Joey ate the Frogs legs, made the Swiss roll, now he's munching Gladbach'.

Measuring 24 feet by 8 feet, and assembled by Kopites Phil Downey and Jimmy Cummings, the banner had snowballed as the Reds had progressed in Europe that season.

Phil, a die-hard Red revealed: "Originally it was just the 'Frogs Legs'. The 'Joey makes the Swiss roll' was a natural for the Zurich semi-final, but we puzzled for hours over what to do for the final.

"Then my mum came up with a solution - run them all together. That's how it came about."

The man himself was staggered when he first clapped eyes on the tribute.

"There was one or two banners at Wembley that had made me laugh, but when I walked out in Rome's Olympic Stadium and saw that one it made me feel about ten feet tall."

Joey Jones

JOEY echoed the sentiments of several of his victorious team-mates in the aftermath of victory. He insists they couldn't have done it without the best supporters in Europe.

"The sight of all them Liverpudlians in Rome lifted me more than anything else. I honestly didn't expect there to be that many of them there. They outnumbered the Germans by about three or four to one.

"It was amazing what some of them had done to get to Rome. We couldn't do anything else."

21

Terry McDermott

TERRY McDermott believes the goal he scored in Rome won't rank as the best he scored in a long career, but it was certainly his most important.

However long he lives he will never forget the reception the team got when they first stepped onto the Roman battlefield in front of 30,000 expectant Scousers. Seeing them packed onto the terraces, McDermott remembers thinking they had to do it for the fans.

"Rome will never fade from my memory. I'll always remember it until the day I die, walking out into the stadium and seeing the red and white chequered flags, I've never seen anything like it and I've never seen anything again since. It was an amazing atmosphere and an incredible feeling to see those fans.

"There must have been at least 30,000 Scousers there, probably more, and it was just phenomenal. We walked on to the pitch about an hour before and thought 'Christ, how can we get beat for these lot' and obviously we didn't.

"My goal I remember perfectly well. I've seen it that many times on television. Although it wasn't the best, it was the most important. Cally passed the ball to Heighway and he's played a great through ball to pick out my run.

"I've got Wolfgang Kneib - he was about 9ft 2in - running out at me. I thought, 'Aye aye, hit it before he comes and clatters me.' It could have gone anywhere, but it went in the back of the net."

John Smith (Chairman)

"THIS is not only the most memorable night in the club's history but it completes the most memorable year since the club began in 1892.

We have established ourselves as the leading club side in Europe, if not the world. This was achieved by our simplicity of outlook as we showed in the way we played against the German side.

We have the best manager in Europe and we count ourselves very lucky that he is with us. Our players are a magnificent set of dedicated men who were playing for the city of Liverpool and the country itself."

Ronnie Moran

RONNIE Moran believes the spur of losing to Manchester United in the FA Cup final in the week preceding the European Cup final in Rome gave the Reds the motivation to wipe the floor with a much-fancied Moenchengladbach.

Defeat in the North West showdown meant it was just a double and not an historic treble Liverpool were going for in the Italian capital but that took none of the shine from a famous victory.

"We'd lost in the FA Cup final, the previous Saturday, and everyone was disappointed about that, not just the players.

"We knew we had the big game in Rome on the Wednesday, so it was a matter of pulling our heads up. We didn't need to kick anybody up the backside, they just rallied around again, which is why we got the good result in Rome."

Bob Paisley

FIVE words were all it took for Bob Paisley to sum up his feelings of 90 thrilling minutes in Rome's Olympic Stadium:

"This is my greatest moment.

He added: "To come away from Wembley and play like that was a feat in itself. Then our spirit was further tested when we made a mistake and gave away a brilliantly taken goal.

"Their response speaks volumes for the players and shows just what great professionals they are. We've done the country proud.

"Tommy Smith was marvellous, though I would not like to single anybody out."

LIVERPOOL FOOTBALL CLUB AND ATHLETIC GROUNDS CO. LIMITED

EUROPEAN CHAMPION CLUBS' CUP COMPETITION - FINAL TIE

LIVERPOOL v BORUSSIA MOENCHENGLADBACH

AT THE OLYMPIC STADIUM, ROME

WEDNESDAY, 25th MAY, 1977.

KICK-OFF 20.15 HOURS

ITINERARY

Hotels:-

Night of Tuesday, 24th May, 1977

The Cavalieri Hilton,
Via Cadlolo,
101 Rome.
(Telephone Rome 3151)

Night of Wednesday, 25th May, 1977

The Holiday Inn, (St. Peter's),
Via Aurelia Antica,
415 Rome.
(Telephone Rome 5872)

Tuesday, 24th May, 1977

Meet at Liverpool Airport

Plane Leaves Liverpool Airport
(B.A. Charter Flight)

Lunch on Flight

Arrives Rome Airport

Motor Coach from Rome Airport to The Cavalieri Hilton

Wednesday, 25th May, 1977

An afternoon sightseeing tour of Rome will be arranged.
Details will be announced in the Hotel.

Motor Coach Leaves The Cavalieri Hilton for the Olympic Stadium 18.15 hours

KICK-OFF 20.15 HOURS

Motor Coach after match from the Olympic Stadium
to The Holiday Inn

Thursday, 26th May, 1977

Motor Coach Leaves The Holiday Inn for Rome Airport

Plane Leaves Rome Airport 14.00 hours
(B.A. Charter Flight)

Meal on Flight 15.30 hours

Arrives Liverpool Airport 17.15 hours

LIVERPOOL 1978 EUROPEAN CUP WINNERS

THE EMPIRE STADIUM, WEMBLEY

No ticket genuine unless it carries a Lion's Head watermark below

EUROPEAN CHAMPION CLUBS' CUP COMPETITION

FINAL TIE

WED., MAY 10, 1978

KICK-OFF 7.15 p.m.

YOU ARE ADVISED TO TAKE UP YOUR POSITION BY 6.45 p.m.

CHAIRMAN: WEMBLEY STADIUM LTD

STANDING £2.50

TO BE RETAINED

TURNSTILES J or K

ENTRANCE 53

725

WEST UPPER STANDING ENCLOSURE

SEE PLAN AND CONDITIONS ON BACK

EUROPEAN CHAMPION CLUBS' CUP

CLUB BRUGGE KV

LIVERPOOL F.C.

Wembley Stadium

Wednesday 10th May 1978 · Kick-off 7.15 · Official Souvenir Programme 40p

Kings of Europe

EUROPEAN CUP

KENN... ...ES HIST... FOR ... ...HTY REDS

Mr magic...the man with a killer touch

INSIDE

THE FOREVER

LIVERPOOL KINGS OF EUROPE

IS MAGIC

LIVERPOOL THE GREATEST

And in the year of '77 did Sir Robert Paisley take the men of Liverpool on the Second Crusade into Europe: he was a gallant; honoured by the Queene; Lord of the Manors of Hetton & Woolton and a Canny Ladde withal: and on the field of Wembley in '78 did Liverpool beat ye olde offside trappe of the Bruges men 1-0.

UEFA

PROGRAMME OFFICIEL

Vendu au profit des oeuvres sociales de la FFF

FINALE DE LA COUPE DES CLUBS CHAMPIONS EUROPEENS

REAL MADRID - C. de F.

LIVERPOOL F.C.

10 F

LIVERPOOL 1981 EUROPEAN CUP WINNERS

FEDERATION FRANÇAISE DE FOOTBALL

Nº 001012

UNION DES ASSOCIATIONS EUROPEENNES DE FOOTBALL

onze onze onze onze onze onze onze

FINALE

DE LA COUPE DES CLUBS CHAMPIONS EUROPÉENS

Mercredi 27 mai 1981 à 20 h 15

au PARC DES PRINCES

TRIBUNE AUTEUIL

Prix : 23 F

Droit de location : 2 F

Total : 25 F

Taxes comprises

Ce billet ne peut être repris, ni échangé, ni revendu.

DAILY POST

CHAMPIONS

PA...EY!

RÉPUBLIQUE ...

L'ANGLETERRE PARIS

LONDRES BRUXELLES

ANFIELD WATERLOO

It was a hard year: Many battles: Many wounded and hors-de-combat ... the young men held the line: with skill, defeating the Bulgars: but the Scribes cried "Woe! and thrice woe - Liverpool will triumph no more" ... And the Germans mocked ... but they fell ... and so did the might of Spain ... and with one voice men cried "Hail Paisley! truly thou art the Greatest"

LIVERPOOL FOOTBALL CLUB

EUROPEAN CHAMPION CLUBS' CUP COMPETITION
FINAL TIE
A.S. ROMA v LIVERPOOL
AT THE OLYMPIC STADIUM, ROME
WEDNESDAY, 30th MAY, 1984
KICK-OFF 20.15 HOURS

ITINERARY

Tuesday, 29th May, 1984	LOCAL TIME
Motor coach leaves Anfield Ground for Liverpool Airport	11.30 hours
OR, if travelling direct to Liverpool Airport, check in not later than	12.00 hours
Charter plane leaves Liverpool Airport (Flight No. EI 7950) 4952	12.45 hours
Lunch on flight	
arrives Rome (Leonardo da Vinci Airport)	16.25 hours
Motor coach from Leonardo da Vinci Airport to Headquarters:- Holiday Inn, St. Peters, via Aurelia Antica 415, Rome.	
Telephone 06 5872 Telex 680195	

...y, 1984

Holiday Inn for Olympic Stadium	18.15 hours
KICK-OFF	20.15 hours

Club Personnel will be held at a Villa in (23.00 hours to 4.00 hours). The motor ...ect to the Villa from the Olympic Stadium. ...at the Villa for ladies to change dresses, etc.

...1984

...oliday Inn for Rome (Leonardo da	11.15 hours
Leonardo da Vinci Airport	12.45 hours
...ool Airport	14.10 hours

Directors, Officials, Players and Wives will ...irport between 15.00 hours and 17.00 hours

...l commence from Liverpool Airport at 17.45 hours ...our will terminate back at Liverpool Airport at

Continued.......

ROMA MIA

Periodico di Sport, Cultura, Arte e Spettacolo per i tifosi giallorossi

Anno IV - n. 12 - 30 maggio 1984 - COPIA OMAGGIO dell'Editrice Pablo Production

ROMA-LIVERPOOL

NON PASSA LO STRANIERO

SPECIALE COPPA DEI CAMPIONI

ISTITUTO TECNICO COMMERCIALE PARIFICATO

G. LEOPARDI

CORSI ANTIMERIDIANI, POMERIDIANI, SERALI. ESAMI IN SEDE

Via del Pettirosso, 3 Tel. 26.53.55 - 26.02.98 - 26.30.19

...RPOOL FOOTBALL CL...

AND ATHLETIC GROUNDS...

LIVERPOOL FC v A.S. ROMA

Dear Supporter,

We are sure that, like us, you are looking forward to our great night in The Olympic Stadium in Rome on Wednesday the 30th May 1984.

The Management and players have always taken great pride in the reputation our fans have built up in Europe over the years. In spite of this, and because of the adverse reports on British fans generally in Europe, we have been warned by Europe's football ruling authority, E.U.F.A., that they propose to make an example of any clubs whose fans misbehave in the future.

We appeal to all fans travelling to Rome to remember what we expect of them, which is to uphold the good name of the Club and its supporters and, as a result, to ensure our continued involvement in European Football.

Once again the eyes of the world are focused on Liverpool Football Club and its supporters. Let's show 'em that our excellent reputation has been well earned.

Have a safe journey and a happy visit.

Joe Fagan, Manager

Graeme Souness, Team Captain

Bata | Coca-Cola | Canon | FUJI FILM | CAMEL | MIA | CINZANO | JVC

...RPOOL F.C.
...AVEL STEWARD
ACCOMPAGNATEUR
ACCOMPAGNATORE
ROME 1984
RoBBiE

FINALE DE LA COUPE DES C... CHAMPIONS EUROPÉENS F... OF THE EUROPEAN CHAMP... CLUBS' CUP ENDSPIEL DES ... KALS DER EUROPÄISCHEN ... STERVEREINE FINALE DEL... COPPA DEI CAMPIONI

LIVERPOOL 2005 EUROPEAN CUP WINNERS
BRONX Club presents
Liverpool Fan Party
YOU'LL NEVER WALK ALONE IN ISTANBUL
"a special night dedicated to reds"
live music THE DEED
brit rock cover band
THE FINAL
WEDNESDAY, MAY 25, 2005
AC MILAN
Fatih Terim's interview
Discovering the magic of Istanbul
The Atatürk Olympic Stadium
All information about Milan and Liverpool teams
CHAMPIONS LEAGUE
İstanbul The Final 2005
BLOCK
ROW
SEAT
VIP GUEST
CHAMPIONS LEAGUE WINNERS
ISTANBUL 2005
daily news
ectacular final:
erpool champ
LIVERPO
ŞAMPİYO
3-3
ECHO
GERRARD: I'LL STAY A RED
WE DID IT!
THE GREATEST COMEBACK IN FOOTBALL HISTORY
LİVERPOOL ŞAMPİY
FENER ATEŞE DÜŞ
Benitez: Yüreğimizle oynadık ve kazandık
Information Leaflet
LIVERPOOL v AC MILAN
CHAMPIONS LEAGUE FINAL 2005
25/5/05
LIVERPOOL CHAMPIONS LEAGUE WINNERS 2005
HAMPIONS LEAGUE FINAL
ERPOOL MILA
ISTANBUL
25-5-2005

How the Liverpool fans rewrote history . . .

OF BANNERS

78

81

84

Jamie Carragher was "made up" when LFC magazine took its special tribute banner up to Liverpool's Melwood training ground to show him for the first time. It was the week before the final in Istanbul. The lads wished him the best of luck and he said how proud it would make him to bring the trophy back and see the banner in the museum like the famous 'Joey Jones ate the frogs legs' one. Well done Carra... mission accomplished!

SUPERCROATIGORBISCAR
USEDTOBEATROCIOUS

★★★★★ THE FUTURE BELONGS
TO THOSE WHO BELIEVE
IN THE BEAUTY OF
THEIR DREAMS
25.5.05

LIVERPOOL FC
SOME SAY IM
A DREAMER
BUT IM NOT THE
ONLY ONE
LEVELEYS

L.F.C. GLADIATOR
Success Is A Journey
Not A Destination

GIMME
5

THE RAFALUTION
IS HERE

1977 1978 1981 1984
RAFA'S RED ARMY
Istanbul 2005
ALL HAIL
KING CARRA
DICKO'S ON TOUR
CHAMPION'S LEAGUE
WE'RE HAVIN' KEBABS
IT IS LEFT TO GREAT MEN
TO DO GREAT THINGS
77
78
81
84
IF YOU CAN IMAGINE
YOU CAN ACHIEVE
IF YOU CAN DREAM
5 TIMES TONITE
TURKISH
DELIGHT
OUR EYES
HAVE SEEN THE GLORY
THE TTW&R COLLECTIVE
BELIEVE
REDMEN
YNWA
96
STEVEN GERRARD
JAMIE CARRAGHER
"THE ITALIAN JOB"
MAKING FOREVER HISTORY
L.F.C.
KINGS OF EUROPE
77 78 81 84
LIVERPOOL F.C.

WELCOME TO HELL
MY ARSE IF YOU
THINK THIS IS HELL TRY THE
GRAFTON
ON A FRIDAY NIGHT

CRAZY
HORSE

KEBABS
AND 1
EUROPEAN
CUP

WE DARE NOT FORGET
TODAY, THAT WE ARE
THE HEIRS OF THAT
FIRST REVOLUTION

IS
BOS-PH

¡HALA
ROJOS, A
GLORIA!

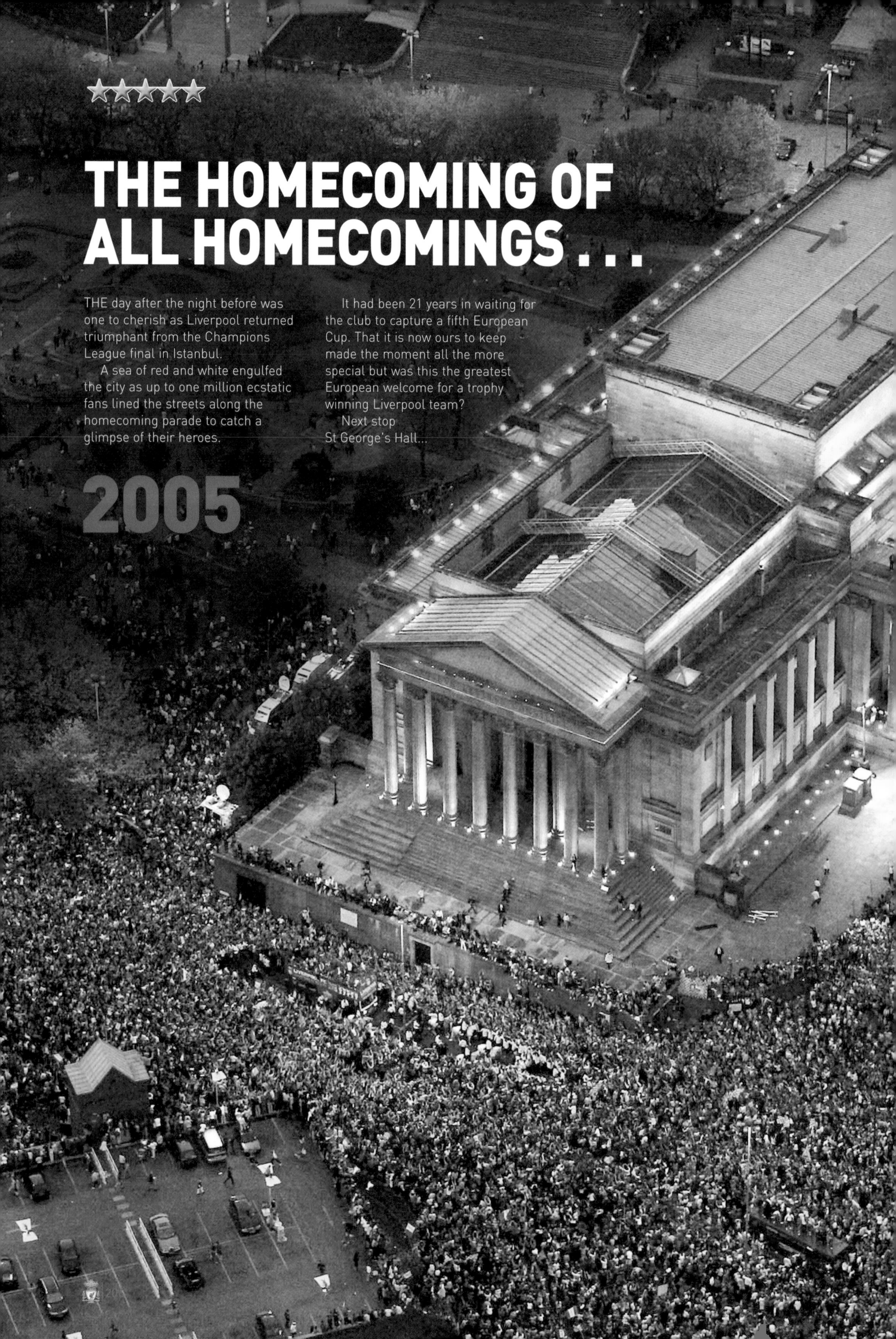

THE HOMECOMING OF ALL HOMECOMINGS . . .

THE day after the night before was one to cherish as Liverpool returned triumphant from the Champions League final in Istanbul.

A sea of red and white engulfed the city as up to one million ecstatic fans lined the streets along the homecoming parade to catch a glimpse of their heroes.

It had been 21 years in waiting for the club to capture a fifth European Cup. That it is now ours to keep made the moment all the more special but was this the greatest European welcome for a trophy winning Liverpool team?

Next stop St George's Hall...

2005

1977

MAGIC! Liverpool's favourite word (or at least it was in 1977) was the only one which could describe the tremendous night when the conquerors of Europe came home.

Everyone - from the record 750,000 crowd right up to the Queen herself - came together to salute and hail the mighty Reds.

The figure was the highest ever recorded in this country of ours for the homecoming of a football team. Every inch of the 11-mile route from Liverpool airport to Picton Library was a mass of red, with a sprinkling of blue as Evertonians too turned out to cheer a night of glory for all Merseyside.

Onlookers were up in the trees, on the bus shelters and even on traffic lights - all turned to red for the night. From the moment the plane touched down on the tarmac to the last reluctant departure of Emlyn Hughes at Picton after eight o'clock, the cheering, singing and dancing of the red and white thousands never ceased.

1978

AN estimated 500,000 jubilant supporters came out to welcome the Kings of Europe back to the city in what was billed as the biggest celebration in Liverpool since V.E. Day.

The banner-waving, cheering crowds showed their appreciation to the team as they made their way through a 14-mile route parading the trophy from an open-top bus.

Police paid tribute to all concerned after reporting no trouble and no arrests.

"It was great. The fans behaved marvellously," said a delighted Superintendent Tom Hanley, who was in charge of the police operation.

"Everyone was there, from babes in arms to grannies and there was no trouble at all. I am very pleased with the way things went," he said.

Every inch of the route was packed with incident - an impromptu peal of bells was provided at St Andrew's, Clubmoor, a cricket match came to a halt as the team passed by and firemen set off their sirens on Mather Avenue.

THE ROUTE...

THE Reds enjoyed a bigger and better route for their triumphant homecoming than they had sampled 12 months earlier .

City officials extended the victory parade by three miles to enable more fans to catch a glimpse of their heroes.

The team bus set off, complete with motorcycle outriders, from Allerton Station at 6.30pm before waving its way through 14 miles of streets lined with well-wishers before finishing at the junction of Queens Drive and Prescot Road, Stoneycroft.

Unlike 1977, there was no grand finale reception at Picton Library but plans were being drawn up for a Town Hall reception later in the year.

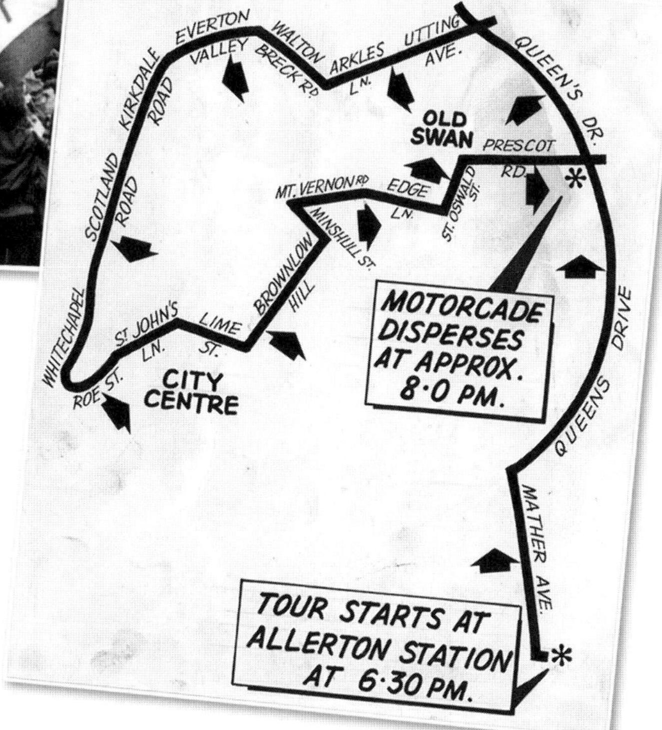

1981

UP TO 500,000 people were estimated to have lined the 16-mile homecoming parade route.

Youngsters climbed on to trees, lamp-posts, bus shelters, roofs and road signs to get a glimpse of their heroes.

A 25-strong police motor-cycle escort guided the cavalcade through the city's streets.

Goalscoring hero Alan Kennedy received the loudest cheers, with his nickname 'Barney Rubble' spelt out on hundreds of banners. A four-foot teddy bear named 'Barney' was passed up to the coach by an adoring fan.

Starting from Liverpool Airport, the parade passed through Allerton, Anfield, Kirkdale, Scotland Road and Lime Street, before ending in Aigburth Vale.

Retired city social worker Jack Connor instructed his solicitor to reclaim the cost of his garden wall, which was flattened as the parade passed through Queens Drive in Clubmoor.

As two members of the team bus made a dash for Mr Connor's toilet, they were mobbed by youngsters and in the melee, down went the £250 wall.

1984

WHAT a victory, what a season and what a welcome home.

The European Cup final penalty shoot-out in Rome had capped an amazing treble-winning campaign for Liverpool and the 300,000 or so delirious fans that came out to greet their heroes was fitting of such an achievement.

A nun wearing a red and white scarf, babies in scarlet romper suits and disabled people, their wheelchairs decked out in ribbons, were among the masses who all but stopped the cavalcade as it crawled along the 16-mile victory parade.

Alan Kennedy was king for the day after adding to his 1981 European Cup winning goal with the decisive penalty in the Italian capital but as soon as the team touched down at Liverpool airport all thoughts turned to the fans who had come under siege from a section of Roma supporters.

Liverpool chairman John Smith said: "I thought Liverpool fans behaved in an impeccable way.

"I am supported in my view by senior members of UEFA. At the end of the game all of them were delighted with the behaviour of our fans."

In typical fashion, manager Joe Fagan opted to take a back seat in the celebrations preferring instead to let his players take the limelight and it was an hour-and-a-half before he was persuaded to walk to the front of the bus to hold the cup aloft.

Liverpool captain Graeme Souness said: "It's wonderful, it's great and we're all over the moon.

"I start celebrating now and I'm going to continue for the next three days."

FC

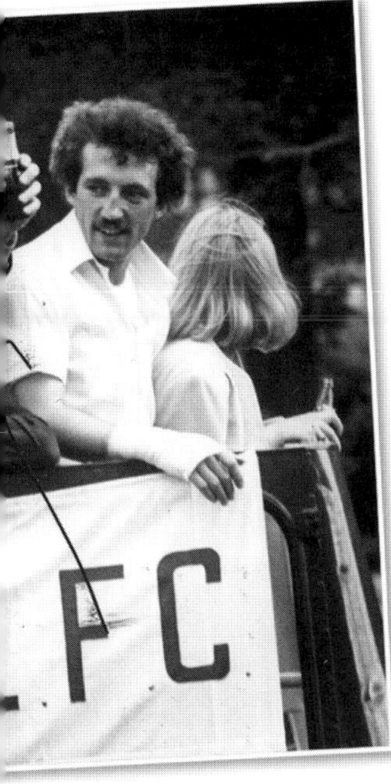

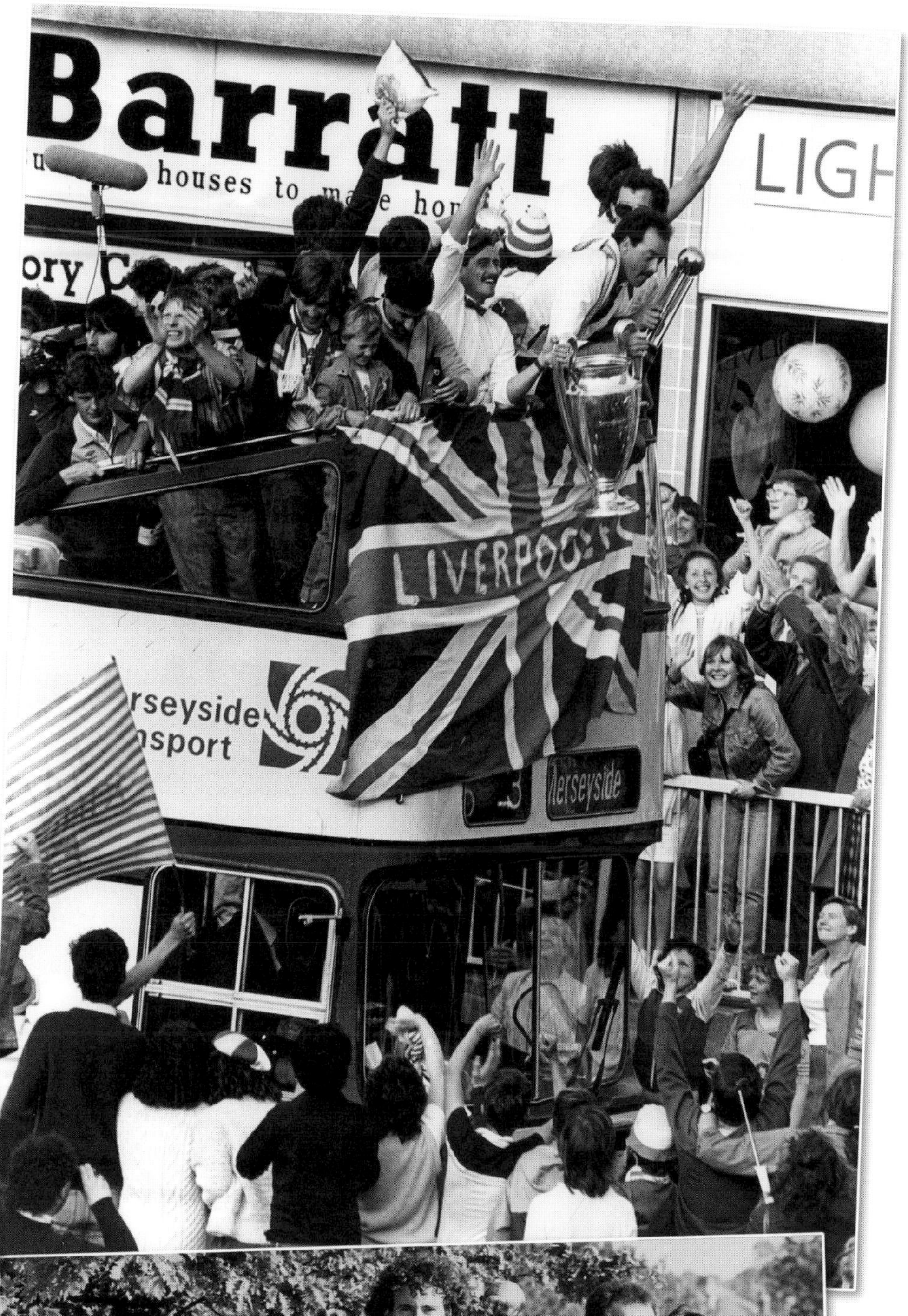
Barratt
LIGH
LIVERPOO
rseyside
nsport
Merseyside

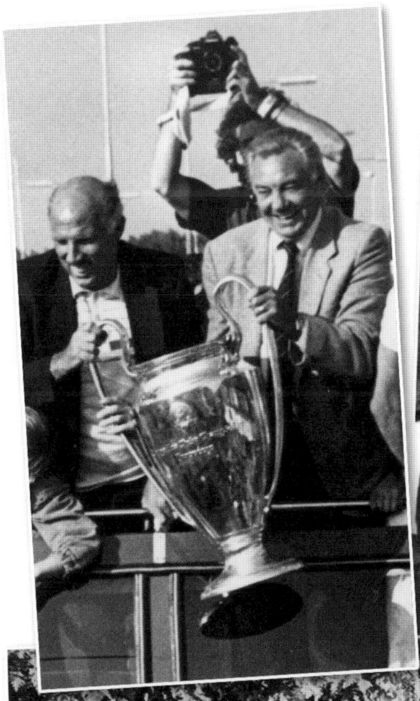

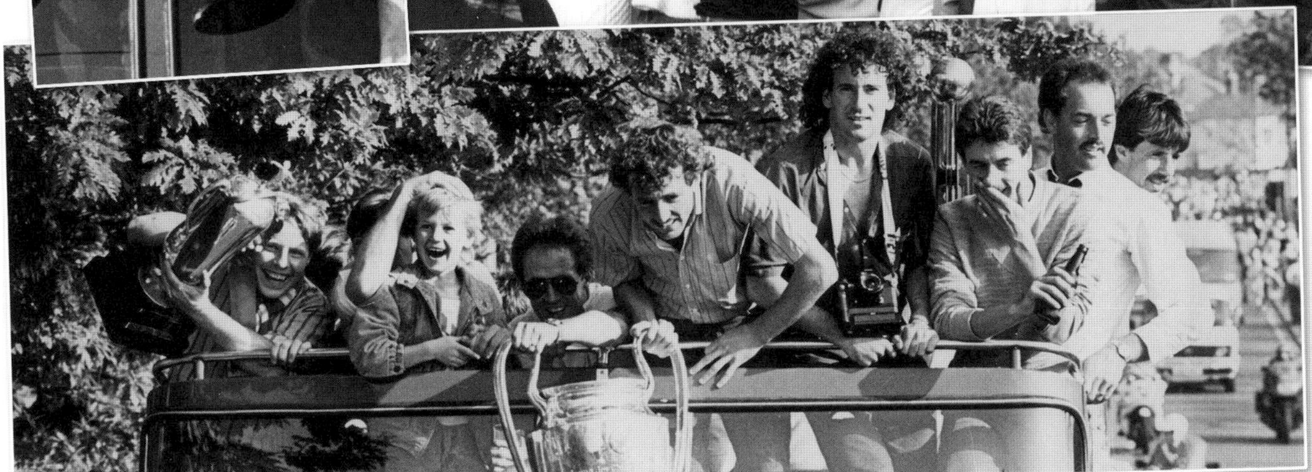

2005

IT had been 21 years in waiting and there was no way up to a million ecstatic Liverpool fans were going to miss the chance to greet the players who had etched their name into the club's illustrious history.

It took over four hours for the parade to make a six-mile journey from the M62 to the city centre due to the sheer volume of people who took to the streets with their banners, flags and scarves.

Up to 300,000 fans gathered outside St George's Hall for a glimpse of our legends as the city came to a stand still.

The eruption of noise and colour on their arrival was met with scenes of celebration from the players who took it in turns to show off the European Cup.

Carlsberg
Reebok
YOU'LL NEVER WALK ALONE
LIVERPOOL FOOTBALL CLUB
EST·1892
08
Liverpool
EUROPEAN CAPITAL OF CULTURE
LIVERPOOL
CHAMPIONS OF EUROPE
LIVERPOOL FC
CHAMPIONS OF EUROPE

Carlsberg
Reebok
LIVERPOOL
CHAMPIONS OF EUROPE
İstanbul 2005
RADIO CITY
St Johns
LIVERPOOL

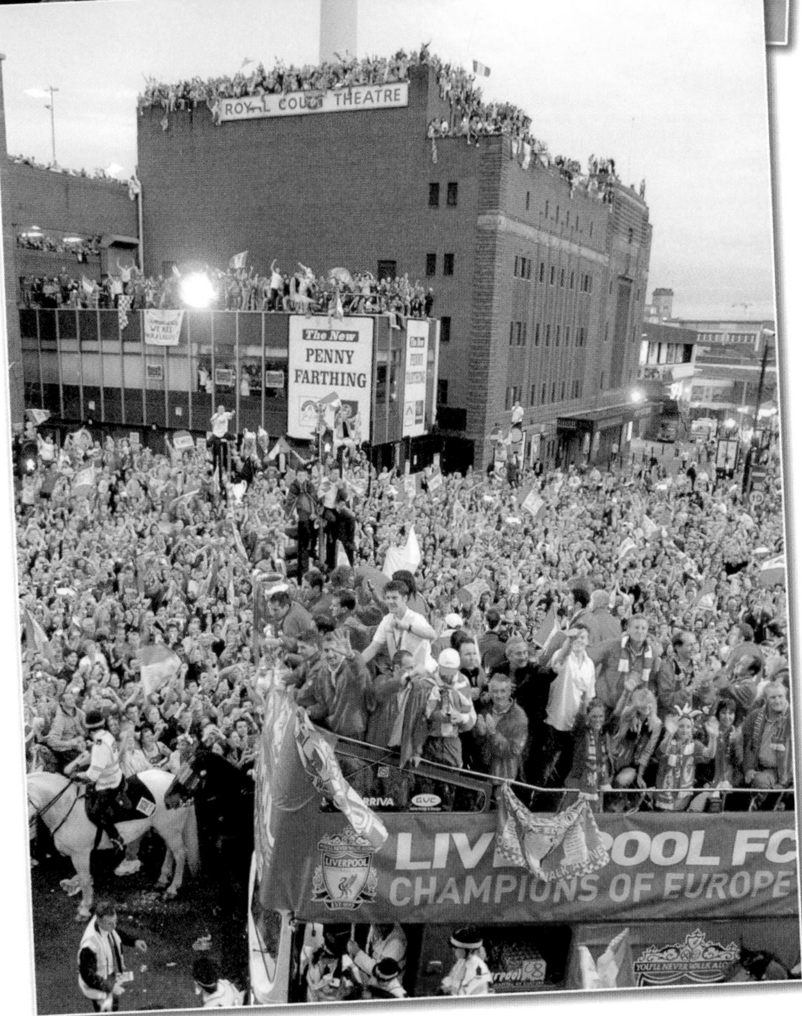

LIFTING the European Cup as captain of the club he has supported all of his life was a truly proud moment for Steven Gerrard.

Bringing the trophy back to his home city saw him realise a childhood dream.

He knew it would be special but even Gerrard was taken aback by the scenes that greeted him and his teammates as they toured the city for the biggest homecoming parade we have ever witnessed.

"It was unbelievable," he said.

"None of the players imagined there would be so many people there, waiting to cheer us on.

"The scenes were incredible. I was sitting on the plane coming home with my medal and thinking 'life can't get any better than this,' and then you saw those fans everywhere.

"Someone told me there was about a million people on the route and it was just so special.

"I can remember the celebrations following the cup treble in 2001, but this was something else. The lads were just buzzing.

"For some of the foreign players it was a real eye-opener but this is Liverpool Football Club, and that's why we never gave in against Milan when it looked like a lost cause.

"The fans in Istanbul were brilliant and the welcome home topped off the greatest night of my life. I'd just like to say thank you to everyone who turned out on behalf of all the players. Those supporters are the best."

Scroll Of Honour

Steven Abbott
Adam Leigh Abdulla
Mark Abigail
P. Abraham
Peter Abram
Dr Mohammad Hilaal Abu Bakar
Andreas Achilleos
Paul Acton
Stephen Adams
Roger Adams
Marc Adams
Kate Adams
Hassan Adia
Jackie Adisorn
James Agius
Reaaz Ahmed
Alam Ahmed
Farhan Ahmed
Max Anthony Ainsworth
Jim Alexander
William Alexander
Mohammed Al-Hashimi
Atif Ali
Annie Allan
Mr Chris Allcock
Jane Allcroft
Philip Allen
Chris Allen
Charlie Allen
Philip Allen
Richard Allen
Peter Allen
Dave Allen
Carol Allman
Mr S.T. Allsopp
Zaid Yahia Al-Qaimi
Dave Alty
Daniel Ambrose
Carl Amo
Jimmy Anderson
Craig Anderson
Craig G. Anderton
Leslie P. Anderton
Chris Andrews
Ken Ankers
Ray Annal
Brian Anthony
Lauren Apamiecki
Leo Appleton
Wayne Appleton
Eric Apter
Daniel Archer
Christopher Argent
Teresa Armitage
Ian Edward Armstrong
David Armstrong
Melanie Armstrong
Johnathan Ashcroft
Mr Tim Ashcroft
Macaulay Ashton
Henry James Ashton
Fred Askew
Paul Aspinall
Jennifer Naomi Asquith
Marc Astick
Marc Astick
Mark Aston
David Atherton
Alistair Atherton
Stephen Atherton
Rany Athwall
Sam Atkinson
C.K. Au
Tony Au Man-yin
Dan Austin
A. Ayman
George Ayscough
Peter Baccino
Tom Bagley
Sheila Bailey

Andy Bailey
Chris Bailey
Sheila Bailey
John Edward Baker
Paul William Baker
Jans Baker
Chinny Baker
Ross Baker
Michael Ball
Sarah Louise Ball
Mr. K.P. Ball
Mr L. Ball
Nigel Ball
Colin Ball
Ed Ball
Daren Balman
Laura Banham
Suleiman Banian
J.L. Banky
M. Bannerman
Paul JW Barber
Malcom Barber
Timothy Barker
Alan Barker
Steve Barker
Frank Barker
Simon Barnes
Luke Thomas Barnes
Gerard Barnes
Anthony Barnes
James John Barnwell
Leo Bartle
R. Bartley
Anne Marie Barton
Martin Barwise
Lee Bashford
Lakhan Basi
Lee Batch
James Battersby
Abraham Baucher
David John Baxter
John Paul Baxter
Daniel Baxter
David Bayer
Steven Bayliff
Clym Baylis
Moray Baylis
Robert Bayliss
Chrissie Bayliss
Matthew Colm Baynes
J.J. Beahan
James Beaney
Neil Beatson
Russell Bedford
Harry Peter Begg
Peter J. Bell
Ashley S. Bell
Gareth J. Bell
Andrew Bell
Mrs Jennifer Bell
Carl Bell
Jonathan Bellamy
Gary Bellis
Stephen Bellis
Glenn Bemment
Terry Benjamin
Janet Bennett
Joe Bennett
Bruce Bennett
Gary Bennett
Dave Bennett
William Bennett
Marc Bennett
Owen Benson
Jamie Benson
Nicola Benson
Daniel Bentzen Li
Craig Berry
Mr I. Berry
Luke Bevan-McCarthy

Joseph James Bibby
Adam Bidston
Matt Bidston
Mark Bidston
Neil Bigelow
Anthony Bigeni
Lee Bignell
Graham Billington
Mark J. Bingley
Jill Birchall
Richard Birtwistle
Rob Bisby
Daniel Robert Bishop
Paul Bishop
Lil Black
Paul Blackburn
Martin Blackmore
Steve Bladon
Karl Gerhard Blain
D.J. Blair
D.J. Blair
Niall Blanchflower
Mark Blaney
James C. Bliss
Suzanne Bloude
Peter Bluck
James Blundell
Malcolm Blyth
Barry Blythe
Frank A. Boardman
Mr T.H. Boardman
David Boland
Mr G.P. Bond
Graham Bond
Joseph Booth
Marc Booth
Walter Henry Booth
Mr Ron Booth
William H. Booth Jnr.
John David Borrows
Danny Bosher
Mr Robert Bott
Joseph Bowdler
Spencer Bowen
Lee Bower
Craig Bower
Steve Bower
Phil Bowers
Wayne Boyce
Nick Boycott
Ciaran Boyle
Jimmy Boyle
Gary Bradburn
Jonathan Braddick
Adrian R.H. Bradley
Timothy Bradley
Sean Brady
Leo Branton
Joy Bratherton
Carl Van Breemen
Lyn Breen
Eddie Breithaupt
Josef Brennan
Patrick Brickley
Mark A.C. Bride
Ian Bride
David Bridge
Steve Bridge
Liam Bridgeman
Gary Peter Brimble
Mr. D.D. Briscoe
Derek Briscoe
Pete Briscoe
Alfred Brittenden
Patrick Brizell
Warren Broadbent
Thomas Broadmore
George-Harrison Brocken
Joanne Louise Brockway
Christina Brockway

Gemma Ellen Brockway
David Stephen Brockway
John Paul Brockway
Sean Anthony Brockway
N. Brogan
Tony Brogan
Lee Brook
Alan G. Broom
Thomas Robert Brothwood
Terry Brown
Fiona J. Brown
Matthew Brown
Mark C. Brown
David Brown
George Brown
Stephen Brown
Claire Brown
Ste Brown
Paul Brown
Jenny Brown
Lee Brown
Thomas Brown
David Brown
Natalie Anna Brown
Mr P. Brownrigg
John Brownson
Ms S. Brunton
Mr. J.W. Bryan
Emma Bryan
Jason M. Bryant
Nancy Bryant
Alan Bryne
George Buckingham
Kevin Buckley
Marie Buckley
Sam Bulley
Yeung Chi Bun
Dan Bunder
George Bundred
Ian Burch
Neil Burchall
Jackie Burgess
Alan Burgess
Martin Burgum
Jeff Burke
John Daniel Burke
Neil J. Burke
Craig James Connor Burke
Ed Burke
Tony Burke
Neil Burlinson
John Edward Burns
Mr. Stanley Burns
Paul M. Burns
Chris Burns
Ian D. Burns
Alfred Burns
Seoras Burns
David Burns
Damian Burton
Tom Burton
Estelle Buscombe
Len Bushell
Warren Butcher
Elsie Butler
Chloe Jade Butler
Sophie Eleonor Butler
Jimmy Butler
James Butler
Megan Butterworth
Mr A. Butterworth
Denis Byrne
Terry Byrne
John Byrne
David Byrne
Gerry Byrne
Lucy Byrne
Michael Edward Byrne
Coner Byrne
Paul Byrne

5-Star Heroes

Daniel Byron
Jimmy Corrio Cabases
Stephen Cable
B.G.S. Caddick
Sam Caddick
Bob Caddick
Joe Cahill
Rory Cahill
Joseph Cahill
Chloe Cain
Mr. Reginald James Cain
Rob Cain
Mrs Kathlen Cain
James Cairns
James Caldwell
Keith Caldwell
Ashley Calland
Matthew Callister
Louise Cambell
Mr R.J. Cameron
James Campbell
Christopher Campbell
Tony Campbell
Vicky Campbell
Alan Campbell
Norman Canavan
Frank Cann
Lucas Finley Cannon
Tim Canty
Chris Capper
Craig Ross Cappie
Graeme Carlile
Dominic Carlin
Mr D. Carney
Jonathan Carney
Benjamin Carpenter
Adam Carpenter
Dr. Peter J. Carr
Kenny Carr
A.D. Carrick
Michael Carroll
Ian Carruthers
Paul Carruthers
Dave Carson
Stephen Carson
Glen Carson
Ian Carter
Dean Carter
Jim Carter
Daniel Carter
David Cartledge
Patricia Case
Simon James Case
John Case
Michael Casey Jnr
Helen Casselden
David Cater
Paul Caton
Mark Caudwell
Davey Caulter
Adam Cavanagh
Deryk Cave
Mark Cawley
Mr J. Cawley
Steven Challinor
Mark Challinor
Peter Chamberlain
Joseph Chambers
Steve Chambers
Dorothy Chambers
Ian Chambers
Billy Chambers
Anthony Philip Chandler
Michelle Louise Chandler
Darren J. Chantler
Alma Chantler-Isa
Andy Chapman
Manuel Charmillot
Ram Kumar Chhetry
Adam Chiocchi
Victoria Chiocchi
Rachid Choaibi
Reeve Christall
Bob Christie
Mark Christopherson
Lloyd Christophorou
Stanley NC Chui

Thomas Chung
Mr Jean-Paul Ciantar
Alexander Ciesco
Marc Clack
Timothy Clapham
Adrian Clare
Matthew Clare
Brendon Clark
Robert Clark
Leslie Clark
Kevin Clarke
James Clarke
Ryan Adam Clarke
Andrew Clarke
Douglas Clarke
Matthew Clarke
Trevor Clarke
James Clarridge
Jill Clay
Christopher J. Clay
Nicholas G. Clay
Robert Clayton
Karl E. Cleary
Steven Clegg
Joseph C. Clem
Macauley James Clifton
Mark C.J. Cloonan
Chloe Bryne Coates-Whay
Jack Cockin
Gerald Cocking
Keith Coker
Mike Cole
Tony Colebourn
Mr A. Coleman
Scott J. Coles
David Colleran
Leslie James Collin
Phil Collier
Liz Collingwood
John Collins
Paul Collins
Andy Collins
Susannah Collins
Matthew Collins
John Collins
Steven Colyer
Douglas Comish
Dane Conneely
Paul Connell
Paul A. Connell
K.T. Connolly
Gabriel Connolly
Archie Connolly
Fergus Connolly
Michael Connor
Mitchell Connor
Mr M. Connor
Sam Connor
Chris Connor
Steven Michael Constanti
George Constantinides
Mr David J. Conway
Carl Cook
Clive Cook
Mr A.R. Cook
James A. Cook
Daniel Coombe
Aaron Cooper
Andrew Cooper
Jack Cooper
David Alexander Cooper
Gill Cooper
Richie Cooper
Paul Joseph Cope
Russell Copland
Alan Corbett
Paul Corcoran M.B.E.
Pamela Corns
Chris Corrie
Tony Corrigan
Mr Anthony Corrigan JNR
Brian G. Corrin
Derek Cosgrave
David W.D. Cosgrove
Christopher Costello
Tom Cottee
Adam John Paul Coughlan

Jimmy Coulton
Mr. Colin Cowell
Kevin Cowley
Kevin Cowley
Matthew Cowton
Mark Cox
Laura Crabb
Charles Bernard Cranny
Paul Cranston
Carl Craven
Steven Paul Crawford
Steve J. Crawford
Helen Crick
Les Crierie
Graham Crilly
W.A. Critchlow
Alisdair Croft
John Edward Crompton
Lol Crook
Mr G. Crook
Ms S.J.E. Crosbie
Alfred F. Cross
Gary Cross
Chris Cross
Daniel James Cross
Neil Crowder
John Cruces
Steven Cruise
Ann J. Crute
Mr Gil Cubells
Marie-Louise Culbert
John Cullen
Terry Culligan
Raymond Cummings
Jason Marlon Cunningham
Stephen Cunningham
Kevin Cunningham
John Cunningham
Jack Cureton
David Curling
Shane Curtin
John Curtin
Anthony Curtis
Billy Curtis
Tony Curtis
Robin Curtis
Dr Daniel J.R. Cuthbertson
Shaun Cutting
Pedro M.C. Da Costa
Pedro Daniel Cordas Da Costa
Ms V. Dagnall
Tonysam Dainty
Paul Daley
J. Dalrymple
Colin Daly
Katy Dalziel
Peter Danaher
Janette Daniel
Steve J. Dannatt
Adrian Darby
Andrew D'arcy
G.R. Dardamanis
S.D. Darwin
Sid Davenport
Danial Pauli Davidsen
Roy Davidson
Dave Davies
Mark Davies
Simon James Davies
Michael Paul Davies
Kevin Davies
Fred F. Davies
Ian F. Davies
Michael Davies
Lauren Elizabeth Davies
John Martin Davies
Michael Ian Davies
James Davies
Nicholas Meredith Davies
Richard Davies
Neil R. Davies
Steven Lee Davies
Phil Charles Davies
Mark Ian Davies
Alan Davies
Ross Edward Davies
Edward Davies

Ian Davies
Deiniol Davies
Saffron Davies
Dave Davies
Louise G. Davies
Peter Davies
Beverley Davies
Graham Davies
Robert Davin
Nick Davis
Ronald Davison
Martyn Frank Dawber
Carole Dawson
Barry Dawson
Joel Day
Paul Day
Adrian Day
James De Blasio
Edward De Burca
Louisa De La Cruz
Andrea De La Cruz
Carlo De Martini
Adam Deacon
Miss Sarah Deakin
Toby Dean
Michael R.J. Dean
Neil Deane
Jonathan Deans
Richard Thomas Dears
E.A. Decker
Kevin Dee
Deegan
Steven Deeks
Stuart Degg
Juergen Dehn
Francis John Delaney
Rupert Dell
Matthew Christopher Denne
Susan Dennett
James Dennett
Spencer Richard Denzey
Arthur Derbyshire
Ann Desposito
Owen Devine
Peter Devine
Andrew Devine
Harmander Singh Dhesi
Manjit Dhillon
Michael Diamond
Alan Mark Daniel Dickaty
Robert Dickinson
Paul John Dickinson
Peter Dickinson
Kiri Jade Dickson
Siobhan Dickson
Joe Diggory
Colin Dillon
Christopher Dillon
Paul Dilworth
Harpreet Diocee
Ian Cameron Disbury
Molly Disley-Jones
Henry Ditchfield
Gregory Phillip Dixon
Simon Dixon
Lee Dobson
Cara Dodd
Gary Doherty
J. Eric Doig
H.W. Dolman
Rob Dolphin
Stevie Donaghey
Terence Donakey
Mr. Jeffrey Philip Donaldson
Carl Donegan
Amy Donnelly
Joe Donnelly
James Donnelly
Anthony Donnelly
Damien Donnelly
Mark Donnelly
Sean Donovan
John Dooley
Peter Dooley SNR
Zak Doran
Alan Dare Douglas
Neil Douglas

★★★★★

Paul Dove
Geraldine Dove
Sean Dove
Alex Dove
Jean Dove
Ian Dow
Steve Dowding
Shaun Dowling
Alexander A. Dowling
Kenny Dowling
Peter Dowling
Shane Downes
Paul Downey
Norman Downs
G. Doyle
Paul Doyle
Richard Doyle
Brendan J. Doyle
Philip Doyle
Mr T.S. Doyle
Mike Draper
James Dray
Gary Dredge
Brian Drever
Emma Susan Driscoll
Danny Driscoll
Phillip Duckworth
Ms H. Dudley
Iain Duff
Ray Duffey
Roy Duffey
B.S.R. Duffy
Steven Duffy
Michael B. Dugdale
Jamie Dumbell
Kelly Mary Dunmore
P.D. Dunn
David John Dunn
Jamie Michael John Dunn
Paul David Dunn
Patrick Dunne
Andy Dunne
Simon Dunne
Eileen Dunne
Andy Dunne
A. Dursham
R.W. Dursham
Pat Dury
Steve Dury
Junior P. Dutton
Christopher Dutton
Mark Dutton
Owen Dutton
Lars Dybwad
Andy Dyson
Ian Dyson
Stale Dysvik
Julian Eardley
Anthony Earl
Martin Eastwood
David George Eccleston
Fred Eccleston
Paul Eccleston
Jamie Eccleston
James Eckersley
Kate Ede
Mr Philip Edgar
Mike Edge
Leonard Edmondson
John Edmondson
Karl Edmondson
Stephen Edwards
Joe Edwards
Trevor Edwards
Adam Edwards
Susan Caroline Edwards
Luke Edwards
Robert Edwards
Michael Edwards
Claire Edwards
Henry Edwards
Gareth Edwards
Mr John J. Edwards
Aaron Edwards
Matthew Edwards
Danny Egerton
Louisa Egerton

Ryan Ekers
Matthew J. Ellams
Matthew Elliott
Martin Ellis
Paul Ellis
Ben Ellis
Brian Ellis Jnr
John Henry Ellison
John Ellison
Joel Guy Emanuel
Per Erik Engh
Pamela England
Edward Joseph English
Stephen L. Ennis
Liam C. Ennis
Malcolm S. Erskine
Heath Essam
Alexander Euassen
Gareth Evans
Chris Evans
Carwyn Evans
John Evans
Simon Evans
John Evans
Dean Evans
Matthew Michael Evans
Mark Evans
Chris Evans
Johnathan David Evans
Jonathan Evans
Neil Evans
Mike Evans
Darren Evans
Clare E. Evans
Martin D. Evans
Mike Evans
Ken Evans
Phil Evans
Claire Evans
Lee Evans
David Evans
Stephen Evans
Robert J. Everett
Gary Eves
Perry Ewance
Carol Ann Ewart
Maureen Eyers
Neil Eyers
Willie Fagan
Leonard Fairbrother
Sharon Fairclough
Chris Falzon
Leile Farah
Neil Farmery
Roland Farncombe
Elizabeth Farrell
J. Farrell
Gerry Farrell
Steven Farrell
Mr Joe Farrelly
Charlie Farrugia
Gary Faulkner
Stephen Fawcett
Ken Fawcett
Barrie Michael Fay
Shahnaz Fazal
Lee Fazal
Michael Fazal
Adam Fazal
Jamie Fazal
Dave Fealey
Tom Fear
Paul Fear
A.W. Fearn
D.A. Fearn
Stephen Fearns
Jack Fearon
Derek Fearon
Seth Daniel Felton
W.H. Fennah
Mr W.H. Fennah
Rebekah Ferguson
Jacob Ferguson
Paul Fergusson
Sarah Fernell
Jake Ferns
Bethany Ferns

Francis Ferris
Robert Patrick Ernest Ferris
David Fidler
Charlie Field
Jake Field
Richard Fielding
Anne-Louise Fielding
Michael J. Finch
Michael Findlay
Richard Finlay
Daniel Finlay-Smith
Mark Finnegan
E.D. Finnegan
Michael Firth
Paul Fisher
Tony Fisher
Josh Fisher
Christopher Fisher
Thomas Fisher
Neil Fisher
Leon Fisher
John Fitz
David Fitzjohn
Sylvia Fitzpatrick
Callum Fitzpatrick
Danny Fitzpatrick
Barry Thomas Fitzsimmons
James Flannigan
Paul Anthony Flattery
David Flavelle
Rachel Fleming
Kevin Fleming
Steven Fleming
Kevin Fleming
David Fleming
Ross Flemington
John Flemming
Alex Stanley Fletcher
Daniel Fletcher
Anthea Flett
Gary Ninder Foat
Thomas Anthony George Foley
Jonathan Foote
C.D. Ford
Joanne Ford
Colin G. Ford
Stephen J. Ford
Lorraine Rachael Forshaw
Paul Forshaw
Jeff Forshaw
Rachel Forsythe
Gareth Forsythe
Robert Forsythe
Ellen Fortune
B. Foster
Roy Foster
Stephen Foster
Brian Foster
Llifon Foulkes
Barry Thomas Foulkes
David Fowler
Steve Fowler
Mr B.A. Fowles
Paul Fox
Martyn Foy
Gillian C. Foy
Adam John Ross Fracz
Victor Fracz
Hazel Frame
Alexander Frame
Theo Franken
Charlotte Fraser
Martin N. Fraser
James Fraser
Kimberley Freeman
Maxine Freeman
L.R. Freeman
Tony Frost
Dean Fry
Jeffrey Charles Fryer
Yuk Ming Fu
Norman Fudge
Robert J. Fulton
Gary Fulwell
Paul Furlong
Joe Fylan
Ste Fyles

Mark Gadsby
Amy Gallagher
John Gallagher
John Galloway
John Christopher Gallwey
Ms Kate Galraith
Mike Galvin
Dave Gamble
Dany Gammall
Jennie Isabel Gammon
J. Gane
Lee Gannon
Jill Gannon
Andrew Gant
Anthony Garcia
Anthony Gardiner
Jody Gardiner
Frederick James Garnett
Joe Garnett
Michael Garnett
Joel Garnett
Johnathan Garrity
Samuel Thomas Jack Garstang
Daniel Garvey
Joseph Gaskin
Richard Gaunt
Martyn Gavey
Scott Gerrard
Eldo Gherbaz
Dr. C. Ghosh
Rima Tatjana Ghubril
Mario Giatt
Amanda Gibbins
Eddie Gibbons
Mark Gibbs
Harold Gibbs
Richard Francis Gibbs
James Peter Gibney
Hannah Leigh Gibney
Joanne Gibson
Michael A. Gibson
Ray Gifford
Michael Gilbert
Simon Gilby
Thomas Patrick Gildea
Kenny Giles
Barry Giles
Steven George Gill
Anmol Singh Gill
Dave Gill
Steve Gill
David Andrew Gillan
Paul Gilland
Anthony Gillespie
Dherran W. Gilligan
Robert Malcolm Gilloes
Ian Gilroy
Jonathan Gilsenan
Sharon Ginnelly
Neil Gladman
Alex Glanville
Rick Gleave
Matthew Gleeson
Ken Goddard
Billy Goldsmith
Kevin Gomery
Mark Gomery
Peter Goodall
John Goodyer
Ian Gordan
Derek L. Gordon
Bill Gordon
Jonathan Gore
Adam Gore
Tony Gormley
Vikesh Nilesh Gosai
Brian Gosling
Becky Gould
David William Gould
Daniel John Goulding
Jeff Goulding
Aaron Gouthwaite
Phillip Goveas
Alan Grace
Robert Graham
Mr. M. Graham
Stephanie Graham

John Graham
Joshua Graham
Georgina Graham
Andrew Paul Graham
John Joseph Graham
John Richard Graham
Nick Graham
Jimmy Graham
James Graham
Harry Graham
John Graham
D.W. Granagan
Jack Grant
Sam Grant
Kenny Gray
George Grears
Andrew Michael Green
Antony Green
Dennis Green
Kevin Green
John Keith Green
Mark Green
Darren Green
Dave Greenhalgh
Anthony Greenland
Danny Greenland
Sian Greenway
Anthony Greenwood
Chris 'Booey' Greenwood
John J. Grego
Darren Gregory
David Malcolm Gregory
Isabella Gregory
David Greig
Matthew Greig
Ian Greig
Jack Grewal
Elliott Grey
Mr Philip Grice
Russell Griffin
Andy Griffin
Paul Griffin
William Griffiths
Adrian W. Griffiths
Richard J.K. Griffiths
Simon Peter Griffiths
Lyla Griffiths
James Griffiths
Mr Brian Griffiths
Sarah Jane Griffiths
David Thomas Griffiths
Matthew Griffiths
Geraint Griffiths
James Griffiths
Daniel Griffiths
Mr J.M. Griggs
David Lawrence Grima
James A. Groves
Adam J. Growther
Gaz Crump
George W. Guinness
Andrew Gunnion
Paul Gurnett
Nicky Gussow
Sigfus Guttormsson
S.C. Guy
Stephen Hack
Sammy Hackett
Raymond Hagan
John Hagan
David Haith
James Peter Hake
Simon Hakeem
James Hale
Julian Hale
Paul Hale
Thomas Hales
Michelle Louise Halford
M. Hall
Kevin Hall
Andrew Hall
Peter Hall
Terry Hall
Mr T.S. Hall
Neil Hall
Terrence Stanley Hall
R. Halliwell

Steven Matthew Hallmark
David Hallowell
Brian Halsall
Paul Halsey
Allan Hambly
Anthony James Hamilton
Mark Matthew Hamilton
Andy Hamilton
Kyle Hamilton
Darren Hammond
Steve Hammond
Mark Hammond-Edis
Jack Hampson
Thomas Hampson
Steven James Hampson
Andy Hand
Brian Hanley
Mr James Hanley
Brian Hanley
Francis Hannah
Mr Nick Hannett
Mr Marcus Hannett
Paul Hanrahan
Stephen Hanrahan
Sandra Hanrahan
Lyndsey Hanrahan
Emma Hanrahan
Paul Hanrahan
David Hanrahan
Tony Hanrahan
Ian Hanson
Stein Hanstad
Robbie Harcombe
John Hardacre
Philip R.M. Hardman
Christopher Hardwick
C.M. Hardy
Mark Harford
Lee Hargreaves
Ann Harkins
Jim Harkins
Stefan Harkon
C.L. Harkup
Thomas Harper
Rob Harper
Gary Harpur
Stephen Harpur
Mr John Harrington
Nicholas Harris
Adam Harris
Dean Harris
Derek Harris
Phillip W. Harris
Steve Harrison
Eddie Harrison
Anthony Harrison
Paul Andrew Harrison
Andrew Harrison
Gail Lee Harrison
David Harrison
Anthony Harrold
Bill Harrop
L.F.C. Harrop
Sinead Harrop
Stuart D. Harrrison
Richard E. Hart
Stephen Hart
Michael Harthen
Fred Hartley
Graeme Hartley
Andrew Hartley
Shaun Harvey
Clare Harvey
Darren Harvey
Max Harvey
Luke Harvey
Christina Harwood
Mr Mohd Hasli Hasan
Martin Hase
Tony Hase
John Hatton
Toivo Haugen
Kieran Haughton
Jeffrey Haver
Mark A. Haver
Rob Hawkes
Lee Hawksworth

Ian Hawthorne
Charlie Hawtin
Stephen Andrew Hay
David Hay
Paul Hayden
Matthew Haydock
Chris Hayes
Christopher James Hayes
Rob Hayes
Steve Haynes
Michael James Hazlett
Gary Healeas
Michael Anthony Healey
John Heaney
Michael John Heaney
Stacey Heaney
Martin J. Hearn
Stuart Heath
Graham Heath
Susan Heavey
Leigh David Hedges
Neil Hedley
Daniel Heffernan
Matthew Hemstock
Stuart Henderson
Stuart Thomas Henderson
Danny Henderson
Andrew Henderson
Steven Heney
Kevin Henney
James Henry
Graham Henshaw
Josh Henshaw
Ethan Henshaw
Billy Henshaw
Paul Henwood
Chris Hersey
Shakeel Herwitker
Sajid Herwitker
John Heston
Peter Hewitson
Duncan Hewitt
David Hewitt
Tony Hewitt
Bernard Hewson
Jamie Riley Hickey
Liam Higginson
David Higham
Stephen Higham
Anthony Higham
Lenny Higham
Ken Hignett
Barry Hilditch
Geoff Hill
Darren Hill
Luke Hill
Patrick Hill
Karen Zowie Hill
Peter Hill
Steve A. Hill
Anthony Hill
Dennis Robert Hillis
Emma Louise Hillis
Joanna Hilton
Stephen Hindley
Ms S.K. Hinds
Dr. N.A. Hindson
Jason Carl Hislop
Matthew Hitchen
Michael Hitchman
Declan Hitchmough
Craig Hitchmough
Tom Dan Hoban
Lee Hobby
Ian Hobson
David Hockey
George Hodgson
Yeo Yien Hoe
Patrick Hogan
Darren J. Holbrook
John Holden
Gary Holden
Craig Holden
Derek Grant Holder
Mr Robert Holding
Simon Holgate
Jack Holland

Master Daniel Holland
Christian Peter Hollerhead
Mr Stephen Hollingworth
Paul Holme
Jamie Holme
Gary Holmes
Neil Holmes
David Holmes
The Holsgroves
David Holt
Emily Jane Holt
John Honeyman
Janice Hoof
Steve Hook
M.T. Hooper
Daniel Hooper
Iain Hooton
Gareth Hopkins
Mr M.R. Hopkins
Duncan Horner
Mark Horner
Wayne Horton
Tom Hosford
Mark R. Hostler
Jimmy Hough
Nicky Hough
Zoe Hough
Kieran Houghton
Colin Howard
Mark Howard
Michael Howard
Alan Howard
Adam Michael Howard
Malcolm Howard
Clayton Howard
David Howard
Daniel James Howard
Ian M. Howarth
Mr J.P. Howarth
Cara Howarth
Robert Howden
Darren Wyn Hughes
Joseph Roy Hughes
G.R. Hughes
Brian Hughes
Chris Hughes
Rebecca Hughes
Dr. A.N. Hughes
Kerri Hughes
David Hughes
Jordan Hughes
Peter Hughes
Debbie Hughes
Thomas William Hughes
Kaylee Hughes
Lesley Ann Hughes
Robin K.T. Hughes
Giles R.W. Hughes
Mark T. Hughes
David Hughes
Richard David Hughes
Mark Hughes
Paul D. Hughes
Johnathan George Hughes
Rose Hughes
Deb Hughes
Barry J. Hulican
Daniel J. Hull
Ron Hulse
Mr Joe Hulse
Harvey Hume
Alan Humphreys
Lorraine Humphreys
Ian Humphries
Kieran David Humphries
Phil Hunter
Ashley Hurd
Liam David Hurley
Julian Hurst
Brian Hutton
Satpal Singh Hyare
George Hyde
H.M. I'Anson
Lawrence Iddison
Pauline Ilsey
Charlie Irvine
Sam Irvine

Stuart Kristian Irwin
David Isaac
Ben Isaac
Stefan Isaacson
Ibdilillah Ishak
Mr Phillip Neil Ivens
Ray Izod
Philip Edward Jackman
Karl Jackson
John Jackson
Neal Jackson
Andrew Jackson
John Grant Jackson
Anthony Jackson
Earle Jackson
Eddie Jackson
Les Jackson
Jason Jacob
Arthur Kenneth Jacob
Abe Jacob
Anthony Jacobs
David Vincent Jady
Susan Margaret Jady
Mr A.E. Jaggs
Matthew James
Hayley Charlotte James
Daniel Paul James
Mr S. James
Mr. R.A. Jameson
Master K.A. Jameson
The James's
Bruce Jamieson
Michael Jamison
Charley Jaques
Trevor Jarman
Andrew Jarvis
Andrew Jeffery
Mary Jeffs
Thomas Jenions
David Jenkins
Alan Jenkins
Michael Jennings
Eric Jennings
Michael Jennion
Dave Jennion
J.K. Jensen
Ulrik Jensen
Lee Jessop
Aaron Scott Jewitt
Gindy Jhuti
Erling Johansen
Donald Johns
Norman Johns
Ben Johnson
Jeff Johnson
Jodhi Johnson
Steven Johnson
Kenny Johnson
Tom Johnson
Jake Johnson
Andrew Johnson
P.T. Johnson
Steven Johnson
Mr R.W. Johnson
Patricia Magaret Johnson
Carol Johnson
Karen Lynn Johnson
Damon Johnson
Ben Le Bon Johnston
Gerald Johnston
William Thomas Johnston
The Johnston Bunch
Eleanor Johnstone
Hayley Jonas
Andrew Jonathan
Carl Jones
Rob Jones
Linda Jones
Joshua Nathan A. Jones
Rhodri Jones
Nigel Jones
Nathan Jones
Maxine Jones
Carolanne Jones
T.W.L. Jones
Bradley Jones
David Alun Jones

John Martin Jones
Kevin Jones
Mr. Gary Ian Jones
Becky Jones
Mrs. June Jones
David Andrew Jones
Karl Jones
Bob Jones
Terry Jones
Peter Wynn Jones
Glyn Jones
Neil Craig Jones
Noel Jones
Barry Jones
Robbie Jones
Amanda Jones
Lesley Jones
Jeff Jones
Alun Owen Jones
Paul Jones
Gavin Jones
George Jones
Heath Jones
Philip Jones
Bob Jones
Craig Jones
Jo-Jo Jones
Richard Jones
Len Jones
Phil Jones
Gareth Jones
David Jones
Gary Jones
Gareth Alwyn Jones
Gary Jones
Kevin M.W. Jones
Steven Jones
Leslie Jones
S.M. Jones
Gareth Jones
David Jones
Andrew Jones
Michael Jordinson
Master C.I. Joughin
Peter Joyce
Liam Judge
Alan Junglas
Nik Azizah Junoh
Ali Kaile
Mustak Karbhari
Katsumi Kashimura
Steven Kattou
Ciaran Kavanagh
Peter Kavanagh
Jaqui Kaye
Martin Kaye
Katie Keane
Anthony Kearney
Andrew J. Kearns
Laura Ann Keen
Stephen Keenan
Paula Louise Keenan
Sue Keil
Eugene E. Kellegher
Linda M. Kellie
David L. Kellner
Graham Philip Kelly
Andrew Ian Kelly
James A. Kelly
Alan Kelly
Billy Kelly
Shawn Kelly
Malcolm William Kelly
Andrew Kelso
Neil Kelty
Sebastian Vito Kemp
Claire Kendall
Miss S. Kennah
Craig Kennedy
James Kennedy
Anthony Kennedy
Paul Kennerley
Shaun Kennerley
Owen James Kenny
Paul Kent
Neil Kenwright
Stephen Keogh

Edward David Kerwick
Tracy Kerwin
Dave Kerwin
Ranj Emrys Khela
Suzanne Kidd
James Anthony Kidd
Liam Kilborn
Declan Kilborn
Luke Kilfoyle
Anthony Killen
Mr I. Killen
Mr GeeSyub Kim
Alison King
Arthur King
Derek King
Danny King
Dean King
Sue King
Steve Kingsman
Rob Kinney
Miss J.R. Kinvig
Brain Kirk
Darren William Kirkham
Greg Kirkpatrick
Roy E. Kirkwood
John Kitching
Andrew Michael Kiveal
Matthew James Kiveal-Duffy
Kevin J. Kneale
Chris Knell
Kevin Paul Knott
Neale Knowles
Simon Scott Knuckey
Tadeusz Kolodziej
Fintan Kolokotrone
Sotiris Korologos
Anand Krishnasamy
Adam Kuflowski
Einar Kvande
Wilson Chan Kwok Hung
Graeme Kynaston
Merseyside Branch L.F.C. O.S.C.
Mick-Liam Laithwaite
Bernard Lamb
Sean Lamb
William Lamb
Ian Lamb
Ron Lamb
Shane Lambert
Ian Robert Lambert
Paul James Lambert
Joy Lampkin
William Landy
Brian Lane
Emma Jane Lang
Thomas Langan
Will Langdon
Stephen J. Lange
Paul Frederick Langton
Kevin Langton
Philip Lappin
Amy Larkin
John Larkin
Daniel Latham
Alan John Latham
Simon Lattimore
George Lawrence
Joe W. Lawrence
Christopher Lawrenson
Deborah Lawson
Llewellyn Layton
Mr M. Leach
Ievan James Leach
Neil Leadbetter
Stuart Keith Leader
Lee Anthony Leaf
David Leahey
Jemma Leary
J.P. Leary
S.G. Leatherbarrow
Ian Leatherbarrow
Daniel Anthony Leatherbarrow
Joseph Alexander Leatherbarrow
Tom S. Leatherbarrow
Craig Leathley
Simon Joshua Lebeau
Rebecca Lee

Royston Gregory Lee
Jason Philip Lee
Angi Lee
Stacey Lee
Jennifer Lee Aspin
Cameron Leece
Barry Leece
Dave Leedham
Ronnie Lees
Lee Leggett
Michael John Leigh
Richard Leigh
Kevin Anthony Leigh
Elaine Leigh
Kevin Lennon
Robbie Lesbirel
Doug Lesbirel
Christoper Leslie
Mr Andrew Leslie
Mikhail Lesnykh
Mr C. Lester
Christopher Levett
Mary Lewis
Dr. John Lewis
Richard Lewis
Mr. Daniel Lewis
Jianwen Li
Petros Liaros
Matthew Lightbown
Paul Lightfoot
Kevin Liken
Helen Lindfield
G.F.M. Lindsay
Kirk Lindsay
Peter Lindsay
Graeme Lindsay
Mark Linnett
Sarah Lipscombe
Alex Lithgow-Smith
Jean Ann Littler
Ian Littlewood
Helen Liu
Chad Livesey
Dave Lloyd
Bryn Lloyd
Elen Mair Lloyd Williams
Vincent Lock
Ali Lock
Ami Lock
Chloe Lock
Jamie Lock
Ian Lockley
Gary Lockwood
Arthur Lockyear
Cian Malcolm Loftus
Graham Neil Logan
Loizos A. Loizou
Harry Lomas
Ryan Thomas Lomax
Bernadette Lonergan
Bernadette Lonergan
Mr M.W.T. Long
The Longthornes
Brian Longworth
Neal Lonsdale
Declan Lord
Mr Gary Lord
Mikael Johansen Loretsen
Robbie Lorey
Darren Lorking
Jimmy Louth
John Low
Chonghao Kelvin Low
Richard Lowe
Elliott Lowe
Matthew Lowe
Jon Lowrie
Paul Lowry
James Lowry
Jimi Lowry
Pam Lucas
Stephen Ludgate
Lubomir Georgiev Lulev
Steve Lumley
Leo Lumley
Matthew Lumsden
Hanns Peter Lundeppen

Tony Lungley
Geraint Lunt
Bernie Lupton
Sally Lupton
T. Lynch
Carl Anthony Lynch
Craig Lynch
Dave Lynch
J.P. Lynn
Gaynor Lyth
William Lythgoe
Angus Macdonald
Billy MacGlashan
John MacGlashan
Joshua Liam Machin
Victoria Macindoe
Jack MacIntyre
Stewart Mackenzie
Helen Mackie
Paul Maddocks
Clive Maddocks
Martyn Maddocks
Lawrence Magee
Robert S. Maguire
Thanarak Mahachaipongkul
Gerry Mahoney
Edward Mahoney
Iain Emlyn Main
Syed Abu Khalid Majid
Andrew Major
Terence Joseph Maley
Richard Malley
Nathan Malley
Michael Malley
George Mallon
Maria Malloy
Paul Malone
Antoinette Malpass
Mr. D.O. Manning
Aaron Manning
Chris Mansfield
Richard John Mansley
Janne Mansukoski
Dan Mara
Nathan Liam Mara
S.R. Markey
David Marley
Colin Marples
Simon Marriott
Chris Martin
Jacob Marsden
Andy Marsden
Derek Marsden
Jonathan Marsh
Vicki Marsh
John Marsh
Catherine Marsh
Rebecca Marsh
Luke Marshall
Ian Marshall
John Marshall
Kenny Marsland Jnr
Thomas Martin
E.C. Martin
Walter Martin
Tracy Martin
Bethan Martland
Ian Mason
Barry Mason
Stuart Mason
Stephen Massey
Aileen Mathews
Paul Mathias
Paul Mathur
Andy Maud
James E. Mawdsley
Guy A. Mawdsley
Rosanne K. Mawdsley
Kenneth May
Stephen May
Stuart May
Ashley Mayers
John Maylor
Helen Maynard
Mr Fred Maynard
Andrea McAdam
Stephen McAleer

Robert S. McAllister
Joshua James McAllister
Benedict Luke McAllister
Matthew John McAllister
John Paul McAllister
David McAreavey
Kristopher McAreavey
Neil McAtamney
Stephen McCabe
Colin McCabe
Tom McCallum
Ron McCann
Steven McCarthy
James Andrew McCartney
Sam McCauley
Mr N.J. McChesney
Frank McConechy
Gavin McConkey
Mr Tommy McConlough
A.G. McConnell
Graeme McConnell
Ray McConville
Ciaran McConville
Joshua McCormack
Paul McCormick
Chris McCormick
Ron McCready
John McCullagh
Anne McCullough
Daniel McCully
Kevin McDermott
Emma Louise McDermott
Alfred Nelson McDermott
Steven McDonald
R.J. McDonald
Andrew McDonald
Keith McDonnell
Sean McDonnell
Robert McDougall
Adam McElhinney
Maureen McElligott
Paul McEvitt
Phillip McEvoy
E. McGarry
Neil McGee
John McGill
William McGinnigle
John Wesley McGivern
Barry McGlynn
Mrs D.A. McGorrin
Andrew McGowan
Dave McGowan
Mark McGrady
Hannah McGrail
Danny McGrail
Jerry McGrath
Karen McGrath
Leslie McGregor
Michael McGrellis
Patrick McGuigan
Alex D. McGuinness
Mark McGurgan
Matthew McGurk
Alan McHuch
Garry McHugh
Fred McHugh
Tony McHugh
Stephen McInerney
Ken McKay
Callum McKean
Mitchell McKenna
Michael McKenna
Colin McKenzie
Paul McKenzie
Rich McKenzie
Mr J. McKeown
Thomas Robert McKeown
Mr Raymond Samuel McKeown
Julie Hayley McKeown
Jamie McKernan
Daniel McKibbin
Michael McLaughlin
John Tsepo McLean
Derek McLean
Pauk McLear
David McLennan
Martin McLoughlin

Andrew McLoughlin
Allen James McMullin
Steven McNairn
Joseph McNally
Billy McNally
Paul McNurny
Jack McPhail
Derek Peter McQuillan Lee
Graeme McTweed
Steven McVeigh
Nicholas Mead
Christopher K. Medway
Paul James Mee
David Melling
David Mercer
Tony Mercer
Steve Mercer
David Mercer
Paul Merrifield
Kim Messenger
Ralph Mestrom
Joan Metcalf
Steven Metcalf
Stephen Midgley
Paul Newton Midgley
Matthew Miedzwiecki
John Mighall
P.J. Miles
Bill Millard
Cllr Peter Millea
John S. Miller
Steve Miller
Derek Miller
Jackie Millhouse
Graham Millie
Richard S. Millington
Adam Mills
Jimmy Mills
Bill Mills-Roberts
Connor Milne
Becky Milsom
Jonathan David Minshall
Hitesh Hetal Mistry
Jason R. Mitchell
Mr P. Mitchell
Paul Jamed Mitchell
Alun Moakes
Patrick Modoux
Steven Moffat
Stephen Francis Moffatt
Karl Mogan
Frank Mohan
Colin Molloy
Adrian Monk
Graeme Montgomery
Alan Montgomery
Mark Montgomery
Florence Moody
Paul Moore
Andrew Moore
Stephen Moore
Paul Moore
Stephen Moorehead
Gregory Moorehead
Joan Moores
Jenny Moores
Tony Moran
Larry Moran
Philip Stephen Morgan
Eileen Morgan
Gareth Philip Morgan
Elizabeth Anne Morgan
John Morgan
Gary Morgan
Leon Morgan
David John Morgan
Paul Morgan
Gareth Morgan
Chris Morgan
Solomon Morgan
Daniel Morgan
Michael Thomas Morgan
John Joseph Morgan
Miyuki Mori
Paul David Moring
Sean Morley
Warren Morley

Patrick Morn
Gary Morrey
Ian Morris
J.B. Morris
Sarah Morris
Stephen Morris
Stuart Morris
Chloe Louise Morris
Michael Morris
Simon J. Morris
Mark Morrisey
Bill Morrison
Mr. John Morrow
Robin Moseley
Andrew Paul Moseley
Peter Moss
Mr N.P. Moules
Dave Moult
Paul Mower
Shaun Patrick Moynihan
Tony Mudge
Paul Muil
Paul Mulhall
Peter Mulhall
Danny Mulhearn
Thomas Edward Mulholland
Ste Mullen
Karl Mullen
James Mullett
Mr. D.K. Mulligan
Peter. G. Mullin
Matthew J. Mullin
Adrian Mumford-Smith
Jack Munnerley
John L. Murney
Patrick Murphy
Steve Murphy
Kelvin Murphy
Eleanor Murphy
Keeahn Murphy
Loraine Murphy
Josh Murphy
Siobhan Murphy
Mr Barry Murphy
John Murphy
Aileen Murphy
Jason Murphy
Darragh Murphy
Dean John Murphy
Lee K. Murphy
Eddie Murphy
Ian William Murphy
Paul M. Murphy
John H. Murray
Brendan J.J.Murray
Matthew Murray
Michael Murray
Luke Murray
Anthony Murray
James Murray
Declan J. Murray
Mr D. Murray
Kevin Murray
Brian Murray
Mark Muscat
Tony Musker
Mark Mutch
Brian Mutch
P. Myers
Michael Myers
Richard Markus Mylius
Ian Naftel
Dr Rieko Nagai
Adam Scott Nagy
Kevin Narramore
Andy Naughton
Daniel Nealen
Micky Neary
Mr Paul J. Neave
Simon Needham
Patrick Needham
Adam Needham
Samir Neffar
Arthur Phillip Neil
Lindsey Neilson
Noel Nelson
Mr. A.W. Nelson

★★★★★

Dale Nelson
Paul E. Nelson
Caleb Neocleous
Dr.S.I. Neophytou
G.A. Neophytou
Mario Neophytou
Paul Netherwood
Robert Neubauer
Will Neville
Anthony Joseph Newcombe
Mark Anthony Newman
M.C. Newton
Netzer Ng
Pauline Nicholas
Andrew Bamber Nixon
Sarah Noble
Paul Noblet
Marc A. Nolan
Patria Nolan
P. Noon
Gary Norgate
D.A. Arkwright Norris
Kevin Norwood
Chloe Norwood
Ansley Nugent
K. Nuntha Kumar
Ali F. Nurmohamed
Mark Nuttall
Arnold Nybo
Peter Oakes
Brian John Oakes
David Oakes
Michael O'Boyle
Eoin O'Brien
Ged O'Brien
Ricky O'Brien
Louise-Antoinette O'Brien
Colin O'Brien
Ian O'Connell
Sean O'Connell
Hugh O'Connell
Shaun O'Donnell
Peter S.J. O'Donoghue
Peter O'Donovan
Stephen James O'Gorman
Ulric Ojeer
Andrew Okin
Fred Oldfield
Steven Oldham
Steven Oldham
Joanne O'Leary
Gareth O'Leary
Miss May Oliver
Andrew O'Loughlin
Scot O'Loughlin
Danny O'Malley
Timothy Oon
Chris O'Prey
Ryan James O'Quigley
Mr David Orledge
John O'Rourke
Lee O'Rourke
Mr B. O'Rourke
Lizzie Osborne
Gavin Lee Osborne
Paul Osborne
Neil Overett
Mo Owen
Philip Owen
Robbie Owen
Fay Owen
Matt Owen
Colin Owens
Philip Owens
John Owens
Allan Owens
Daniel Owens
Louise Owens
Padraig Owens
Angela Oxbrow
A.J. Packenham
Neil Page
Alex Page
Molly Page
Gary Page
Thomas Painter
Nigel John Palmer

Mr Manu Pankhania
Christos Papalexis
Solomon Papaloizou
Chris Pardoe
Keith Parke
Gary Thomas Parker
Alan Parker
Graham Joseph William Parker
Barry Parker
Carl Parker
George Parker
Carole Parker
Owen Thomas Parle
Kevin Parnell
Keith Parr
Harry Parr
Alun Parry
Ken G. Parry
William Emlyn Parry
E.D. Parry
Matthew Parry
John Parry
Don Passey
Sanjay Patel
Vijay Patel
Ketan Patel
Bhavesh Patel
Chetan Patel
Masihullah Patel
Chris Paterson
Shaun Patrick
Andrew Pau
Stanley Peach
Colin Peake
Ryan Joshua Pearce
Peter G. Pearcey
Chris Pearson
David Pearson
Peter Graham Pearson Thompson
Mark A. Peers
Geoff Penn
D.W. Penrose
Michael Peri
Sandra Perkins
Ian Perks
Paul Perry
Joe Peter
Ronnie Peters
Neil Peterson
Paul Petherbridge
Harry William Philcox
David John Phillips
D.A. Phillips
Michael Phillips
Anthony Phillips
Aled Phillips
Lynne Phillips
Matthew Phillips
Mark Phillips
Steve Phillips
Max Pichon
The Picketts
Andrew David Pickles
Rico Pieri
Tamsin Piggott
Alistair Pike
Tony Pinch
Martin Pipet
Francis Andrew Pitt
Gordon Plant
Bob Platt
Paul Platt
Adrian Platt
David Platt
Mark Platt
Susan Plumb
Brian Plumridge
Kevin Pogorzelski
Mark Pogorzelski
Ray Edward Pollard
Samantha Pollard
Lee W. Pollitt
Gary Poole
Michael Poole
Gary Porter
Dave Postlethwaite
David Vincent Postlethwaite

Dave Postlethwaite
R.W. Potsig
Robert Potter
Michael Potter
Richard Alexander Potts
G. Potts
Tony Potts
Neil S. Poulson
Paul Poultney
Keith Powell
Liam Powell
Keith Powell
Rhys Powell
Tony Powell
Joe Power
David Poynton
David Prayle
Mark Prescott
Neil Preston
Mark Preston
June Preston
George William Preston
Ian Price
Denis Price
Kate Price
Phil Price
David Price
Adam Price
David B. Prince
Danni Prince
Joshua Prince
Neil Prince
Robert Pritchard
Gareth Pritchard
Michael Pritchard
Ratnarala Probaharan
Kiel Proctor
John Proctor
Tomos Prys-Owen
Gareth Puckey
Ronald William Pugh
Greg Pugh
Thomas Wyn Pugh
David Pun
Graham Purcell
Anthony Putt
Tom Pye
Kevin Quick
Anthony Quigley
Anthony Paul Quinn
John Quinn
Jim Quirey
Margaret Quirk
Shazan Qureshi
Terry Rabson
David Rad
Alan Radford
Michael Rafferty
Kavi Raja
Paul Ralph
Ms C.A. Ralph
Derek Ralphs
Jattinder Singh Rana
David Randles
Jamie Randles
Dave Rankin
John Francis Rankin
Mark Rasem
Jevaid Rashid
Jon Rathe
Mark Ian Rawlings
Mr Jim Rawlinson
Mrs Stella Maris Ray
Keith Raymond
Laurence Rea
Michael Reason
Bob Reason
Ken Reaveley
Kevin Reavey
Paul Redford
Paul Christopher Redhead
Steve Reeves
Steven Reeves
Mark Rega
Joseph Reid
Alex Reid
Donna C. Reid

Mark Reid
Colm Reilly
Keith Rennie
George Renshaw
Euan Rhodes
William Rice
Ian Rice
Chris Rice
Peter Rice
Garry Richards
Kris Richards
Gareth Richards
Scott Barry Richards
Colin Richards
Andy Richardson
Graham Richardson
Mr R.H. Richardson
John Richter
Mike Riddlesworth
Mark Ridout
Carl Rigby
Rod Riley
Christopher I. Riley
Ethan Michael Edward Riley
Daniel Riley
Amanda Riley
Sean Riley
Tony Riley
David Riley
Christopher I. Riley
Jason Riley
Chris Rimmer
Nicolle Rimmer
Gabriella Rimmer
Allan Rimmer
Jon Rimmer
G.R. Rimmer
Philip J. Rimmer
Samuel J. Rimmer
Jonathan P. Rimmer
Stuart Ritchie
Paul John Ritchie
David Rix
John Roach
Ian Roach
Christopher Roach
Davey Roberts
Eleanor Elizabeth Roberts
Jeffrey Roberts
Ron Roberts
Dave Roberts
Alex Roberts
Stephen Charles Roberts
Sion Guto Roberts
Mark Roberts
Alan Roberts
Harvey Roberts
Christian Roberts
Nathan Roberts
Alan Roberts
Nicholas Michael Roberts
Josh Roberts
Mr W.A. Roberts
Alan Roberts
Nowi Von Roberts
Kenny Roberts
Kim Roberts
Clive Roberts
Mark Roberts
Dewi W. Roberts
Michala Roberts
David Roberts
Sam Roberts
Luke Robertson
Ken Robertson
Lukey Robertson
Brian Robinson
Tony Robinson
Martin Robinson
Francis Robinson
Les Robinson
Thomas Robinson
Shaun Robinson
John Paul Robinson
Andy Robinson
Joy Robinson
Alan Mark Robson

Michael Roche
Terry Roche
Fred Rodaway
Graham Rodgers
Elizabeth Rodrigues
Bianca Feliciana Rodriguez
Paul Rogers
Graham C. Rogers
David Rogers
Nathan Rogers
Michael Rogers
Paul Rogers
Colin Rogers
Andrew Rollins
Graham Ronson
Phil Rooney
Carl Thomas Rooney
Georgina Roscoe
Daniel Cecil Roscoe
Tony Rose
Christopher Rosoce
Ian Ross
Robert Ross
Steven George Rossington
Melissa Charlotte Sarah Roston
Stuart John Round
Sarah Jane Round
Liam Lewis Rourke
Paul Rowan
Jay Rowan
Mark Rowan
Sam Rowe
Martin John Royle
Peter John Royle
Geraldine Alicia Royle
Sebastien Ruch
Ben Runacus
Sheila Ruse
Lee Rushbrooke
Steven Rushe
Geoffrey Russell
Mr. R.W. Russell
Daniel Russell
Samuel W. Russell
Graeme Russell
Stephen Russell
David J. Rutherford
Ann Ryan
Paul Ryan
Kevin Ryan
Mrs S.J. Ryan
Jason Ryan
Maura Ryan
Robert Ryan
M.E. Ryder
Konrad R. Rylatt
Daniel Sabatino
D. Sacco
Joseph A. Sainsbury
William Sainsbury
Galal Saleh
Carl Salters
Jon Sammarco
Saeed Samnakay
Richard T. Samosa
Ritchie Samosa
Pete Sampara
Ryan Sampson
Mr M.C. Sandales
David Sanders
Peter Sandland
Shivraj Sangha
Paul Sankey
Neil Sankey
Nicolette Sarath
Philip John Sargeant
Shaun Sarginson
Jim Saul
Liam Savage
Steven Savill
Matt Savory
Paul Martin Sayer
Mark Saywell
Paul Edward Scanlon
Tim Scanlon
Dawn Scarisbrick
Amy Scholten

Svenja Schroeder
Elke Schuch
Andrew J. Sciarrini
Andrew Scott
David Thomas Scott
Peter Philip Scott
Frank Scragg
Wendy Scragg
Janice Scragg
R.T. Scrivens
Jason Scrymgeour
Gerrard Scully
Craig Scully
Craig Scurr
Robert Scutchings
Alan Scutts
Ron Sigi Seagraves
Matthew Seales
Andy Seasman
Stephen William Sefton
Carla Sergeant
Philip John Sergeant
Himesh Shah
Ian Shakeshaft
Paul Shakespeare
Stephen Peter Shale
Mark Christopher Shale
Sahill Shan
Mark Shannon
Joshua E. Shapira
Ali Sharif
Lalit Sharma
K. Sharp
Trevor Sharp
Jonathan Scott Sharp
Mr Gareth W. Sharp
Graham Shaw
Daniel Shaw
Carl Shaw
Joseph Shaw
Luca Jeremy Shaw
Graham Shaw
Jonathon Shears
Derek Shearson Snr.
Phil Sheehan
Geoffrey Sheen
Darren Sheen
Brian Sheil
Nathalie Shepherd
J. Sheppard
D.J. Sheppard
Sally Sheridan
John Sherlock
Michael Shewell
Keiko Shibata
Richard Shields
John Shimmin
Mr C.W. Sibbald
Natalie Silcock
David Sillitoe
Benjamin Simister
David Simmonds
Laura Simmonds
Andrew Christopher Simms
Jeanette Simpson
Natalie Simpson
Mr Brian Simpson
David Sinclair
Andrew Sinclair
Richard Singh
Gee Aaron Singh
Gary Ninder Singh Benning
Peter Sinnott
Martin Sixsmith
Steve Skelding
John A. Skelhorn
Keith Skerratt
Simon Skillen
Martin Skillen
Samuel George Skinner
Mr Tracey John Skipper
Leif Slaatten
Kevin William Slaven
Stephen Sleigh
Chrisine Sleuman
Andrew Smalley
Andrew James Smart

Callum James Smart
Ian Smith
George James Smith
Stephen Eric Smith
Megan Lucy Smith
John Smith
Michael Smith
Emma Jane Smith
Peter J. Smith
Christopher Smith
Gary Smith
Daniel James Smith
Kevin Smith
Christopher Smith
Simon James Smith
P.E. Smith
Jordan Smith
Rob Smith
Steffan John Smith
Rhodri Llywelyn Smith
Darren Smith
Michael Steven Smith
Michael Andrew Smith
Barbara Smith
Karen V. Smith
Jamie Smith BSC
The Smiths
Andrew Smyth
Edd Snell
Andrew Snell
Graeme Snell
Lorraine Snoddy
Joanne Snow
Dr Kaveer Sohan
Vijay Solanki
Rajiv Soni-Tricker
John Sowerby
Harry Spain
Kate Sparkes
Bill Spasevski
Will Speed-Evans
Andrew Spence
Paul Spencer
Fred Spencer
Chris Spencer
Darren Spencer
Phil Spencer
Gareth Spencer
Chris Spragg
Harpreet Sprawn
Lee Sprung
Neil Kyle Stallard
Richard Stanfield
Linda Stanford
Mark James Stanistreet
Steven Stanley
Steven Thomas Stanley
Richard Stanton
G.E. Stead
Matthew C. Steer
Simon Stein
Chris Stephens
Phil Stephenson
Mark Lee Stern
J.M. Stevenson
Paul Gregory Stevenson
Ian Stevenson
Mr. K.A. Stewart
Nathan Stewart
Beverley R. Stewart
David Stiell
Barry Stinchcomb
Jeffrey Stinchcomb
Neil Stinchcomb
Lee Stinchcomb
Karl Stinchcomb
Stuart Stirling
Tommy Stockdale
Jessica Ann Elizabeth Stocker
Diane Stocksborough
Mark John Stockton
Mike Stoddart
Helen Stoddart
Jonny Stokkeland
Richard Stonyer
Steve Storey
Philip Thomas Stott

David Stowe
John Strabel
Phillip Streeter
Wayne Anthony Stretch
Sam Stringman
Chris Strong
Jamie David Stuart
Lee Stuart
Danny Styles
George Sullivan
Rebecca Sullivan
Lizzie Sullivan
Miss Pei Suen Sum
Paul Sumner
Andrew G. Sumner
Graham Sumner
Craig Sumner
Colin Sumpter
Debbie-Lea Sumpter
Paul Sumpter
John Sumpter
Ian Sumpter
Kevin Sumpter
Nicky Sumpter
Lyndsey Sung
Mr J.L.P. Sutcliffe
Evan Anthony Sutton
Oliver Swallow
Stephen Swallow
Tony Sweetman
Colin Swensson
John Swift
Ken Swift
Mr S. Sykes
Ben Sykes
Richard M. Sykes
Paul Symons
Ken Sysum
H. Tabuchi
James Taggart
Rafiq Tai
Darren Talbot
Joseph Daniel Talbot
Eric S.W. Tangeman
Darren Tanner
Declan Tanner
Craig Tanner
Robert Tarrington
Peter Tavey
Kay Jin Tay
Josh Taylor
John Taylor
M.A. Taylor
Daniel Robert Taylor
L.J. Taylor
Gus Taylor
Darren Taylor
Alexander Taylor
Andrew Taylor
Ian D. Taylor
Dave Taylor
Philip Teeling
James Telford
Paul Tennant
Keith Tennant
Sim Theng Theng
Suren Thiru
Mathew Thomas
Ffion Thomas
Aaron-Lee Owen Thomas
Michael Thomas
Harry William Thomas
Alwyn Thomas
Roger J. Thomas
Mark Stephen Thomas
Richard Thomas
Helen Thomas
David Thomas
Nikki Thomlinson
Joanne Thompson
Peter A. Thompson
Tracey Thompson
Terance Paul Thompson
Helen Thompson
Darren Thompson
Luke Thompson
Joseph Thompson

Stuart Graham Thompson
Geoff Thompson
Jonathan D. Thompson
Sebastian Thompson
Dave Thompson
Hayley Thomson
Luke Cheah Fook Thong
Howard Thornley
Ronald Thorpe
Jay Threlfall
Amy Threlfall
Katy Threlfall
Mr H.D.W. Thurman
Mark Thwaite
Derek Thwaite
Ian Thwaite
Sharon Tierney
Mr Richard Tierney
Jessica Till
Marc Tilley
Richard Timmons
Sue Timperon
Alan Tinsley
Keith Todd
Daniel J. Todd
Matthew R. Todd
Dominic Toller
Owen Toller
Honey-Louise Toller
Jari Tolonen
Liam Toolan
John-Paul Tooley
Michael David Toon
Phillip Daniel Torres
Herman Ekeli Tostrup
Robert Tostrup
J.G. Townsend
Eileen Townson
Keith Trainer
John C. Trayler
Anthony Traynor
Stephen Traynor
Raymond Trewern
Karen Trill
Victoria Tucker
Gareth Tudor
Annie Tufte
Mervyn Turker
Sue Turnbull
Barry Turner
Michael Turner
Roger Turner
Mr D.W. Turner
Mr Simon Turner
Joe Turner
Mia Ellen Turner
Sean Twomey
Geoff Tyrer
Karan Uka
Philip Unsworth
Sarah Utley
Graham Vail
Mr F. Van Laere
Mrs A. Van Laere
Mr K. Van Laere
Richard Vanderplank
Mr Prakash Vara
Oliver James Adam Vasco
Neil Vaughan
Barry Vaughan
Thomas Veidman
Joel Ventre
Jon Vernon
Chris Vernon
Keith David Vincent
Philip Lee Vincent
Stephen Von Bargen
Tracy Waddington
Alan Waddington
Graeme Waddington
Alan Wade
Simon M. Wah
Mark Wakeham
Judy Waldron
Mark Walker
Roy Walker
Michael Walker

Phil Walker
Michael Walker
Craig Walker
Ms H.G. Walker
Simone Walker
Jason Walker
Neil Walker
Lee Walker
Barry Wall
Andrea Wall
Barry Wall
Niall Wallace
Eamonn Wallace
Spencer John Wallis
Claire Louise Walls
Liam Walsh
Cameron James Walsh
Mary Walsh
Paisley Walsh
Jonathan M. Walsh
Peter Walsh
Robert Walsh
Gary Walsh
Miss K.J. Walsh
Robert Walsh
Mrs C.E. Walsh
Mary Walsh
Cameron James Walsh
Harold L. Walters
David J. Walters
Shaun Ward
Cleasie Ward
Christine Ward
John Ward
Ken Ward
Mark Ward
Barrington Ward
Derek Ward
Jade Ward
Jenny Ward
Nick Wareham
Robert Michael Wareing
Robert Warner
S.M. Warrington
Alan Warwick
Keith Watkin
Tommy Watkins
I. Watkinson
Andrew Watkinson
John Watkinson
R. Watson
Cherith Watson
Tim Watson
Dylan Watson
Andrew John Watters
Jimmy Watts
Graham Watts
Ricky Watts
Mr Ian Watts
Karen Way
Josh Weaver
Dave Weaver
Kelly Weaver
Philip Weaver
Alison Webster
Jamie Webster
Paul Webster
Steven Webster
Sam Welbourne
Owen Wells
Russell Wells
Stewart Wells
Jason Wells
Robbie Welsh
Phil West
Simon Westhead
Dr Claire Westmoreland
Christopher Weston
David M. Whaley
Michael Wheatley
Lee Francis Wheeler
William T. Wheeler
Cathy Whelan
Terry Whiley
Malcolm Whipp
Ray White
Michael T. White

William Stephen White
Master Michael T. White
Joe Whitehead
Mark Whitehead
Chris Whitehead
Melanie Whitehouse
Janine Elizabeth Whitehurst
George Richard Whitehurst
Craig Whiteley
Jill Whitfield
Ruth Whitley
Debbie Whitley
Simon Whitley
John Whitlow
Brain Whittle
Andrew Phillip Wholey
Lee Whorton
Nick Wicks
Mr Paul Wiggins
Francis Anthony Wignall
Hugh Wignall
Colin Wilcock
Shaun Wilde
Timothy J.F. Wilding
Paul Wildridge
Alan George Wilkins
Baz Wilkinson
Mark Wilkinson
Tom Wilkinson
Sam Wilkinson
Peter Wilkinson
Pete Willan
Paul Willey
Allan William
Robin William
Mark Williams
John Williams
Tosh Williams
T.P. Williams
David Williams
Joey Williams
Jake Williams
Geoff Williams
Katy Williams
Ian Michael Williams
Thomas Williams
Gary Williams
Edward Charles Williams
Julia K. Williams
Timothy Robert John Williams
John C. Williams
M.W. Williams
Michael Williams
Martin C. Williams
Gemma Alison Williams
James Edward Williams
David Williams
Jack Ryan Williams
Ian W. Williams
Kenneth Brian Williams
Heather Williams
Carl Williams
Colin Williams
Lee Williams
Andy Williams
Ryan Anthony Williams
Chris Williams
Mark Williamson
Robert H. Willis
Henry Brian Willis
Jack Willis
Ben Willis
John William Willis
Tom Willis
Christopher Wilson
Robert Thomas Wilson
Andrew Wilson
W.E. Wilson
Bob Wilson
Paddy Wilson
Allan Wilson
Liam Wilson
Michael Wilson
Graeme Wilson
Peter J. Wilson
Liam Wilson
Kenneth Wilson

Roy Wilson
Alex Wilson-Daniels
David Robert Winn
Edward James Winrow
Ian Winrow
Paul Winrow
Billy Winrow
Richard Winson
Lisa Winstanley
Alex Wisidagama
Debby Wolf
Colin Wolfson
Hans Wong
Peter Yiu Wong
Dominic L.Z. Wong
Nicholas James Wonnacott
John James Wood
Andrew Wood
Callum Wood
Barry Wood
Carol Woodards
Frederick Woodcock
John Woodcock
Jamie Woodend
Richard Woodger
Ben Woodger
David Stanley Wooding
Gavin Woodrow
Kate Woods
Barbara Woods
Graham Woods
Karen Woods
Brain Woods
Stevie Woods
Daniel James Woodward
H. Dennis Woodward
Michael Woodward
Paul Woolcott
Mark Woolford
Mike Woolrich
Hope Woolven
Neill Woosey
Mark Woosey
Paul Worrall
Jake Paul Worrall
Mrs P.M. Worthington
Lee Wrench
Andrew Wright
Thomas James Wright
Patrick Owen Wright
Kerry Wright
Steve Wright
Mr E.C. Wright
Andrew Wright
Eric Wright
Leslie Wright
Andrew Wylie
Fred Wyniger
Gaynor Wynne
Mr Masahiro Yamashita
Jack Yarlett
Yuko Yasui
Mark E. Yates
Helen Yates
Jennifer Yeardsley
Emma Yeates
Wong Kar Yeow
Bernard Yeung
Alf Yeung
Ritsuko Yoda
Thomas John Youds
Kath Young
Nick Young
Ian Young
Malcolm Young
Robin Young
John Young
Dean Young
Jamie Young
David Yoxall
Tom Yoxall
Caetano Zahra
Aaron Zeverona

*** This Scroll Of Honour features names of fans who pre-ordered 'Liverpool's 5-Star Heroes'**